Origin and significance of the Frankfurt School

International Library of Sociology

Founded by Karl Mannheim

Editor: John Rex, University of Warwick

Arbor Scientiæ
Arbor Vitæ

A catalogue of the books available in the **International Library of Sociology** and other series of Social Science books published by Routledge & Kegan Paul will be found at the end of this volume.

Origin and significance of the Frankfurt School

A Marxist perspective

Phil Slater
Visiting Lecturer at The Centre
for Arts and Related Studies,
The City University, London

Routledge & Kegan Paul

London, Boston and Henley

First published in 1977
by Routledge & Kegan Paul Ltd
39 Store Street,
London WC1E 7DD,
9 Park Street,
Boston, Mass. 02108, USA and
Broadway House,
Newton Road,
Henley-on-Thames,
Oxon RG9 1EN
Reprinted in 1979
Reprinted and first published
as a paperback in 1980
Set in Times
and printed in Great Britain by
Redwood Burn Ltd
Trowbridge & Esher
© Phil Slater 1977

ISBN 0 7100 8438 2 (c)
ISBN 0 7100 0490 7 (p)

For the children of 110 Daubeney Road

Contents

A note on translation

Although as a general principle existing translations have been consulted and employed for the purposes of quotation, two exceptions should be noted: first, translations, particularly partial translations, that have appeared in obscure journals have not been made use of as a rule; second, translations that were made on the basis of later editions than those of the period under consideration have, on the whole, been ignored, since these editions frequently involve not merely stylistic but also conceptual and ideological modifications. This was particularly true of Reich's work, but also of Horkheimer's programmatic essays.

In addition, the liberty has been taken of modifying the translators' renderings so as to achieve a uniformity in the translation of key concepts (for example, alienation), as well as to improve on passages where the original dialectical quality has been lost in translation.

Acknowledgments

My thanks go, first and foremost, to Wilfried van der Will and Stuart Hall, who, in their different ways, gave me invaluable help as well as welcome criticism, but also constant encouragement throughout my research. Second, I should like to thank all those people at the Institut für Sozialforschung, Frankfurt am Main, and the Internationaal Instituut voor sociale Geschiedenis, Amsterdam, who were of assistance to me in my archival work. Of the figures directly or indirectly associated with the Frankfurt School, I was privileged to meet Max Horkheimer (shortly before his death), Felix Weil, Alfred Schmidt, and Herbert Marcuse. Marcuse, more than any of the others, was genuinely receptive to the criticisms I had to level against the formative years of the Frankfurt School. Last but not least, a special word of thanks to Alfred Sohn-Rethel, whose work was so important for my critical analysis of the Frankfurt School, and who encouraged me in this direction from first to last.

The author wishes to express his gratitude for permission to reprint certain materials from the publications listed below:

From Theodor W. Adorno: *Negative Dialectics*, trans. by E. B. Ashton (Routledge & Kegan Paul, 1973). Published in the USA by The Seabury Press, Inc. English translation Copyright © 1973 by The Seabury Press, Inc. Reprinted by permission of the publishers.

From Max Horkheimer and Theodor W. Adorno: *Dialectic of Enlightenment*, trans. John Cumming (Allen Lane The Penguin Press, 1973) pp. xiv, xv, 36f, 135, 160. Copyright © 1944 by Social Studies Association, Inc., New York. Reprinted by permission of Penguin Books Ltd.

From Herbert Marcuse: *An Essay on Liberation* (Allen Lane The Penguin Press, 1969) pp. 46, 56f, 59, 66. Published in the USA by

Beacon Press. Copyright © 1969 by Herbert Marcuse. Reprinted by permission of Penguin Books Ltd and Beacon Press.

From Herbert Marcuse: *Counterrevolution and Revolt* (Allen Lane The Penguin Press, 1972) pp. 23f, 39, 44f, 48f, 86, 98, 107, 123f, 128, 132. Published in the USA by Beacon Press. Copyright © 1972 by Herbert Marcuse. Reprinted by permission of Penguin Books Ltd and Beacon Press.

From Herbert Marcuse: *Negations* (Allen Lane The Penguin Press, 1968) pp. xi, xii, xv, 95, 102f, 108, 121, 124, 131, 134, 135, 158, 282. Published in the USA by Beacon Press. Copyright © 1968 by Herbert Marcuse. Translations from German copyright © 1968 by Beacon Press. German text © 1965 by Suhrkamp Verlag, Frankfurt am Main. Reprinted by permission of Penguin Books Ltd and Beacon Press.

From Herbert Marcuse: *One-Dimensional Man* (Routledge & Kegan Paul, 1964). Published in the USA by Beacon Press. Copyright © 1964 by Herbert Marcuse. Reprinted by permission of Routledge & Kegan Paul Ltd and Beacon Press.

From Herbert Marcuse: *Reason and Revolution* (Humanities Press, Inc.). Published in Great Britain by Routledge & Kegan Paul Ltd. Reprinted by permission of the publishers.

From Herbert Marcuse: *Soviet Marxism: A Critical Analysis* (New York: Columbia University Press, 1958). Published in Great Britain by Routledge & Kegan Paul Ltd. Copyright © 1958 Columbia University Press. Reprinted by permission of the publishers.

From *The Crisis of Psychoanalysis* by Erich Fromm (Jonathan Cape, 1971). Published in the USA by Holt, Rinehart & Winston. Copyright © 1970 by Erich Fromm. Reprinted by permission of Jonathan Cape Ltd and Holt, Rinehart & Winston, Publishers.

From *Three Essays on the Theory of Sexuality* by Sigmund Freud, © Sigmund Freud Copyrights Ltd, Basic Books, Inc., Publishers, New York. Reprinted by permission of the publisher.

Introduction

The term 'Frankfurt School' has come to be used widely, but loosely, to designate both a group of intellectuals and a specific social theory. The intellectuals concerned were associated with the Institut für Sozialforschung (Institute for Social Research) which was established in Frankfurt am Main in 1923. It was, however, only with the appointment in 1930 of Max Horkheimer as Director of the Institute that the basis was laid for what was to become known as the 'Frankfurt School'. Horkheimer (1895–1973) gathered together a team that included such now famous figures as Herbert Marcuse (born 1898), the radical philosopher and later ally of the student movement; Theodor W. Adorno (1903–69), philosopher, sociologist, and aesthetic theoretician; and Erich Fromm (born 1900), the psychologist of international repute.

Despite the role of other figures in the Institute (such as Friedrich Pollock, Leo Löwenthal, Karl August Wittfogel), it is essentially the work of Horkheimer, Marcuse, Adorno and Fromm which constitutes the core of Frankfurt School theory. And it was between 1930 and the early 1940s (when the team split up) that the Frankfurt School took shape and produced its most original work on the problem of a 'critical theory of society'.

The present study focuses on this period, and stresses the intended Marxist orientation of the Frankfurt School's formative years, an orientation which is distorted in the vast majority of the commentaries at hand today, where the Frankfurt School's work in its early years is either condemned for 'revisionism' and 'eclecticism' (by the 'orthodox' Marxist-Leninists), or else 'saved' from the 'slanderous' label of 'Marxist' (by bourgeois intellectuals). Both perspectives are inadequate: what is needed is a *differentiated* analysis. The following study propounds the following thesis: the Frankfurt School of the 1930s and early 1940s made a serious contribution to the elucidation and articulation of historical materialism but, *at the same time*, failed to achieve the relation to praxis which is central to the Marxist project.

Thus, the present study attempts a metacritique of the Frankfurt School's social theory in its formative years. It is worth stating, in anticipation, that a metacritique is a critique framed within a context that transcends the object under scrutiny. In the case of the Frankfurt School, such a procedure is both complex and problematical: they acknowledge as their frame of reference the method, categories, and political orientation of historical materialism, yet their analyses fail to concretise these categories, particularly as regards the problems of economic manipulation and revolutionary social praxis. Thus, immanent critique and metacritique, in the case of an analysis of the Frankfurt School, fuse.

No attempt is made in this study to explain the weaknesses of Frankfurt School theory by a sociological study of the respective individuals, since this study is concerned not with these individuals themselves but with the practical significance of their theoretical productions, which are at present finding an ever-increasing readership in Britain and America. Similarly, no extensive biographical or institutional history of the Frankfurt School is provided here. Such a history is available in the form of Martin Jay's *The Dialectical Imagination*.[1]

Jay's study, while providing a detailed account of the Frankfurt School's history, as well as mapping out their major areas of research, avoids the task of a critique of the Frankfurt School's relation to the theory-praxis nexus. Instead, Jay makes a familiar simplification:

> 'Men of ideas' are noteworthy only when their ideas are
> communicated to others through one medium or another. The
> critical edge of intellectual life comes largely from the gap that
> exists between symbol and what for want of a better word can
> be called reality. Paradoxically, by attempting to transform them-
> selves into the the agency to bridge that gap, they risk forfeiting
> the critical perspective it provides. What usually suffers is the
> quality of their work, which degenerates into propaganda.[2]

As a result, Jay can easily justify the very state of affairs that demands a systematic and critical analysis:

> It will be one of the central contentions of this work that the
> relative autonomy of the men who comprised the so-called
> Frankfurt School of the Institut für Sozialforschung, although
> entailing certain disadvantages, was one of the primary reasons
> for the theoretical achievements produced by their collaboration.[3]

Jay does not operate with a scientifically defined notion of 'propaganda', and actually fails to do justice to the most advanced demands made on their work by the Frankfurt School themselves. The 'disadvantages' involved in their 'relative autonomy' are not specified. The present study, by contrast, evaluates 'critical theory of society' in terms of the historical materialist theory-praxis nexus, and defines its terms in their significance for the class struggle. In this sense, the following analysis answers many of the programmatic questions outlined by Douglas Kellner in his review of Jay's book.[4]

It is essential to realise, however, that the metacritique undertaken in the present study is not 'purely' theoretical. In fact, a fundamental critique of this nature is possible only on the basis of a close study of the Frankfurt School's failure to establish links with the working-class movement in the 1930s, and, subsequently, in connection with the *practical* critique the Frankfurt School underwent at the hands of the student anti-authoritarian movement in the 1960s. Since, however, the latter movement stressed the need for a critical *appropriation* of Frankfurt School theory, the urgency is underlined, once again, for a *differentiated* evaluation in the present study.

A crucial, if controversial figure related to the Frankfurt School is Walter Benjamin (1892–1940), who was a strong influence on Adorno, and who was engaged in some work for the Institute, but who at the same time, largely due to the influence of his close friend Bertolt Brecht, kept a certain critical distance from the Institute's mainstream activity. The precise relationship between Benjamin and the Frankfurt School cannot yet be finally established, due to the secrecy surrounding the Institute's files, but, in any case, a discussion of Benjamin's work throws a good deal of light, much of it critical, on the Frankfurt School's work in the period under consideration.

Although the later split between Horkheimer and Marcuse is discussed here at length, since it reveals a great deal about the contradictory nature of the team's formative years, none the less the specific concern with the period from 1930 to 1942 means that certain problems falling outside this period could not be incorporated into the present study explicitly without sacrificing the succinctness of presentation essential to the theoretical metacritique. Thus, the present study does not cover the empirical work of the later 1940s (the anti-Semitism project), nor does it discuss the later revision of 'critical theory of society' by Jürgen Habermas, except by way of a note.

However, these gaps are not as serious as they may seem. First, the anti-Semitism study was not an Institute project; and second, more importantly, these studies betray the same general line of ideological degeneration as revealed in Horkheimer's and Adorno's publications of this period. The latter are, for the reasons outlined above, discussed here at length. In the same way, Habermas's work since the 1960s can be seen in the same light of a progressive alienation from the more Marxist perspective of the formative years. In any case, Habermas's ideas are discussed at great length, if only by implication, in the section on Albrecht Wellmer. Notes provide the necessary references in both instances.

1 The historical background of the Frankfurt School

Section One: the pre-Horkheimer tradition of the Institute

1 The founding of the Institute

The Frankfurt Institute for Social Research, the home of what later came to be known as the 'Frankfurt School', was founded in 1923 and officially opened in June of 1924.[1] The chief architects behind this creation of what was, in those days, a unique institute, were Felix Weil (born 1898), Friedrich Pollock (1894–1970), and Max Horkheimer, later Director of the Institute. These colleagues of the early 1920s showed a mutual interest in this ill-defined field, and Weil, together with his father, Hermann Weil (a big-business man), donated the necessary funds for establishing the relevant buildings and maintaining its paid staff.

In September 1922, Felix Weil produced a 'Memorandum on the Creation of an Institute for Social Research',[2] addressed to the Curator of Frankfurt University; in this document, which is the first evidence of a conception in the vein of what later became famous as the 'Frankfurt School', Weil centralised, as the proposed institute's objective, 'knowledge and understanding of social life in its totality', from the economic base to the institutional and ideational super-structure. Weil's examples of pressing problems (revolution, party-organisation, immiseration, etc.) made it clear that the concern was historical materialist,[3] but Weil did not fail to stress that the In-stitute's work would proceed 'independently of party-political considerations'.[4] As it turned out, the assurance was honoured: never, not even after Horkheimer's appointment in 1930, did the Institute form organisational ties with any political party.

At the time of the Institute's foundation, neither Weil, Hork-heimer, nor Pollock qualified for a professorship, and since the statutes demanded that the Director of the Institute be a professor of the University of Frankfurt, the three young intellectuals had no chance of actually taking control of the new institution. However, Weil was in a position to promote an acceptable candidate, which he did before actually handing over the grant. But although Weil's suggestion, Kurt Albert Gerlach, was acceptable to the University, Gerlach died suddenly, and a new candidate had to be found. Weil's negotiations with Gustav Mayer came to nothing, largely because of ideological differences, and Weil turned to Carl Grünberg, the Austro-Marxist historian of international repute. Agreement was reached among all parties concerned,[5] and Grünberg (1861–1940) became the Institute's first Director, also assuming a Chair in Economics and Social Science at Frankfurt University, in late 1923.

2 Grünberg's directorship

Grünberg's inaugural lecture made the Institute's sympathy with Marxism explicit. The Director avowed himself an opponent of the prevailing socio-economic order, and freely admitted that he be-longed to the 'adherents of Marxism'.[6] He continued that this position would dictate the method, stressing that this was not to be a purely personal matter, but institutional policy: 'the method taught as the key to solving our problems will be the Marxist method'.[7] Basic differences in method and ideology, Grünberg went on, would not be tolerated among his team, since such differences led either to wishy-washy compromises or else to violent disrup-tions. By contrast, the Institute would apply a uniform method: Grünberg emphasises the point by the expression 'dictatorship of the Director'.[8]

However, this hard line need not be taken too seriously. Weil has since explained that in looking over Grünberg's draft for this lecture, he (that is, Weil) had added certain formulations so as to dispel any idea that Grünberg was a mere puppet.[9] Weil's claim can be accepted at face-value, particularly if one compares Grünberg's interests and goals on the one hand, and the actual work of the Institute during his directorship, on the other: while the method employed in the Institute certainly was Marxist, as Grünberg had stated it would be, the interpretation of the Marxist method often went far beyond any-thing Grünberg himself envisaged. But this contention requires a detailed look at the latter's inaugural lecture.

Grünberg's lecture was certainly provocatively left-wing; he ex-plicated his Marxism not only by referring to the famous thesis of base and superstructure, but, in addition, by paraphrasing the equally famous opening sentence of the *Communist Manifesto:*

> And just as the historical materialist interpretation of history
> views all social phenomena as reflexes of economic life
> in its respective historical form, so that, in the last instance,
> 'the production-process of material life determines the social,
> political and intellectual life-processes,' so also all history
> (apart from primitive history) reveals itself as a procession of
> class-struggles.[10]

However, like Weil, Grünberg did not neglect to stress that all reference to Marxism was to be understood 'not in a party-political sense, but strictly in a scientific sense'.[11]

But far more significant is the fact that much of Weil's memorandum is, in Grünberg's lecture, missing, or at least underemphasised. Whereas Weil had spoken of social life 'in its totality', Grünberg was preoccupied with the more tangible aspects of this totality: 'above all, the study and presentation of the working-class movement', and 'the pursuit of basic socio-political questions'. Superstructural problems (ideology, even class-consciousness) are not listed with anything like the same clarity; instead, Grünberg merely concludes, in a vague manner, with the need for a 'genetic illumination of social theories, both socialist and otherwise'.[12] Ideology-critique, which Weil had implicitly thematised, and which was to be the corner-stone of the Institute's work under Horkheimer, had no great significance for Grünberg.

Although Grünberg did state that the production-process was the ultimate determinant of the ideational superstructure, he did not outline any need for a closer analysis of the complex mediations in this process. The lack of concern with the psychological dimension in particular marks a basic difference between Grünberg and Horkheimer, as will be shown below. Another crucial difference is the respective attitudes to philosophy; while Grünberg is correct to deny that historical materialism is a philosophy or metaphysic,[13] he fails to specify the dialectical *relation* between philosophy and scientific socialism. Instead, he speaks, far too generally and far too abstractly, of a 'fertilisation' of the Institute's work by philosophy, putting the role of this discipline on a par with the equally vague 'relation' to history and jurisprudence.[14]

Another qualifying feature of Grünberg's 'Marxism' is his lack of emphasis on the theory-praxis nexus. His archival and chronicling work, together with his book reviews, do, it is true, ensure a certain topicality, but he does not acknowledge the need to relate actively to any critical social praxis. Grünberg repeats the assurance that his team will keep their distance from party politics: the Institute will abstain from all 'day-to-day politics'. And any impact that the

Institute might have 'will be, in both form and extent, none other than that which scientific work as a whole exercises'.[15] The Marxian notion of scientific socialism as a class-weapon of the proletariat plays no role in Grünberg's conception of the intellectual's task.

Yet, within the context of the lecture as a whole, Grünberg's orthodox academic stance is quite logical: he speaks of the present-day transition from capitalism to socialism as a scientifically verifiable, and irrefutable 'fact'.[16] Given this premise, 'Marxist' science can indeed rest content with the task of clarifying and registering such 'facts', since this economistic mechanism ignores the very aspect of society which Grünberg earlier designated as the key to history: namely, class-struggle. Thus, while Grünberg's 'Marxism' is not altogether lacking in coherence, neither is his overall position free of internal contradictions. Weil has since maintained[17] that these questionable aspects of the first Director's 'Marxism' were expedients of the Institute's inauguration, ensuring academic recognition for it. Be that as it may, the fact remains that the Institute never fulfilled a conscious agitational role. The conception of the theory-praxis nexus was, under Horkheimer, raised to a far higher, more differentiated level; yet the Frankfurt School's actual productions (with the exception of Marcuse's work since the late 1960s) fell far behind their own conception. Critical social praxis was not a concretised constituent of their 'critical theory of society'.

3 The Institute's work in the 1920s

The work of the Institute under Grünberg's directorship (which in the late 1920s, due to ill-health, was only nominal) shows, first, that Grünberg's empirical interests did play an important role, but also, second, that much of the Institute's work went beyond the Director's theoretical horizon, and worked in the spirit of Weil's earlier memorandum. In 1929, Weil produced another memorandum,[18] this time outlining the Institute's progress so far (and, thus, implicitly outlining the tradition that any new Director would have to satisfy). Six major departments of study were listed: first, historical materialism, and the philosophical basis of Marxism; second, theoretical political economy; third, problems of planned economy; fourth, the position of the proletariat; fifth, sociology; sixth, the history of social doctrines and parties. Most significant of all is the order: in first place stands the question of the relation of scientific socialism to philosophy, a question fundamental to the Frankfurt School's critique of ideology.

The first of the Institute's major publications was Henryk Grossmann's *The Law of Accumulation and Collapse in the Capitalist System*,[19] a good illustration of the high theoretical level that the Institute was capable of. Grossmann (1881–1950) argues that the

Marxian critique of political economy cannot be taken for granted, but is, rather, a highly complex method which itself requires serious consideration if it is to be appropriated and continued. Grossmann stresses that Marx has recourse to the power of abstraction:

> The object of analysis is the concrete, empirically given world of appearances. But this world is too complicated to be grasped directly. We can approach it only by stages. To this end, we make numerous simplifying presuppositions, so as to be able to recognise the object under analysis in its *essential nature*.[20]

But these characteristics, achieved via a process of abstraction and simplification, are not to be taken as the definitive results of the Marxian analysis; rather they are a *stage* in the dialectical presentation of capitalist economy. As the presentation unfolds, each simplification is revised by an ongoing reference to the complexities of socio-economic life; what was neglected is now brought into consideration, and in this way, Grossmann argues, the theory gradually comes to express that reality 'adequately'.[21]

Grossmann's concern over Marx's method is due to the confusion surrounding the law of the falling rate of profit. Grossmann maintains that this confusion is the result precisely of a failure to distinguish the stage-by-stage method of presentation employed by Marx. Thus, Grossmann attempts to reveal not just the law itself, but also, and of necessity, the force of the law: what makes this law into a 'law' in the first place, and how does a 'law' operate? Marx, it may be recalled, outlined 'The Law as such', followed by 'Counteracting Influences', and then revealed the dialectical conflict of all the factors involved; this constitutes his 'Exposition of the Internal Contradictions of the Law'.[22] Marx himself qualifies the 'law' as follows:

> ... the same influences which produce a tendency in the general rate of profit to fall, also call forth counter-effects, which hamper, retard, and partly paralyse this fall. The latter do not do away with the law, but impair its effect. ... Thus, the law acts only as a tendency.[23]

Such is the method of Marx's critique of political economy; Marx called it 'the method of rising from the abstract to the concrete', a method Hegel had employed but idealised, and which, stripped of its idealist distortion, constituted, in Marx's eyes, 'the scientifically correct method'.[24] It is a tribute to Grossmann that he clearly appreciated this procedure at a time when the majority of Marx's explicitly methodological works were still unpublished.

The second major theoretical publication of the Institute was Friedrich Pollock's *Experiments in Economic Planning in the Soviet Union 1917–1927*.[25] The author describes this work as a 'report', to

5

be complemented at a later time by an evaluative commentary on this empirical material.[26] The latter work never materialised, unfortunately, but even this first volume has one outstanding merit: the economic developments in the USSR are not viewed in abstracto, but in conjunction with the socio-economic conditions out of which the proletarian dictatorship arose. Simultaneously, Pollock re-examines the Marxian concept of communism in the light of this concrete historical experience. This puts Pollock's work in a class other than Grünberg's predominantly archival publications, and also marks it off from the later Institute's attitude to the USSR; as will be shown in Chapter 3, Horkheimer's team failed to keep up the explicit relation to socialist praxis which Pollock had attempted in the late 1920s.

The last major undertaking to be completed under Grünberg's directorship was Karl August Wittfogel's *Economy and Society of China*,[27] which was not published until 1931. It is a largely empirical study, a report, in fact, like Pollock's study of the USSR, never complemented by the promised second volume, which was to have analysed superstructural questions, including those of ideology and class-consciousness.[28] However, even here, Wittfogel (born 1896) does touch on superstructural problems, and he has a number of informative historical materialist observations to make. Although he accepts the Marxist doctrine of the ultimate determining force of the economic base, he emphasises the dialectical intricacies of the Marxian perspective. For example, the cultural features of a society are determined not only by the *nature* of the production-process, but also by the length of *time* during which this particular mode of production has operated: this is crucial in explaining the problems of superstructural lag and heterogeneity.[29]

However, Wittfogel has no desire to attempt to formulate an articulate historical materialist psychology, and he thus rests content with pinpointing several clear parallels between the economy and its science. Many of these observations are highly perceptive, for example, the relation between state-power and astronomy;[30] but it can be stated in conclusion that although the work of Grossmann, Pollock and Wittfogel are not simply subsumable under Grünberg's archival, purely empirical concern, the work of the early Institute did not extend to the problem of the significance of depth-psychology for Marxism, a problem which, under Horkheimer, was to become crucial.

4 The 'Grünberg Archive'

Before coming to Frankfurt, Grünberg had already made a considerable name for himself as editor of the *Archive for the History of Socialism and the Labour Movement*,[31] or the *Grünberg Archive*, as it was popularly known. It was, of course, inevitable that the concerns of this major periodical would play a significant role in the work of the Institute, at least while Grünberg was Director. Not surprisingly, the inaugural lecture listed as top priority the study and presentation of the labour movement; and Felix Weil reported in the late 1920s that this concern did indeed play a major part in the Institute's work.[32] A study of the *Grünberg Archive* is thus necessary both to appreciate the tradition of Grünberg's historical research, as well as to establish the continuity or discontinuity between this journal and the later journal of the Institute in its 'Frankfurt School' period.

Grünberg saw his journal as a means to fill a major gap in the social sciences: the history of the labour movement and of socialism. Five main departments of study were built into the journal: first, theoretical problems; second, original or obscure material; third, chronicling the previous year's events and relevant programmes; fourth, book reviews; and, fifth, a full bibliography.[33] The significance of such material was not merely academic, Grünberg stressed, but, in addition, 'practical-political'.[34] However, as in the inaugural lecture, and as in Weil's 1922 memorandum, Grünberg precluded any party-bias, and even went as far as to relinquish any claims to editorial control of an ideological nature[35] (further evidence to substantiate Weil's assertion that he, not Grünberg, had written in the talk of a directoral 'dictatorship' into the inaugural lecture).

As regards Grünberg's own studies, this pluralism was of little account: concerned, as he was, with an archive and chronicle of the labour movement as a whole, theoretical and ideological evaluation played no role. Apart from book reviews (over one hundred bear his name), his work consisted in collecting, sorting, checking, and presenting documents related to the working-class organisations. Grünberg never featured a theoretical work from his own pen; even when he presented the basic juridical document of Soviet Russia, he was not inclined to evaluate the material. Since the authenticity of the document was beyond question, the minimum words served as an adequate introduction. Grünberg does stress that interest in this material should be particularly keen 'at the present time, when in Germany too, the argument is raging over the question: National Assembly or Soviet System?'[36] But there is no suggestion on Grünberg's part that this question should be used by social historians as an agitational weapon in favour of either alternative; rather, the role of the historian is to 'present material for debate'.

The theoretical work of the *Archive*, as in the case of the Institute, went beyond Grünberg's conceptual horizon. In fact, around the time of Grünberg's appointment in Frankfurt, his journal featured one of the most crucial works ever written on the problem that was subsequently, under Horkheimer, to become a burning issue for the

Institute: this was Karl Korsch's *Marxism and Philosophy*.[37] Korsch's work will be discussed at some length below; for the present, it is more important to point out that questions such as the philosophical genesis of Marxism had, from the beginning, assumed a respectable position within the *Archive*. Emil Hammacher, for example, had discussed the important problem of the relation of scientific socialism to Hegelian dialectics (as well as to Kant and Fichte), and done much to reveal the explosive contradictions within Hegel's philosophy, stressing that scientific socialism had abolished philosophy only in the dialectical form of sublation (*Aufhebung*)* in theory and praxis.[38]

However, the vast majority of conclusions drawn on such problems in the journal is highly questionable. Hammacher is a case in point; he concludes by holding up aspects of 'True' Socialism (Hess and Grün) in a favourable light against Marx and Engels, who are criticised for being 'undialectical'.[39] The true relation of historical materialism to the idealist values of philosophy will be discussed in detail in the subsequent chapter; for the moment, it is sufficient to say that Hammacher fails to appreciate the real nature of the sublation involved. Fortunately, the other outstanding theoretician in the *Archive* apart from Korsch, namely Georg Lukács, demolished Hammacher in a short, sharp reply to any attempt to 'correct' the Marxian evaluation of 'True' Socialism. Lukács's article, 'Moses Hess and the Problems of Idealist Dialectics',[40] is essentially a class-based critique of Hess's failure to integrate his ideals and his class-sympathy in a practical-critical theory of emancipation.[41]

As for the explosive contradictions in Hegel's dialectics, Lukács was in complete agreement, although he located and formulated the basic dichotomy far more succinctly; it was the fact that in Hegel's phenomenology 'historical and supra-historical conceptualisation intertwine, intersect, and uproot each other'.[42] In a startling anticipation of Marx's critique of Hegelian dialectics (which was as yet unpublished), Lukács designated as Hegel's greatest achievement:

... that Hegel grasped the objective forms of bourgeois society in their ambivalence, in their contradiction: as moments of a

* 'Sublation' is a makeshift translation, actually used by the Frankfurt School in their English publications, of the dialectical concept of *Aufhebung*. Hegel explicates the concept in the following manner:

That which is sublated, does not thereby become Nothing; Nothing is *unmediated*, whereas something that has been sublated is *mediated*. It is the Non-Being which is the *result* of the action of a Being, and as such it still carries with it the determination of whence it came. Sublation has the double meaning, in German, of preserving, i.e., *retaining*, and causing to cease, i.e., *ending*. ... Thus, that which has been sublated has also been preserved; it has lost its immediacy, but has not thereby been destroyed. (G. W. F. Hegel, 'Wissenschaft der Logik', Erster Teil, in *Werke*, V. Frankfurt: Suhrkamp, 1969, pp. 113–14.)

process in which man (Spirit, in Hegel's mythological terminology) comes to himself through externalisation, to the point where the contradictions in his existence are pushed to their extreme, providing the objective possibility of qualitative change, of a sublation of these contradictions.[43]

This anticipated the subsequent evaluation of Hegel by the Frankfurt School, and is indicative of the heights to which the *Archive* could rise, even under Grünberg's editorship.

But, as with the Institute's work in the 1920s, the *Archive* draws a complete blank on psychology, which was to be raised to a place of honour in Horkheimer's subsequent publications. That some sort of gap existed in historical materialism's explanation of consciousness, was admitted by the later Engels; interestingly enough, Korsch's *Marxism and Philosophy* quotes Engels's statement to this effect:

> We all laid, and were bound to lay, the main emphasis on the fact that political, juridical and other ideological notions *are derived* from basic economic facts and that this also applied to actions mediated through these notions. We stressed the content and neglected the form, i.e. the ways and means by which these notions came about.[44]

Korsch was in no position to provide an adequate historical materialist psychology; indeed, his concern was not with psychology in the sense of the Frankfurt School's later work. But his differentiated study of the complex phenomenon of ideology meant that he steered clear of any idealist make-shifts, whereas lesser theoreticians like Hammacher, who failed to appreciate the historical materialist sublation of 'values', slipped into a psychological idealism, appending a number of 'humanist' categories to an otherwise 'deficient' Marxism. However, in conclusion, despite outstanding theoreticians like Korsch and Lukács, the *Archive*, like the early Institute, saw no need to consider the significance of Freudian depth-psychology. The change came with Horkheimer's appointment in 1930.

5 Horkheimer's appointment as Director of the Institute

From 1927, Grünberg made no contributions to his *Archive*, and was inactive as regards the Institute. By 1929, Pollock was effectively directing the latter,[45] but a full-time Director had to be appointed, in conjunction with a professorship at the University. This posed problems; Grünberg had been acceptable to Weil because, despite his somewhat narrow conception of Marxism, Grünberg had been willing to leave Weil and similarly minded scholars to pursue more far-reaching theoretical tasks. A replacement of equal tolerance would be hard to find, and what made things worse was that Grün-berg's Chair had been in Economics and Social Science, where the ideological tradition was far removed indeed from Weil's conception of the Institute's task. After heated, often unpleasant exchanges be-tween the Minister of Culture, the Faculty, and the University Senate, on the one hand, and Felix Weil, on the other, during which the Weils implicitly threatened to cut off the grant unless their 'rights' (that is, Felix's) were recognised, agreement was finally reached on Max Horkheimer, an old colleague and friend of Weil.

Horkheimer had successfully submitted a professorial dissertation in 1926, and thus could satisfy the statutes regarding the Institute's Directorship. The impasse vis-à-vis the faculty was resolved by transferring the Director's Chair to Philosophy, Horkheimer be-coming the first Professor of Philosophy and Social Philosophy.[46] It should, therefore, be remembered, when trying to label Horkheimer's subsequent work, that the term 'Social Philosophy' did not con-stitute a new self-understanding by the Institute, but, rather, was an expedient devised in order to get as Director a man sympathetic to Weil's original plans for his Institute.

Horkheimer's inaugural lecture bore an obvious title: 'The Present State of Social Philosophy and the Tasks of an Institute for Social Research'.[47] It outlined the general conception of social philosophy as 'the philosophical interpretation of men's fates in as far as these men are not just individuals, but members of a community'. The object of this discipline was nothing less than 'the entire material and spiritual culture of mankind as a whole'.[48] A polemical note is soon struck; Horkheimer attacks the transfigurative function of this philosophical 'interpretation', and he exemplifies this with the case of Hegel: in the face of the assurance that man's 'essential being, the Idea' reigns supreme in world history, the fate of the individual (and, in fact, the fundamental constituents of material culture) appear to be 'devoid of philosophical significance'.[49] Social philosophy, while claiming to analyse *social* reality, reserves all the 'reality' for its philosophical component. In the context of glaring contradictions between man's supposed 'substance' (which is 'freedom') and his social reality (alienation, unemployment, conscription), the philo-sophical transfiguration of social being is an accomplice in class-domination.

Horkheimer, who, as will be seen, is no friend of positivism, none the less attacks the self-satisfied manner in which social philosophy deals with the individual sciences. They become 'sublated' (in a purely idealist process) into a conceptual whole, over which philo-sophy rules imperiously, pronouncing the 'ultimate truth' on the findings of the various branches of enquiry.[50] Thus, the term 'social philosophy' does not indicate philosophy's relinquishing of its self-appointed hegemony, but, on the contrary, involves a defence and reinforcement of that hegemony. As for the material aspects of this social 'reality', nothing changes.

Horkheimer counterposes to this picture a dialectical conception of the relation between philosophy and the individual sciences:

> The chaotic specialisation of knowledge is not overcome by undertaking poor syntheses of specialist research-findings; nor is an impartial empiricism to be achieved by trying to eradicate the theoretical element. Rather, the problems of empirical research and theoretical synthesis can only be achieved by a philosophy which, concerned with the general, the 'essential,' provides the respective research-areas with stimulating impulses, while itself remaining open enough to be impressed and modified by the progress of concrete studies.[51]

In short, collaborative work should be organised 'on the basis of topical philosophical problems'.[52]

The use of the term 'philosophical' may cause grave concern to many historical materialists, but one has to remember the occasion of the lecture, as well as the title of Horkheimer's Chair. As regards concrete programmes of study, the new Director strikes a new note altogether; the focal point of the Institute's first major enterprise will be the following question:

> What connections can be established, in a specific social group, in a specific period of time, in specific countries, between the economic role of this group, the changes in the psychic structure of its individual members, and the thoughts and institutions that are a product of that society, and that have, as a whole, a formative effect upon the group under consideration?[53]

The appropriate method of analysis is neither 'vulgar-Hegelian' ('the basis of the world and of history is Spirit'), nor 'vulgar-Marxist' ('the human psyche, personality, as well as law, art, and philosophy are the mere mirror-image of the economy'), but one that grasps the dialectical interaction of material reality and mental reality. The 'complicating role of psychic connecting links' is not to be explained away, but laid bare.[54]

Horkheimer emphasises that the study of the economic base is a sine qua non for an adequate depiction of social reality.[55] But he does not regard this study as particularly problematical: he seems to view this part of the programme as self-evident. What really emerges as a consciously problematical departure is the interest in psychology and philosophy. As to the former, the need for an adequate psychological component in social theory is stressed heavily, and with an awareness that next to nothing has been done in this field so far; the actual articulation of the psychological categories is left for the Institute's future work. But the concern with philosophy, as a non-mystificatory component in the evolution of a social theory, is discussed at length by Horkheimer. This reveals the new Director's major interest, but also creates massive problems.

Grünberg's assertion that Marxism was not a philosophy or metaphysic, was a simple, but correct assertion, particularly in the face of philosophical bastardisations of historical materialism. Of course, Marxism was derived in part (but only in part!) from Hegelian dialectics, but to speak in the twentieth century of organising studies, be they ever so stimulating, 'on the basis of topical philosophical problems', is dubious. Even allowing for Horkheimer's tactical manoeuvrings, one is struck by the fact that he does develop his argument via a dialogue with philosophical categories. This is more than an expedient; it reveals a great deal about Horkheimer's future development. Although he outlines a historical materialist project for his Institute, and although the term 'social philosophy' gives way to the more concrete 'science of society',[56] philosophy becomes a crucial object of study within this social theory.

This role of philosophy, which is to be an *object* of study rather than the method of study, is best illustrated by a look at Horkheimer's 1930 publication, *Origins of the Bourgeois Philosophy of History*.[57] The author describes this book as 'a collection of studies written down for the purpose of self-clarification'. Horkheimer believes that the current reflection upon history (and this reflection is itself a historical phenomenon) can learn something 'of practical value' by looking at some major exponents of the philosophy of history, a philosophy which to this day provides many significant elements of a method for grasping society.[58] Horkheimer is not concerned to 'revitalise' philosophy qua philosophy; rather he is convinced that a reflection upon philosophy will reveal not only the latter's historically determined distortions of reality, but also, and thereby, a great deal about that reality, particularly in its mental representation. These studies, which are a prototype of Horkheimer's essays in the 1930s, thematise what was to become the Frankfurt School's first concern: ideology-critique. Despite the humble respect paid to his predecessor, Horkheimer had radically new plans for the Institute.

The transition is totally distorted in Paul Kluke's account of the Institute's history. Kluke remarks on the new Director's intimate debate with philosophy, as well as upon Horkheimer's failure to repeat his predecessor's confession of (Marxist) faith. But Kluke implies that Horkheimer is thus not a Marxist: not only does Kluke show a total unacquaintance with Marx's early polemical writings, but he actually proceeds to reduce historical materialism to a crude (and thus clearly untenable) economic determinism:

> Even where Horkheimer ... considered the significance of economic conditions for social development as a whole, he did not, as his predecessor had done, make an a priori declaration in favour of historical materialism, but argued for a reciprocal influence of economic and psychic structures.[59]

As 'proof', Kluke quotes precisely that 'focal point', outlined by Horkheimer, which implicitly declares the Institute's intention not to relinquish the historical materialist method but to implement it and further articulate it in the sense of Engels's later writings. Horkheimer's concern with philosophy and psychology certainly constitutes a departure from Grünberg's work and from Grünberg's 'Marxism', but Horkheimer conceived of his new tasks as urgent needs of historical materialism itself. How far he and his team were *successful* in their adventure can only be assessed by a serious analysis of their subsequent development, but there can be no doubt about their conviction that Marxism was the only method adequate to the purpose of analysing society.

But one striking similarity can be observed between Grünberg and Horkheimer: despite their different interpretations of the 'Marxist' method, both Directors conceive of the Institute's work as academic in an orthodox sense. Grünberg's assurance to this effect may have been inserted by Weil, but it was by no means alien to the Director's own position, as a brief look at his editorial preface to the *Archive* shows. Horkheimer's position is no different: he is concerned to overcome the unsatisfactory split between the empirical sciences and social philosophy, but he does not indicate that the Institute's work should be directed to formulating a practical-critical theory of social change. Of course, it is possible that Horkheimer, who at that time was a relatively unknown figure, was making concessions to his audience. But the problems thrown up by his inaugural lecture are very serious ones, and will have to be followed through systematically in assessing the Frankfurt School's first great period of intellectual production.

6 The Institute's work under Horkheimer

The first major work published under the new Director was Franz Borkenau's *The Transition from the Feudal to the Bourgeois World View*.[60] Borkenau (1900–57), who had been a minor contributor to the *Archive*, had been working on this book for some years under the auspices of the Institute. It was thus not indicative of the new Director's interests. But in an editorial preface, Horkheimer pointed out that Borkenau's work was related to the new concerns of the Institute, in that this study of the bourgeoisie's revolutionary natural science dealt with 'the fundamental problem of the relation between economy and intellectual culture'. This, said Horkheimer, was 'a problem, the treatment of which is also of particular interest for the Institute's own research.'[61]

None the less, the real physiognomy of the new Institute was revealed far more clearly in the next major publication, the *Studies in Authority and Family*,[62] conceived, planned, and produced under Horkheimer's direction. This work is obviously the product of the 'focal point' outlined in his inaugural lecture, and Horkheimer confirms that the analysis of the 'relation between the various areas of material and mental culture' has assumed an important role in the Institute's work.[63] And the 'psychic connecting links' appear in the form of the 'masking of authority'; this, and not the discrepancy between bourgeois ideology and proletarian reality, is the real concern of the *Studies*.[64]

But the primary medium for the new Institute was its periodical, the *Zeitschrift für Sozialforschung*.[65] Serious analysis of the *Zeitschrift* is left until later (as is discussion of the *Studies in Authority and Family*), but the continuity and/or discontinuity between this journal and the *Archive* should be established now. A prospectus for the new journal announced it as a 'sequel' to the *Grünberg Archive*, but added that 'compared with Grünberg's Archive, the subject-matter has been considerably broadened'.[66] As regards the continuity (largely formal), the publishing house remained Hirschfeld until Nazi rule put an end to this privilege, and the format was much the same as in its predecessor; the journal divided up into theoretical essays and book reviews. But Grünberg's archival and chronicling work (which had, in any case, been progressively neglected as Grünberg's health deteriorated) were dropped. But the *Zeitschrift* was a new departure in a much deeper sense too. In fact, the very title, *Journal of Social Research*, emphasised the broader scope, which was closer to Weil's original conception than to Grünberg's.

Even more significant, perhaps, is that Horkheimer chooses this title in preference to *Journal of Social Philosophy*. The editorial preface to the first issue reaffirms the inaugural lecture's outline of the central problem as 'the relationship between the individual cultural spheres, their interdependence, and the laws governing their change'. And the general move to a more concrete designation is reflected in Horkheimer's gradual evolution of a new label for his work; the term that emerges is 'theory of society'.[67] It is only a small step to 'critical theory of society', which was to be the most articulate expression of the Institute's method, and which was to make a major contribution to the historical materialist analysis of society.

But at this stage, Horkheimer's conception of the theory-praxis nexus remains inarticulate. Like Grünberg, he sees the Institute's work as 'of interest', but not as a practical, political class-weapon. True, Horkheimer does say: 'But, no matter how far history enters as a constituent into all theory, nonetheless, the findings of research must stand up to theoretical criteria if those findings are to prove themselves in society'.[68] But this 'proving themselves' (*Bewährung*) remains undifferentiated; there is no distinction between what Horkheimer was later to term the 'traditional' and 'critical' positions (see Chapter 2), and there is no reference to the living agents of social change. Instead, the reproduction and revolution of social reality is to be 'grasped', and although Horkheimer promises to keep up the 'reference to current problems', and to undertake 'enquiries into the future direction of historical development',[69] the interpenetration of theory and praxis appears, at this stage, as a one-way process. The future may not be a given quantity, but theory is not viewed as an agitational weapon in deciding how the contradictory constitution of the present will be decided.

This conception of the role of theory for Horkheimer's team was subsequently radicalised, and the relation to class-struggle became, for the Institute, a methodological imperative. Thus, before tracing the development of Frankfurt School theory, it is essential to provide a rudimentary picture of the socio-economic and political development of the Germany out of which this theory arose, and into which it was to penetrate as a practical-critical weapon. An outline of this period will, simultaneously, enable a more concrete presentation of the Frankfurt School's own economic and political interpretation of the constellation in which its theory operated.

Section Two: the Weimar Republic and the rise of fascism

The radicalisation of Horkheimer's conception of the social function of his theory is, in essence, a materialist articulation of the theory-praxis nexus. In 1935, Horkheimer asserted (and acknowledged) that the value of theory 'depends on its relation to praxis'.[70] The socio-political consequence of this relation was that an adequate social theory had to be linked to the existing revolutionary forces within society; in 1934, Horkheimer wrote: 'the value of a theory is determined by its relation to the tasks taken up, at the given moment in history, by the most progressive social forces.'[71] The full dialectical implications of the theory-praxis nexus in, and for, the Frankfurt School, are discussed in the following chapter. But, even now, it is

15

clear that an understanding, let alone a metacritique, of the Institute's work in the 1930s is impossible without an acquaintance with the 'tasks' and 'progressive social forces' of that period.

These questions in turn presuppose a knowledge of the economic development; Horkheimer stated categorically, in the first volume of the *Zeitschrift*: 'if history divides up according to the different forms in which the life-process of human society is carried out, then the basic historical categories are not psychological, but economic.'[72] The presentation of the economic development of Germany was left to Pollock, while the major figures of the Institute concentrated on superstructural analyses. But at the back of all these analyses is the critical intellectual's omnipresent awareness of the descent of Germany into barbarism. The clearest expression, in the period under consideration, of this development is provided in Marcuse's *Reason and Revolution*,[73] published in 1941 and dedicated to Horkheimer and the Institute; Marcuse writes:

> The roots of Fascism are traceable to the antagonisms between growing industrial monopolisation and the democratic system. In Europe after the first World War, the highly rationalised and rapidly expanding industrial apparatus met increasing difficulties of utilisation, especially because of the disruption of the world market and because of the vast network of social legislation ardently defended by the labour movement. . . . The emerging political system cannot develop the productive forces without a constant pressure on the satisfaction of human needs. This requires a totalitarian control over all social and individual relations, the abolition of social and individual liberties, and the incorporation of the masses by means of terror.[74]

Without a brief sketch of monopoly capitalism and of the class-struggle that resulted in fascism in Germany, one cannot understand the socio-political experience against which Frankfurt School theory was an uninterrupted, if often implicit, protest.

1 Monopoly capitalism

'Monopoly', in the sense of monopoly capitalism, designates a stage of capitalism where, even given a number of large corporations operating within the same market, a monopoly operates, in as far as prices are fixed (jointly, by the corporations), and price-war is seriously curbed. A monopoly is exercised by the corporations, in unison, and prices show a manipulated, steadily upward trend. The Frankfurt School entertain no illusions on this score; they refer constantly to 'post-competitive capitalism',[75] and 'the tendency of

16

present economy to eliminate the market and the dynamics of competition'.[76] The systematic analysis of this phenomenon, however, was delegated to Pollock.

Pollock explains the genesis of monopoly in terms of the production process: economic concentration and the rising organic composition of capital (that is, rising overheads) made uninterrupted production a *need* of capitalism itself.[77] This is what Horkheimer and Adorno mean by their cryptic reference to 'dictatorship of production';[78] it is not just a reiteration of the basic historical materialist thesis, but focuses on the capitalist societation of production and the latter's totalitarian power. As Marcuse wrote, years later:

'Consumer society' is a misnomer of the first order, for rarely has a society so systematically been organised in the interests which control *production*. The consumer society is the form in which monopoly state capitalism reproduces itself at its most advanced stage.[79]

While it is true that the Frankfurt School never elaborated a systematic theory of manipulation in *production* (and this gap had serious consequences for their superstructural analysis of the dialectics of manipulation and liberation), there is no denying their explicitly anti-capitalist motivation, which was informed by no mean understanding of many of monopoly capitalism's mechanisms. And Marcuse's outline, in *Reason and Revolution*, of the economic development in Germany, is absolutely correct to locate the consolidation of monopolism in the years following the First World War. It was here, in the Weimar Republic, that, to use Horkheimer's terms, the 'most progressive social forces' took up the 'task' of smashing capitalism; and it was as a result of their failure that fascism seized power.

2 The Weimar Republic and the German working class

For the Marxist, capitalism's own development is the objective key to its own revolutionary overthrow. Marx wrote:

Along with the constantly diminishing number of the magnates of capital ... grows the mass of misery, oppression, slavery, degradation, exploitation; but with this too grows the revolt of the working-class, a class always increasing in numbers, and disciplined, united, organised by the very mechanism of the process of capitalist production itself.[80]

Horkheimer, looking back, in the 1960s, to the Frankfurt School's formative years, clearly subscribes to the Marxian interpretation of crisis and immiseration: 'In the first half of the century, proletarian uprising was a plausible expectation in the European countries, passing as they were through crisis and inflation.'[81] This assessment requires serious consideration, if the theory-praxis nexus is to be thematised with regard to the Frankfurt School's first period of production.

In the economic chaos that followed the First World War, the establishment of the Weimar Republic, and the imperialist Treaty of Versailles, vast capitals were accumulated in Germany. Debts were paid off with worthless currency, and large enterprises bought out smaller ones at ridiculously low prices. Thus, the growth of monopoly advanced in leaps and bounds. But actual operating capital was lacking, as was any guarantee of the Republic's capitalist base. The necessary capital to stabilise this Republic came from America, which viewed the defeated Germany, with its high production capacity, as a lucrative investment. The Dawes Plan of August 1924 was followed by the massive Dawes Loan, and numerous individual loans.[82] Mass-production on a monopoly base was taken up in earnest.

Germany was to recover economically, so as to be able to pay out, along with fantastic reparations, a further slice of its national wealth, in the form of interest, to the Americans. The profits that German monopoly capitalism had to generate were thus phenomenal, as were the concomitant burdens to be shouldered by the country's working class. An examination of these burdens will give a concrete picture of the revolutionary potential of Weimar Germany, and show just how far Horkheimer's talk of 'proletarian uprising' as a 'plausible expectation' is justifiable.

The experience of the German workers can be reduced, basically, to the phenomenon of 'rationalisation'. This meant the transfer of American production techniques to the German factory, along with a staggering rise in the intensity of labour.[83] A parallel, and tell-tale rise is to be found in the accident-rate: fatal accidents increased relatively to the number of workers employed, and non-fatal accidents increased absolutely.[84] And official statistics of health show a marked deterioration in the general standard of health,[85] partly due to the increased intensity of labour, and partly due to the low level of the wages paid to the labourer.

Wages did rise nominally between 1924 and 1930, but this is misleading: first, the rate of rise soon dropped, and second, the rise was never sufficient to reach the recognised subsistence-minimum, let alone pass it.[86] And deductions from the wage-packet in the form of taxes and insurance rose, between 1914 and 1927, by 200 per cent, only to reach 300 per cent by 1932.[87] Needless to say, this drop in real wages led to an increase in the *extensity* of labour; while the

Social Democrats defended the principle of the eight-hour day, over-time or a second job became a need of every worker.

But rationalisation meant hard work for a *reduced* number of workers; for the rest, it meant unemployment, which from 1924 to 1932 was higher than pre-war years. And hand in hand with this high unemployment went short time, which in the second half of the 1920s accounted for one-tenth of workers employed.[88] The economic crash, of course, meant mass unemployment and short time well beyond any 'norm'. And, as Pollock reported in the *Zeitschrift*, 1930 saw the beginning of sharp absolute drops in wage-levels.[89] Thus, as regards the production sphere, immiseration was a steady but ex-plosive fact of working-class existence in the Weimar Republic.

Of course, burdens of this nature can be eased by social welfare, but this was not the case in Weimar Germany. Not until 1927 was any serious attempt made to provide unemployment benefit; in fact, the government never really established the extent of unemployment; whether or not it appreciated the extent of short time is less im-portant, since people on short time were not eligible for benefit any-way. The fund set up was inadequate to the needs of the totally unemployed; it provided for three-quarters of a million, with an 'emergency' fund for a further 400,000. Clearly, the provisions were inadequate to an economy whose most favourable unemployment figure was well over a million, and which by the late 1920s was approaching 3 million.[90] Successive governments either made token concessions to the masses (taxing luxury items), or else, as under Brüning, actually cut expenditure in the public sector (at a time of widespread social hardship), leaving industry intact and even pump-ing in government aid, convinced that Germany's problems could only be solved off the backs of the labour-force.[91] In reality, the 'solution' only came with Hitler and the Nazi reign of terror.

3 Fascism and capitalism

Hitler's 'solution' to the economic débâcle of Weimar Germany raises the question as to the relation of fascism to capitalism. The Frankfurt School have no doubts; Horkheimer wrote in 1938: 'Fascism is not opposed to bourgeois society, but, under certain historical conditions, the latter's appropriate form'.[92] Thus, a year later, Horkheimer asserted that 'he who does not wish to speak of capitalism, should also be silent on fascism'.[93] Fascism can only be understood in terms of the class-struggle within the respective countries: 'The alliance between the bourgeoisie and the fascist organisations arises from fear of the proletariat.'[94] Once again, the economic articulation of this deep conviction was left to Pollock.

Pollock referred the specific phenomenon of fascism to the general phenomenon of monopoly capitalism and state monopoly capitalism. In the first issue of the *Zeitschrift* he wrote:

> Today, a large number of industrial enterprises and banking concerns have grown so enormously that no state, no matter how laissez-faire it pretends to be, can sit back idly and watch one of them collapse. Beyond a certain level of capital accumulation, the respective enterprises and concerns may continue to claim the profit unilaterally, but they can pass on the risk to the mass of tax-payers, since the collapse of one such giant would have the most disastrous consquences for the entire economic, and thus also political sphere.[95]

This is the economic rationale behind the growing interference of the state in the economy, as well as of the growing interference of the monopolies in the state.[96] This, Pollock stresses, is no fascist 'aberration', but inherent in the present stage of capitalism.

But Pollock is concerned not just to emphasise the capitalist base of fascism; he wants to *analyse* fascism, not just denounce it, and he thus tries to lay bare the peculiar nature of fascist economy. A key aspect is the role of the profit-rationale; while fully aware of the continuing significance of the profit-motive, Pollock evolves a concept of state monopoly capitalism, in which the nature of economic command surpasses the concept (Pollock's) of simple monopoly capitalism:

> The monopolistic organisations no longer operate as disturbing intruders but take over the market functions as government agents. What formerly were more or less voluntary supra-entrepreneurial organisations have become compulsory and comprehensive. Instead of each specific group fighting for maximum profits at the expense of more and more frequent interruptions of production, they collectively assume the responsibility of coordinating the whole economic process and thereby of maintaining the existing social structure.[97]

Pollock does differentiate 'democratic' and 'totalitarian' forms of state monopoly capitalism, at least as ideal-types, but he constructs his concept of state monopoly capitalism from an analysis of its 'totalitarian' form as exemplified in Nazi Germany. This is because Pollock is not sure that anything but a 'totalitarian' form is possible.[98]

But Pollock's theory of fascism did not go unchallenged within the Institute; Franz Neumann's *Behemoth*[99] was an attack on the entire notion of state monopoly capitalism, which was seen as a tendential denial of fascism's capitalist economic base. Neumann (1900–54) was concerned to emphasise the continuation of the antagonisms of capitalist production, and, making use of the economic theory of the Social Democrat Rudolf Hilferding, attacked the concept of 'state monopoly capitalism' as a contradictio in adiecto: if the state were to own all the means of production, Neumann argued, then there cannot be any talk of capitalism.[100] In fact, of course, Pollock had never implied that state monopoly capitalism referred to any monopoly *ownership* by the state of the means of production. But Neumann's mind was made up: Pollock's theory of 'state monopoly capitalism' was an example of the progressive denial of the Third Reich's capitalist nature.[101]

The major figures of the Institute tended to side with Pollock. Weil, in a letter of 15 August 1942 to Karl Korsch,[102] criticised Neumann for his tendentious argument and his 'stubborn determination to ignore the *new* order'. Neumann's forced argumentation lands him in contradictions; while refusing to look at what aspects of fascist capitalism *were* new, his findings did suggest, none the less, that Pollock's thesis was right. Weil further complained about Neumann's 'vanity', which 'prevented him from consulting his colleagues at the Institute'. All in all, Weil concluded, 'we' (presumably the Institute as a whole) are 'glad that his book did not appear as an Institute publication'.

Marcuse too seems to have sided, implicitly, with Pollock; in his last contribution to the *Zeitschrift*, he wrote: 'The Third Reich is indeed a form of "technocracy": the technical considerations of imperialistic efficiency and rationality supersede the traditional standards of profitability and general welfare'.[103] This was in no way a denial of fascism's capitalist base; it was merely an attempt to understand the peculiar physiognomy of this base. Indeed, the most frightening thing about Pollock's theory was the very fact that fascism was explained in terms of a general trend in capitalism:

> Under a totalitarian form of state capitalism the state is the power instrument of a new ruling group, which has resulted from the merger of the most powerful vested interests, the top ranking personnel in industrial and business management, the higher strata of the state bureaucracy (including the military) and the leading figures of the victorious party's bureaucracy. Everybody who does not belong to this group is a mere object of domination.[104]

This being the case, one can assume that Hitler's Germany, far from 'solving' the problems of the Weimar economy, merely increased the burden on the working class. This was indeed the case.

4 The Third Reich and the German working class

Although unemployment faded with astounding speed, the new-found work had little attraction. Its intensity, as well as extensity, rose sharply,[105] and the accident-rate increased by 200 per cent in only five years.[106] In addition, the mass of wage-deductions (largely for the war-machine) soared,[107] production for personal consumption dropped,[108] and a progressive rationing and debasement of food and clothing set in.[109] This sad state of affairs was only surpassed by the cynicism of the Nazi ideology; as Marcuse reported: 'Today, when all the technical potentialities for an abundant life are at hand, the National Socialists "consider the decline of the standard of living inevitable" and indulge in panegyrics on impoverishment'.[110] And, of course, this economic impoverishment presupposed a political impoverishment: the smashing of the German labour movement.

Having rounded up all active communists, Social Democrats, and militant trade unionists, repressive labour laws were progressively enacted for the purpose of immobilising working-class organisation as a whole and reconstructing the terrorised workers around the needs of the war-machine. The agricultural labourers were prevented from migrating to the towns, and subsequently, the authorities began expelling numbers of white-collar and factory workers who had come to the urban areas during the last generation. And in 1935, systematic labour conscription was begun,[111] a development made even more oppressive by the cancellation, in 1936, of all holidays.[112]

And, lastly, the imperialist intentions of the Nazis, and of their sponsors in heavy industry, meant, ultimately, yet another form of impoverishment: death by war. The armaments industry meant not only slave-labour and the squandering of potential plenty; it meant that the terrorised workers were producing the weapons for their own destruction. Thus, the Nazi 'solution' to the problems of the German economy brought the working masses less than nothing. As Horkheimer wrote in 1939: 'The work columns designated to the armaments industry, to the construction of newer and newer highways, to building underground railways and community houses stand to gain little from the mobilisation, except a mass grave'.[113] Immiseration in its Nazi form went to its extreme conclusion as millions of soldiers and civilians died. And Horkheimer's 'mass grave' was given an ironic twist by the mass extermination of the Jewish people, from whom Marcuse, Adorno, Fromm, and Horkheimer himself were descended.

5 The problem of manipulation

The history of Nazi Germany proves that immiseration, even in its most extreme form, does not trigger off automatically a revolutionary upsurge. The Frankfurt School, in exile, could not help but be impressed by the strength of the Nazi rule of terror. Whereas Neumann saw this rule as the 'Behemoth', Pollock, whilst admitting the legitimacy of the question as to whether there was a Nazi 'state', stressed that this regime could hold together; despite internal rivalries, common interests bound the sections of the ruling class together. And it was wrong to expect Nazi Germany to collapse internally as a result of economic contradictions.[114]

Horkheimer supported Pollock's repudiation of the 'wishful idea' of fascism's inevitable economic collapse; the Director was convinced that 'such a society can endure for a long and terrifying period'.[115] As for the prospects of revolutionary class-struggle, proletarian uprising might be a 'plausible expectation', but Horkheimer had no faith in any potential for centralised political leadership. To Horkheimer, it was 'totally naive for the outsider to exhort the German workers to rise up'. The regime of terror was far too efficient; that had to be recognised, and anybody who could 'only play at politics, should abstain from it'.[116]

The Frankfurt School's theory of political organisation is discussed in Chapter 3. For the moment, it is necessary to see how the history of Germany thematised for the Institute a specific problem: manipulation. The whole tenor of Frankfurt School theory (at least up to Marcuse's radicalisation in the late 1960s) is that as they write, revolutionary prospects increasingly recede. This feeling is summed up in Horkheimer's contribution to the *Studies*, where we read that revolutionary moments are 'rare and short', and that:

the obsolete social order is quickly patched up (seemingly renewed); the periods of restoration last long, and in them the antiquated cultural apparatus, in the form of the mental state of society's members as well as the network of concrete institutions, gains new force. What is needed now is the exact and systematic analysis of this apparatus.[117]

This analysis, as stated previously, was largely superstructural. The psychological and 'aesthetic' components are discussed below (see Chapters 4 and 5 respectively); but despite the weaknesses of the Frankfurt School's theory of manipulation, it is vital to understand that the concern with this problem was conceived not as an 'appendage' to historical materialism, but as the most pressing question facing the historical materialist in the given socio-political context.

Of course, the first question to be answered was: how could the Nazis, even before the reign of terror, enjoy such popular support? Horkheimer implicitly indicated his answer when, in his inaugural lecture, he focused the Institute's attention on the labour aristocracy and the white-collar workers.[118] And in this regard, Horkheimer's team could draw on the pioneering work of two outstanding figures: Siegfried Kracauer and Wilhelm Reich. If the latter was more important for the evolution of the scientific categories, the former provided what was indubitably the first serious study of the modern white-collar workers, *The Clerks*.[119]

This was more than an account of the effects of the inflation upon small savings; it was a study of a social group whose 'proletarianisation' had taken place on the basis of *stabilisation* and expansion. The white-collar component in industrial production had more than doubled between the late nineteenth century and the late 1920s.[120] Germany now had $3\frac{1}{2}$ million clerical workers (including more than a million women), and over one-third of these were employed in industry.[121] The reasons are obvious: larger scale of production; expansion of the distribution apparatus; increased accounting for a growing volume and speed of circulation. But the qualitative change in the clerical work was equally outstanding; and once again, rationalisation was at the root of it:

> This rationalisation has meant the penetration of the machine and of 'conveyor-belt' methods into the clerical offices of the large companies. Thanks to this transformation (modelled on America, and far from complete), large sections of today's white-collar masses are assigned functions in the labour-process which are vastly reduced vis-a-vis earlier. . . . The 'N.C.O.s of capital' have become a state army numbering more and more interchangeable 'privates.'[122]

Proletarianised clerical work means interchangeability of semi-robotic mental labourers, and, in addition, exposure to all the vicissitudes of the labour-market. And wages are actually inferior to those of the blue-collar workers.

But why did these clerks not join the working-class parties, SPD or KPD? Why did their vote, a massive vote, go increasingly to the fascists? Why do Kracauer's interviews reveal that for the clerks, the differences among themselves were as nothing compared with the gulf separating them ('thank God!') from the proletariat.[123] Kracauer attempts to explain this sentiment in terms of an ideology which, though undermined in economic substance, lives on in the minds of the clerks; they are 'spiritually homeless' objectively,[124] but their former home lives on in their heads.

Kracauer outlines the hierarchical structure of the clerical labour-force and explains that almost all of these workers have some opportunity to play the 'little master' in some capacity, aping the entrepreneur's 'master-in-my-house' attitude. A superb metaphor is coined to express this: 'Under conditions analagous to military discipline, it is at least to be expected that a cycling mentality will develop. "Cyclist" is a common nickname for certain military ranks—with their backs they stoop; with their feet they tread hard'.[125] The psychological component of this analysis is made explicit by Kracauer's talk of this

hierarchy providing a 'gratification of their instincts'.[126] In the subsequent work of the Frankfurt School, this theory was used to explain
the psychological mechanisms of authoritarianism generally.

But in this latter undertaking, too, the Frankfurt School had a
forerunner: Wilhelm Reich. Looking back at the collapse of Weimar
Germany, and of liberal democracy, as well as at his own very bitter
experiences with the Stalinists, he wrote:

> It is, of course, necessary to expose the objective function of
> Social Democracy and of fascism. But experience teaches that
> this exposure, though repeated a thousand times over, did not
> convince the masses, which proves that the socio-economic
> perspective alone is not enough. Surely, the question emerges
> as to *what goes on in the masses* which makes them unable, or
> unwilling, to recognise this function of Social Democracy and
> fascism?[127]

Reich clearly overestimates the attraction fascism held for the workers,
but as far as the psychological categories of an ever-developing
historical materialism are concerned, his work unquestionably leads
into that of the Frankfurt School. It remains to be seen whether
Horkheimer's team, too, let their psychological theory blur the
reality of the Weimar Republic's class-struggles. It also remains to
be seen whether this theory of manipulation succeeded in satisfying
the demands made in Horkheimer's most radical conception of the
theory-praxis nexus. Above all, it is necessary to provide a more
detailed account of the class-struggles of Weimar Germany, as well
as of the precise manipulative nature of the modern production process, and to lay bare the distortions in Frankfurt School theory
which result from their inadequate attention to these questions.
These critical reflections are systematically presented in the con-
cluding three chapters, particularly Chapter 3. But before that, it is
necessary to introduce in adequate detail the Frankfurt School's
overall frame of theoretical reference: 'critical theory of society'.

2 'Critical theory of society': the historical materialist critique of ideology

The label of 'Frankfurt School' is a loose term, applied ex post facto. The label evolved by Horkheimer's team themselves was 'critical theory of society'. The nature of this theory was presented most clearly in a 1937 essay by Horkheimer, entitled 'Traditional and Critical Theory',[1] supplemented in the same year by a joint article by Horkheimer and Marcuse, entitled 'Philosophy and Critical Theory'.[2] This lengthy discussion reflects the significant role of the term 'critical theory', which featured heavily in subsequent essays in the *Zeitschrift*, and in Marcuse's work to this very day. In 1938, Marcuse explained 'critical theory' as 'the theory of society as presented in the expository essays of the *Zeitschrift für Sozialforschung* on the basis of dialectical philosophy and the critique of political economy'.[3] And when Horkheimer's essays were reprinted in the 1960s, the former Director of the Institute let them appear under the collective title of *Critical Theory*, explaining, in the preface, the significance of his work in terms precisely of 'critical theory of society'.[4]

In what will henceforth be referred to as the Frankfurt School's 'manifesto', Horkheimer explains that the word 'critical' is here intended 'not so much in the sense of the idealist critique of pure reason, as in the sense of the dialectical critique of political economy'.[5] The formulation is precise: the Kantian sense of 'critical' *does* play a role, but one subordinate to the Marxian meaning of the word. The convergence between the two is related by Horkheimer, in the sequel to this essay: 'critical theory of society' regards men as the producers of their cultural totality, and thus of their ideational artifacts: 'The attempt to relate the material of seemingly irreducible truths ... to human production is a point on which critical theory of society is in agreement with German Idealism'.[6] As will be demonstrated, the Frankfurt School saw one of its major tasks in the systematic presentation of those components of German Idealism

26

which had been preserved and materialised, or sublated, in 'critical theory of society'.

1 The 'manifesto' of 1937

The essay 'Traditional and Critical Theory' introduces the role of theory as the medium through which the findings of the various scientific branches are gradually united, by being referred to common principles. The specific form that this takes in 'traditional theory' on the one hand, and 'critical theory' on the other, is vastly different; and the difference transcends the sphere of theory itself. Basically, an ideological conflict is involved. Horkheimer wishes, however, not merely to take sides, but to reveal this conflict in detail.

In 'traditional theory', Horkheimer proceeds, the basic demand is that 'all constituent parts are linked up, in a thorough-going frame of reference, and free of contradiction'.[7] This attempt to achieve harmony via a purely intellectual labour reflects an uncritical attitude to the material production-process out of which it arose, Horkheimer maintains; the insidious function of this perspective lies in its absolutisation:

> Wherever the concept of theory ... is made autonomous (as if this concept were established by reference to the 'essence' of knowledge, or by some other a-historical procedure), the concept is transformed into a reified, ideological category.[8]

Horkheimer demolishes this a-historical notion by outlining the socio-historical determinants in the realm of knowledge and research: the scientific spheres are guided and financed by industry and the government; their brief is largely that of the production-process; and, most important of all, the object of perception is historically given, and the subject of perception (man) is historically, and socially, determined as regards his methodological and categorial apparatus.[9]

The 'manifesto' reveals the full dialectics of this historical determination in its relation to the dichotomy between conscious and unconscious social action; Horkheimer problematises the whole notion of 'society' and the 'individual':

> Where the latter experiences himself as passive and dependent, the former, which is, after all, made up of individuals, is an active, even though unconscious and thus inauthentic subject. This distinction in the existence of man and society is an expression of the deep divisions that have marked all historical forms of social life up to the present. The existence of society has either depended on direct oppression, or else it has been the blind result of contradictory forces; in any case, certainly

not the outcome of the conscious, spontaneous actions of free individuals. . . . Under bourgeois conditions, the activity of society is blind but concrete; that of the individual is abstract but conscious.[10]

Thus, true self-knowledge and true self-fulfilment are not purely intellectual acts, but presuppose a practical concern with reconstructing society; the 'critical theory of society' is 'shot through with an interest in reasonable conditions'.[11] Theory is thus sublated in a double sense.

The first aspect of this sublation is the adequate reflection of the historical determinants of 'knowledge' in its given form; 'knowledge' is relativised, although only in a historical materialist sense.[12] Clearly, this sublation does not resolve the problem; the contradictions and one-sidedness which the various spheres of investigation reveal (when subjected to this metacritique) are viewed by 'critical theory of society' as necessary products of the division of labour. This is particularly so as regards class-antagonisms, which are not 'resolved' in theory, but deliberately developed to full consciousness.[13] 'Critical theory of society' describes forces and counter-forces, and hopes, in raising these to self-consciousness, to heighten the social tension: 'The theory . . . that pushes for the transformation of society as a whole, has as its immediate result a sharpening of the struggle with which it is linked.'[14] Thus, the ultimate sublation of the contradictions of science is a practical act of social reconstruction; the mediating link in this process is a theory linked to the class-struggle. That is why Horkheimer calls the theory 'critical and oppositional'.[15]

In reality, of course, the theory-praxis nexus is far more complex than outlined here by Horkheimer. Everything hinges on whether the theory really is 'linked' to the relevant 'struggle', and that presupposes two things: first, that 'critical theory of society' recognises the full dialectical nature of the fundamental struggles, and, second, that the theory is mediated to those involved in them in a practical way. Merely showing the necessity of contradictions and making them conscious is not enough; a real revolutionary theory involves a theory of *organisation* and *political action*. What is needed is a *practical-critical* theory. And precisely this is lacking in the Frankfurt's School's conception. However, a metacritique of this nature can only be performed adequately after a detailed analysis of 'critical theory of society' as a whole. Before its weaknesses can be pinpointed, its strengths must be fully appreciated; and Frankfurt School theory has many strengths.

Apart from anything else, the 'manifesto' marks an advance on the conception of the role of theory as evidenced in Horkheimer's inaugural lecture and editorial preface to the *Zeitschrift*. There, the future was regarded, at least implicitly, as a thing that was un-decided, but not as something which could be decided by an alliance between revolutionary theory and revolutionary class. Instead, social theory carried on the academic task of 'predicting' the future. According to the 'manifesto', the future lies in man's hands, or, more precisely, in the hands of whichever class carries the day. Horkheimer speaks, at one and the same time, of capitalism develop-ing into barbarism, and of revolutionary change, both in terms of a logical, necessary upshot of economic contradictions.[16] This is not evidence of confusion in Horkheimer's thought; it reveals his awareness that the blind tendency towards barbarism can only be checked and defeated by organised political struggle and the revolutionary reconstruction of the production-process.

Another feature of 'critical theory of society' is its careful and conscious distance from pragmatism. Horkheimer stresses that the relation to practice, if it is not socially differentiating, is purely 'traditional'. Indeed, pragmatism is inherent in 'traditional theory' as a whole. The 'critical' perspective on practice is radically different:

> Even though the critical position emerges out of the structure
> of society, it is not concerned, either in its conscious intention
> or in its objective significance, that anything within this
> structure function more efficiently. Rather, the categories of
> efficiency, utility, suitability, the values 'productive' and
> 'valuable,' in their meaning for the status quo, are themselves
> regarded by the critical theoretician as dubious; they are by no
> means extra-scientific premises to be taken for granted.[17]

Clearly, 'critical theory of society' can draw here on the legacy of Classical German Idealism, particularly in its Hegelian form; indeed, Horkheimer employs Hegelian categories to explain the dialectical evolution of 'truth'.[18] But these categories are now materialist, and it is the Marxian critique that forms the corner-stone of 'critical theory of society'. The latter, says the Director, begins 'with the depiction of an economy based on exchange'.[19]

As regards the reference of theory to specific stages of social development, Marx's critique of political economy and Hegel's logic are, says Horkheimer, 'examples of the same method'.[20] The dialectical, critical thrust of Hegel's method is preserved in the Marxian method: 'In contrast to the procedure of the modern specialised science of economics, critical theory of society remained philosophical, even in the form of the critique of political economy'.[21] The use of 'philosophical' here should not be misunderstood, and Horkheimer's 'manifesto' outlines the moment of abolition too, contained in the Marxian sublation of Hegel's dialectics: the goal of 'critical theory of society' is the 'abolition of class-society'. This is, so to speak, the 'materialist content of the idealist notion of Reason'.[22] In this sense, Horkheimer says, modifying and extending Engels's famous closing words to his study of Feuerbach, 'critical theory of society' retains (and realises) the heritage not just of German Idealism, but 'of all philosophy'.[23] The hypostatisation of theory itself is annihilated: theory becomes a moment of revolutionary social struggle.

The transition from philosophy to social theory is the key to the corner-stone of Frankfurt School theory: namely, the critique of ideology: 'Modern dialectical philosophy upheld the view that the free development of the individual depends on the reasonable constitution of society. In analysing the basis of contemporary conditions, this philosophy turned into the critique of economy'.[24] 'Critical theory of society' does not demolish the values of German Idealism; rather, it radicalises the materialist aspects of this philosophy and demonstrates the objective perversion of the values concerned.

The critique of political economy reveals the transformation of the dominant economic concepts into their opposites: of free exchange into the increase of social inequality; of free economy into monopoly; of productive labour into conditions that stifle production; of the reproduction of social life into the immiseration of whole nations.[25] Man does indeed make his own history, and to this extent, reason exists in society; but man's world is, so far, a world of alienation, similar to that of blind extra-human nature: 'this world is not their world, but the world of capital.'[26] Thus, the materialist critique of Reason becomes the revolutionary demand for reasonable, that is, classless society.

2 The pre-'manifesto' formulation of 'critical theory of society'

The essay 'Traditional and Critical Theory' was not so much a new departure as a distillation of the various components worked out in the *Zeitschrift* from its inception. 'Traditional theory' had been under attack from the first issue as well. In 1935, Horkheimer polemicised against pragmatism, saying that the epistemological theory of truth being life-promoting and of 'rewarding' thought being true, contained a 'harmonistic delusion', unless this epistemology was part of a theoretical whole in which 'tendencies towards a better, truly life-promoting life' could find expression.[27]

The role of Hegelian categories was, equally, a feature of the *Zeitschrift* from its early days. In 1934, the Director of the Institute formulated his critique of 'traditional theory' thus:

The individual sciences only provide the elements for the
theoretical construction of the historical process, and these

elements, once subsumed under the latter construction, do not remain what they were in the individual sciences, but receive new meanings, of which previously there was no mention. Thus, all genuine thought can only be understood as a continuing critique of abstract determinations; such thought contains a critical, or, as Hegel puts it, a sceptical moment.[28]

But the critique of ideology in its broadest sense also strikes German Idealism itself; the incongruence between the 'principle' of bourgeois society and the objective reality of the latter can only be revealed by a theory that is 'materialist'.[29] This latter designation is not as precise as the later 'manifesto', but, even here, the sublation of dialectical philosophy is clearly thematised: Hegel (and Kant) viewed Reason as the unity of subjective and objective freedom; this was correct, but 'the theory of its realisation leads from philosophy to the critique of political economy'.[30] Idealist scepticism becomes a *practical* scepticism. Not even 'critical theory of society' is the final resolution; rather, this theory is a 'premise of correct action'.[31] Dialectical ideology-critique is a stage in the self-transcendence of theory. And the Hegel-Marx transition is fundamental to the Frankfurt School's conception of their theory.

3 Hegel's dialectics: 'critical theory' in philosophy

Reason and Revolution, the most articulate statement by the Frankfurt School on the Hegel-Marx transition, designates two forms of critical theory:

> Hegel . . . recognised the social and political order men had achieved as the basis on which reason had to be realised. His system brought philosophy to the threshold of its negation and thus constituted the sole link between the old and the new form of critical theory, between philosophy and social theory.[32]

The Frankfurt School go to great pains to evolve their theory and categories by reference to this genetic process, and while they ultimately repudiate Hegel's idealism, they attempt to lay bare the full critical content of his dialectical philosophy.

Before joining Horkheimer's team, Marcuse published a major work, entitled *Hegel's Ontology*.[33] This study, though a largely immanent reappraisal of Hegel's work, was moving in the direction of the Frankfurt School's evaluation. Adorno, reviewing the book in the *Zeitschrift*, praised Marcuse for moving away from Heidegger's existentialist phenomenology: Marcuse was moving from the 'Meaning of Being' to the 'analysis of what is', from ontology to the philosophy of history, from 'historicity to history'.[34] Marcuse was

31

initially concerned to demonstrate that the critical force of Hegel's philosophy resided in its dialectical, historical quality:

> The basic meaning of Being, and the meaning which determines the first step in the concept of Being, is the original *unity* of the antitheses of 'subjectivity' and 'objectivity' (Being-for-Self, and Being-in-Itself, Being-Objective). In that this unity is conceived by Hegel as a *uniting* unity and as the action precisely of what is, *movement* is recognised as the fundamental characteristic of Being.[35]

The study of the activity in which alone what is, *is*, becomes the study of the *history of what is*. Thus: 'The history of man does not just take place "in" the world (as if in something essentially different), but occurs as one with the outcome of the world, without thereby losing its essential peculiarity'.[36] Phenomenology is sublated into historical materialism.

Marcuse claims that Hegel's assertion of the process of objectification (*Vergegenständlichung*), and of its transpiercing, as the activity which constitutes the *Being* of Life, is Hegel's 'greatest discovery, the source (clouded over all too soon) of the new view of the historical process, a view made possible by Hegel'.[37] Thus, Hegel's achievement, as well as his ultimate failure, lie precisely in his conception of the process of Being as a development in which objectification plays a crucial, and, for Hegel, fated role.

To Hegel, Spirit is the subject, the substance, and the goal of all Being, all history. Spirit, which is, in itself, the *essence* of Being, becomes, through the *process* of Being, 'for itself', that is, constituted as its own result, and recognised by itself as such. This takes the form, according to Hegel's mystified account, of Spirit first alienating itself, assuming an alien form, that is, becoming objective (*gegenständlich*). At the same time, however, this *alienated* Spirit remains *Spirit*, and once this subject recognises itself for what it is, then Spirit sublates its own alienation, and has become, through this process as a whole, in-and-for-itself.[38]

Despite the idealist terminology, this process involves the concrete social praxis of man's dialectical interaction with his surroundings. The idealist terminology has a materialist dimension; thus, the Concept, or Notion (*Begriff*) is only adequate to itself when it has become 'perfectly realised'.[39] And Reason is not merely mental labour, but 'purposive activity'.[40] Thus, the 'freedom' of the stoics is no freedom in any real sense: 'Freedom, as a thought, has only pure thought as its truth, and thus lacks the concrete fulfilment of life. It is, therefore, merely the notion of freedom, not living freedom itself.'[41] 'Living freedom' can only be established on the basis of a rational production-process. Hegel thus turns his attention to the latter.

The product of labour is the 'work' (*Werk*), which, for Hegel, is the reality that consciousness gives to itself. The idealist analysis stresses that the 'work' is cast into the realm of society as a whole, and that this reality is thus not merely an individual relationship on the part of the producer. Without giving any concrete details, Hegel then traces the development of the 'work' to full societation, with the resultant 'true work' (*das wahre Werk*, or *die Sache selbst*). Thereby, the subject of work, man, is himself subsumed and fulfilled by the general subject, that is, by the community.[42] Hegel certainly fails to specify the material dimension of this progress to classless society, and his idealism actually demolishes this potential critique of political economy (see p. 34), but it remains an outstanding achievement of dialectical idealism that it focused attention on the production-process, stressing socialisation as a *need* of human society.

To the Frankfurt School, however, the critical significance of Hegel's phenomenology lay not merely in its materialist component; the idealist conception of history as ultimately the work of Spirit was a critical reflection of the real alienation of man's productive powers. Horkheimer stressed that Marx and Engels too did not accept man's immediate consciousness and volition as the basic driving-force of history up to the present: 'They held ... to the Hegelian conviction of the existence of supra-individual dynamic structures and tendencies in historical development, but discarded the belief in an autonomous spiritual force at work in history'.[43] 'Spirit' was thus reduced, by Marx and Engels, not to 'man' pure and simple, but to the alienated human powers active in class-society, and thus, as regards contemporary society, to capital.

4 Hegel's idealism: 'traditional theory' in philosophy

Although the idealist view of history had a critical significance, this could only be appropriated via a materialist metacritique. Horkheimer's inaugural lecture had attacked the transfigurative nature of Hegel's idealism. This was developed at greater length in the essay 'Concerning the Problem of Truth':

> Hegel's belief that his thought grasped the essentials of all
> being, and that his system united all these essentials in a perfect
> and self-sufficient hierarchy, unaffected by the developing and
> passing-away of individuals, means ... the eternalisation in
> thought of the basic secular conditions. Dialectics assumes a
> transfigurative function. The social order, in which, according
> to Hegel, mastery and slavery, as well as poverty and misery,
> all have their place, is sanctioned, in as much as the con-

ceptual framework into which they are absorbed is represented as a higher value, as the Divine and Absolute.[44]

Hegel's Reason, which was to be actualised, has 'become affirmative before the objective reality can be affirmed as reasonable'.[45] In this sense, even *dialectical* idealism is subsumed under 'traditional theory'.

The distortions within Hegel's dialectics are viewed, by the Frankfurt School, in terms of capitalist ideology; Marcuse wrote: 'German Idealism uses bourgeois society as a model for its exposition of the concept of universality; in this sense, its theory constitutes a new justification of social slavery.'[46] This being so, the idealist conceptualisation is an ideological escape from the class-antagonisms of capitalist society: labour becomes exclusively intellectual labour, because any concrete labour at the contradictions would become political revolution.

Hegel's Ontology stresses, from first to last, that the idealist logic progressively undermines all the historical, and thus critical, categories, in favour of the timeless idea of 'Absolute Knowledge'. Since everything is Spirit, and since Hegel has 'recognised' this, then alienation has 'ceased to exist'. This reveals the insidious function of a base-superstructure theory within the framework of idealism; the specific stage at which the objective world is sublated (not to a higher form of production, but away from it altogether) is totally arbitrary. Without explaining how the master-slave relation has been resolved in real terms, and with no materialist expression of socialisation, Hegel presses on towards 'Absolute Knowledge', which is a purely ideational construct. It is, as Hegel himself admits, 'transfiguration'.[47] Unfortunately for Hegel, this transfiguration does *not* mean the 'annulment' of time.[48] The idealist history of the world may be complete, but real history continues, as do the contradictions of class-society.

5 The Marxian critique of political economy

For the Frankfurt School, theory's only possible line of progress beyond this point, is a progress beyond philosophy. Marcuse summed this up at the close of the first great period of Frankfurt School production, when he wrote:

Philosophy reaches its end when it has formulated its view of a world in which reason is realised. If at that point reality contains the conditions necessary to materialise reason in fact, thought can cease to concern itself with the ideal. . . . Critical thinking does not cease, but assumes a new form. The efforts of reason devolve upon social theory and social practice.[49]

Thus, the term 'critical theory of society' marked a radical advance beyond the Director's inaugural lecture and the latter's talk of 'social philosophy': the new label reflected a closer articulation of the materialist theory-praxis nexus.

Marcuse's contribution to the programmatic presentation of 'critical theory of society' was his essay 'Philosophy and Critical Theory' (written jointly with Horkheimer, but largely by Marcuse). Paraphrasing Marx, Marcuse wrote:

> At the time of its origin, in the thirties and forties of the nineteenth century, philosophy was the most advanced form of consciousness, and, by comparison, real conditions in Germany were backward. Criticism of the established order there began as a critique of that consciousness, because otherwise it would have confronted its object at an earlier and less advanced historical stage than that which had already attained reality in countries outside Germany.[50]

Thus, the Marxian critique of political economy began with the Marxian critique of Hegel; and the Frankfurt School go to great lengths to stress and elucidate this genetic aspect of their 'critical theory of society'.

Marx's *Economic and Philosophic Manuscripts of 1844*,[51] appearing in 1932, had vindicated Lukács's and Korsch's stress, taken up by the Frankfurt School, on this philosophical genesis of Marxian thought. And Marcuse's assessment in *Hegel's Ontology* had its direct parallel in these early writings of Marx, where Hegel's 'outstanding achievement' is regarded as the dialectical depiction of human self-realisation via alienated objectification and the transcendence of the latter.[52] This dialectical categorial apparatus, along with the values it contains, is appropriated by Marx, but only through a materialist metacritique; Marx says of Hegel:

> It is not the fact that the human being *objectifies himself inhumanly*, in opposition to himself, but the fact that he *objectifies himself* in *distinction* from and in *opposition* to abstract thought, that constitutes the posited essence of the alienation to be sublated. . . . The *reappropriation* of the objective essence of man, begotten in the form of alienation [is regarded] therefore not only as the annulment of *alienation*, but of *objectivity* as well. Man is thus regarded as a *non-objective, spiritual* being.[53]

To Marx, of course, the production-process (objectification) was not per se alienation; production was the activity through which man realised his human potential. But Marx recognised that the equation of objectification and alienation reflected an objective fact of

35

capitalist production: wage-labour.[54] Hegelian categories revealed some fundamental truths about modern commodity-production, as well as containing a protest against this system. As Marcuse wrote, 'problems bearing on the potentialities of man and of reason could now be approached from the standpoint of economics'.[55] But only an economics informed by the method and categories of Hegelian philosophy!

But, as *Reason and Revolution* stresses, the critical core of dialectical idealism is sublated not merely into a new theory, but into revolutionary social praxis. Marx, comparing his use of the dialectic with Hegel's, described his own, 'rational' form of this method as 'critical and revolutionary'.[56] Marx does not 'sublate' alienation, but only the inadequate theoretical expression of this phenomenon. Alienation continues; what has been achieved is theoretical clarity as to its social forms, as well as to the material preconditions for its transcendence. Alienation can only be reversed through the practical overthrow of capitalism, and of all class-society. Marx expressed this clearly in his earliest critiques of Hegel:

> As the determined adversary of the prevailing mode of German political consciousness, criticism of the speculative philosophy of right does not remain within itself, but proceeds on to tasks for whose solution there is only one means—praxis.[57]

This is why Marcuse, while stressing the 'philosophical' component of historical materialism, adds that the goal of Marxian theory is 'practical and revolutionary': namely, the 'overthrow of capitalist society by the proletariat'.[58]

Yet, to grasp fully the Frankfurt School's theory, it is necessary to understand that, even for Marx, the dual aspects of the sublation of philosophy are inextricably fused. Marx wrote, in the 1840s, with the coming revolution before his eyes: 'you cannot transcend philosophy without actualising it'.[59] This precept, more than any other, is the corner-stone of the Frankfurt School's reading of Marx; Horkheimer, who quotes frugally (to say the least!) from Marx, refers emphatically to this very passage.[60]

6 Dialectical versus undialectical thought

If the Hegel-Marx transition is central in the Frankfurt School's explication of their 'critical theory of society', then the contemporary theoretical debate to which they wished to relate actively, precisely via such an explication, was the debate that had originated in Karl Korsch's violent exchanges with the theoreticians of the Third International (Comintern). This raging controversy, though seldom named by the Frankfurt School, is a crucial key to their beginnings in the 1930s; it is a controversy that could only be resolved adequately through a complete understanding of the Hegel-Marx transition.

Comintern built its argument, entitled 'orthodox Marxism-Leninism', on Lenin's major 1909 work, *Materialism and Empirio-Criticism*[61] (although, by the time the argument with Korsch developed, Lenin was incapacitated and at death's door). Lenin had argued, in this extensive study on Marxist epistemology, that the natural sciences, to this day, shared the materialist standpoint, according to which, sensation was the 'image' of an 'external world'.[62] Lenin had also stressed the need for the natural sciences to adopt *dialectical* materialism (as Marx and Engels had always argued),[63] adding that in the theory of knowledge, 'we must think dialectically'.[64] Unfortunately, Lenin did not get down to a historical materialist critique of natural scientific materialism; in his tirades against Mach and the Machians, he contented himself with the distinction between materialism and idealism:

> Materialism is the recognition of 'objects in themselves,' or outside the mind; ideas and sensations are copies or images of those objects. The opposite doctrine (idealism) claims that these objects do not exist 'without the mind'; objects are 'combinations of sensations.'[65]

At one point, Lenin forgot dialectics altogether, and referred to 'Marx's philosophy, i.e., materialism'.[66]

As shown earlier, Horkheimer, too, occasionally used the term 'materialism' pure and simple to designate his method. But Horkheimer always stressed that this meant the variety of materialism that had been 'schooled in Hegel's Logic'.[67] And Horkheimer did more than state this; he, and his team as a whole, went to great pains to *reveal* this schooling. Lenin did not; while referring to the *'valuable* fruit of the idealist systems, Hegelian dialectics',[68] Lenin never specified the critical significance of this 'fruit' vis-à-vis naive materialism. While this gap was not of great consequence for this work of 1909 (which was, after all, an attack on neo-idealism), it had disastrous implications when, in the mid-1920s, *Materialism and Empirio-Criticism* became the classic work of 'orthodox Marxism-Leninism', and the definitive statement on all Marxist epistemology. This 'holy text' found an explicit opponent in Korsch, as well as a largely implicit opponent in the Frankfurt School.

Korsch's *Marxism and Philosophy* of 1923 did not yet have to face the dogmatic code of 'orthodox Marxism-Leninism', and was thus formulated as a critique of an as yet unidentified group of 'more recent Marxists' who have been misled into 'interpreting the Marxist abolition of philosophy as the replacement of this philosophy by a series of abstract and undialectical positive sciences'.[69] However,

Korsch left little room for doubt as to his evaluation of Lenin's 1909 work: 'The naively metaphysical standpoint of sound bourgeois common sense considers thought independent of being and defines truth as the correspondence of thought to an object that is external to it and "mirrored" by it.'[70] This statement made Korsch a marked man within the Third International.

In 'The Present State of the Problem of "Marxism and Philosophy"' of 1930 (the year of Horkheimer's appointment), Korsch recounted the denunciation of his work by Zinoviev, who labelled it a 're-visionist heresy'.[72] Korsch, in turn, showed that this attack was based on a crude interpretation of Marxist epistemology. But since his enemy was the so-called 'orthodox Marxism-Leninism', and since this was based uncritically on Lenin's *Materialism and Empirio-Criticism*, Korsch now swung into a direct and thorough refutation of the latter.

Korsch claimed that the dominant trend in contemporary bourgeois science was not idealist, but was inspired 'by *a materialist outlook that is coloured by the natural sciences*'.[73] Lenin had failed to appreciate the true sublation involved in the Marxian critique of idealism:

> Lenin regards the transition from Hegel's idealist dialectic to
> Marx and Engels' dialectical materialism as nothing more than
> an *exchange:* the idealist outlook that lies at the basis of
> Hegel's dialectical method is replaced by a new *philosophical
> outlook* that is no longer 'idealist' but 'materialist.' He seems
> to be unaware that *such* a 'materialist inversion' of Hegel's
> idealist philosophy involves at the most a merely terminological
> change whereby the Absolute instead of being called 'Spirit' is
> called 'Matter.'[74]

Thus, 'orthodox Marxism-Leninism' is inadequate to the task of a historical materialist critique of natural scientific materialism and of the latter's logic; that is, 'orthodox Marxism-Leninism' is inadequate to the task of repudiating what Horkheimer calls 'traditional theory'. In a sense, 'orthodox Marxism-Leninism' is itself 'traditional'.

The Frankfurt School's sympathies, as regards the Lenin-Korsch debate, lay clearly with Korsch. As early as 1931, Marcuse, before joining the team Horkheimer was assembling, maintained that 'The Present State of the Problem of "Marxism and Philosophy"' threw valuable light on the genesis of Marxism. Marcuse quoted enthusiastically from Korsch's work, including the accusation that the crude materialist theory of knowledge now being promulgated (Marcuse does not repeat Korsch's explicit reference to Lenin) '*drags the whole debate between materialism and idealism back to a historical stage which German idealism from Kant to Hegel had already surpassed*'.[75]

Years later, in *Soviet Marxism*,[76] Marcuse did not hesitate to name Lenin, whose *Materialism and Empirio-Criticism* 'replaced the dialectical notion of truth by a primitive naturalistic realism, which has become canonical in Soviet Marxism'.[77] This, not least of all, accounts, in part, for the Frankfurt School's critical distance from the Third International, a problem that will be discussed at length in Chapter 3. And the distance from 'orthodox Marxism-Leninism' must also be recognised as one of the major factors behind the Frankfurt School's choice of the label 'critical theory of society'; Adorno, in his *Negative Dialectics*[78] of the 1960s, wrote:

> Marx had drawn a line between historical materialism and the vulgar-metaphysical variety of materialism. . . . Since then, materialism is no longer an arbitrary counter-position, but the methodological essence of the critique of idealism, and of the critique of the reality for which idealism opts by distorting it. Horkheimer's formulation 'critical theory' seeks not to make materialism respectable, but to use it to bring to theoretical consciousness the precise point at which materialism distinguishes itself from amateurish philosophies as well as the 'traditional theory' of science.[79]

The whole problem can thus be reduced to the double sublation of idealist dialectics and undialectical materialism. This explains the Frankfurt School's preoccupation with the Hegel-Marx transition.

7 The historical problematicity of the sublation of philosophy

Marx's claim that 'you cannot transcend philosophy without actualising it', reveals the tight dialectical unity of theory and praxis within the Marxian conception: not only does 'critical theory of society' (as the higher form of theory) push determinedly towards praxis, thus transcending the bounds of theory itself, but that praxis realises the critical content of philosophy. And only at this stage is philosophy finally transcended at all. The precarious balance within theory before this actualisation is not specified by Marx. To the Frankfurt School, critical intellectuals of the Weimar Republic, this balance became a crucial problem.

Alfred Sohn-Rethel, a peer of the Frankfurt School, recently explained the phenomenon of 'critical theory of society', as formulated by Horkheimer's team, in terms of the question of the proximity, or distance, of revolutionary social praxis: Sohn-Rethel (born 1899) asserted:

> Strange as it may sound today, I have no hesitation in saying that the modern Marxist development in Germany, for example,

the Frankfurt School, arose out of impulses from that period
[1918–23] and thus, in a certain sense, out of the theoretical
and ideological superstructure of the failed German revolution.[80]

Weimar Germany, as shown in Chapter 1, was not only a period of
capitalist monopolisation, undermining the economic basis of 'free
exchange'; it was also the period of transition to fascism, where the
values of liberal society were not only not sublated, but actually
wiped out. Thus, the whole idea of sublating, or actualising,
philosophy was recast in a radically new constellation.

The essays in the *Zeitschrift* reveal a conscious attempt to master
this constellation; Marcuse wrote, looking back at his own contributions from the perspective of the 1960s, that these essays had
had a seemingly anachronistic note: 'the concern with philosophy
expressed in these essays was already, in the thirties, a concern with
the past: remembrance of something that at some point had lost its
reality, and now had to be revitalised.'[81] Adorno, in *Negative
Dialectics*, expressed this by means of an indirect reference to that
very Marxian passage which had been central to the Frankfurt
School's theory of the 1930s: 'Philosophy, which once seemed
obsolete, lives on because the moment of its actualisation was
missed.'[82] These words reflect a theoretical concern traceable to the
Frankfurt School's earliest days: the concern to defend, criticise,
and, ultimately, materialise the critical legacy of philosophy.

8 The historical materialist truth is the whole

In this context, the struggle for the sublation of philosophy, even on
the theoretical level, became a permanent, conscious endeavour. In
particular, the fight had to be carried to all theoretical currents which
were undialectical 'resolutions' of German Idealism. Naturally,
since fascism was interpreted in terms of the contradictions of
capitalism, the enemy was not just fascist ideology, but the 'traditional theory' that was the superstructural stronghold of capitalism
generally. This theory, fingered out in the 'manifesto', was a con-
tinuous object of attack for the Frankfurt School theoreticians.

A major component of 'traditional theory' was regarded as
'positivism' (a term used by the Frankfurt School to designate not
merely those who consciously subscribed to that label, but also any
theoretician who was broadly subsumable under the category of
'traditional theory').[83] Of course, positivism had played a progressive role in the revolutionary rise of capitalism; as Marcuse
stresses, positivism's 'appeal to the facts then amounted to a direct
attack on the religious and metaphysical conceptions that were the
ideological support of the ancien régime'.[84] But by the second half

of the last century, this definition of science was proving, as Horkheimer outlines, to restrict scientific activity to the 'registration,
classification, and generalisation of appearances, without regard to
any differentiation of the essential and inessential'.[85] This differentiation is no metaphysical problem, but a vital need of human
society: 'Science and technology are only elements in an existing
social totality, and it is quite possible that, despite all their achievements, other factors, and even the totality itself, could be moving
backwards. . . .'[86] On the theoretical level, what is needed is an
overall critical perspective; positivism cannot provide this.

What has happened, however, is that positivism has been absolutised: technological advance has become the model of all rational
activity. This, Marcuse maintains, precludes 'the interpretation of
these "data" in terms of a comprehensive *critique of the given itself*'.[87]
In this sense, science falls behind the dialectical force of abstraction,
even as manifested in its idealist form. Of course, Hegel's dictum
that 'the truth is the whole'[88] had ultimately resulted in an idealist
distortion, but the Marxian critique of society had rescued the
totality-perspective, by materialising it. This was at the root of
Marx's criticism of 'the abstract materialism of natural science, a
materialism that excludes history and its process'.[89] And it is highly
significant that Engels had the following to say for natural science:

> Only by learning to assimilate the results of the development of
> philosophy during the past two and a half thousand years will
> it be able to rid itself on the one hand of any isolated natural
> philosophy standing apart from it, outside it, and above it, and,
> on the other hand, also of its own limited method of thought,
> which was its inheritance from English empiricism.[90]

It is in this sense that Marcuse speaks (in the context of the critique
of political economy) of 'philosophy':

> Philosophy thus appears within the economic concepts of
> materialist theory, each of which is more than an economic
> concept of the sort employed by the academic discipline of
> economics. It is more, due to the theory's claim to explain
> the totality of man and his world in terms of his social
> being.[91]

But, last, even this 'truth' is no mere theoretical reflection of society;
it is a 'truth' whose full implication is only realised via the revolutionary reconstruction of society. The critique of political economy
reveals the blind economic determinism of capital; and, as Engels
stressed, this determinism could only be smashed via a socialist
revolution.[92] 'The truth is the whole' turns from an idealist transfiguration into the call for critical social praxis.

41

Adorno's famous dictum: 'The whole is false',[93] would seem to repudiate this methodological precept, but appearances, as always, are deceptive. Adorno's cryptic remark is levelled not at the historical materialist notion that 'the truth is the whole', but at the idealist corollary that 'the whole is the truth', where 'the whole' becomes the self-sufficient ideational expression of the dialectical process. As Marcuse wrote, somewhat later: ' "The whole is the truth," and the whole is false.'[94] 'Critical theory of society' could only be true by expressing this falsity adequately; the falsity itself could only be eradicated by revolution. As Horkheimer stated in the *Zeitschrift*, the 'truth' of 'critical theory of society' hung in the balance of class-struggle:

> In contemporary society, there exist real socio-historical forms, the irrationality of which has already been grasped by thought. The dialectic is not at rest. No harmony exists between thought and social reality. Rather, contradiction proves, even today, to be the driving force. . . . The transcendence of this state of affairs is thus effected in the real historical struggle. . . .[95]

9 Ideology-critique and the Marxian critique of society

One of the aspects of this 'real historical struggle' is the ideological struggle. The ideology-critique undertaken by the Frankfurt School was informed precisely by the dialectical notion that 'the truth is the whole', and, as such, distanced itself from any evaluation of ideology as 'pure lies'. As the Second World War drew to a close, Adorno implicitly summed up the direction of the Frankfurt School's ideology-critique when he wrote:

> Among the motifs of cultural criticism, one of the most long-established and central is that of the lie: that culture creates the illusion of a society worthy of man, whereas, in reality, no such society exists. . . . This is the notion of culture as ideology. . . . But to act radically in accordance with this notion, would be to extirpate, along with the false, all that was true also; all that, however impotently, strives to escape the confines of universal practice; every chimerical anticipation of a nobler state; and so to bring about directly the barbarism that culture is reproached with furthering indirectly.[96]

The extent to which the Frankfurt School succeeded in this endeavour to differentiate their critique of ideology, is related in the subsequent pages of this chapter. The ultimate failure to criticise ideology adequately is analysed in the next chapter. For the moment, the analysis should pause and consider the precise implications of the intention of 'critical theory of society'; formulated in terms of an explicit relation to Marx's critique of political economy, Frankfurt School theory aimed at a metacritique of 'traditional theory' and of all notions derived from it. The Marxian method was the one chosen; its categories, and objects of analysis were extended, but the basic principles were affirmed. The Frankfurt School of the 1930s considered themselves Marxists.

The attempt to understand the precise relation between 'critical theory of society' and the Marxian critique of political economy, is confounded by the fact that the only serious discussion of this problem so far, Albrecht Wellmer's *Critical Theory of Society*,[97] distorts Marx, the Frankfurt School's reading of Marx, and thus the Frankfurt School itself. Wellmer's argument is threefold: first, Marx's version of historical materialism shows serious metaphysical and crypto-positivist deviations; second, the Frankfurt School, under Horkheimer, were aware of this in the 1930s already; and third, their work of that period was a conscious attempt to rectify the science of historical materialism, which Marx had distorted! Each and every of these assertions is, in fact, false.

The first claim by Wellmer goes back to Marx's critique of Hegel's dialectics: the critique was not radical enough, and Marx failed to de-philosophise the problematic he wished to appropriate. As a result, the presentation of the proletariat's revolutionary role has an a priori, 'logical' characteristic.[98] This metaphysical deviation is complemented, of necessity, by a crypto-positivist reduction of the emergence of class-consciousness to the mechanism of capitalist production, thereby making active ideological struggle redundant.[99] It is in this light that Wellmer criticises the basic Marxian premises:

> On the one hand, they determine the revolutionary *function* of critical theory as that of a post-ideological, 'positive' science, and on the other hand they lead to the camouflaging of the distinction between the *inevitable* and the *practically necessary* transformation of capitalist society. . . .[100]

Such, claims Wellmer, was Horkheimer's critical evaluation of Marx in the period of the *Zeitschrift*. Unfortunately, Wellmer's claim is incorrect, as is his own evaluation of Marx.

Marx's life-work was a dialectical critique of political economy, including the latter's theoretical representation in Classical Political Economy, which, Marx asserted, had 'investigated the real relations of production in bourgeois society',[101] but had 'never arrived at a consciousness of the results of its own analysis'.[102] Marx's critique was thus ideology-critique from first to last. It is impossible to give here a full account of the progression of this ideology-critique in *Capital*, which is Marx's definitive statement on political economy. Instead, Wellmer's argument can be refuted by reference to a passage in the *Grundrisse* which forms one of the main supports of this distorted picture of Marx. Unavoidably, the following argument, since it involves precise textual analysis, calls for lengthy quotation from both Wellmer and Marx.

Wellmer's accusation that ideology-critique is circumcised in Marx's critique of political economy, is substantiated by Wellmer as follows:

> Later, in the *Grundrisse* . . . he speaks of the 'error of those socialists, especially the French, who would interpret socialism as the realisation of ideas of civil society that were not discovered by the French Revolution, but brought into circulation in the course of history,' and then explains unequivocally: 'What distinguishes these socialists from bourgeois apologists is on the one hand their feeling for the contradictions of the system, and on the other the utopianism which consists in not grasping the necessary difference between the real and the ideal forms of civil society, and therefore in undertaking the superfluous task of trying to actualise all over again what is the ideal expression, the transfigured and reflected image thrown off by reality as such itself.'[103]

Unfortunately, despite his freedom from any reluctance to quote at length, Wellmer does not give a clear indication as to what Marx was talking about. Between the two passages quoted by Wellmer, there is a precise economic argument by Marx, which, far from abandoning ideology-critique, actually endeavours to rationalise the latter, thus precluding any idealistic or positivistic distortions. For the sake of clarity on this crucial passage, Marx's argument is here given in full:

> Hence the error of those socialists, especially the French, who would interpret socialism as the realisation of ideas of civil society that were not discovered by the French Revolution, but brought into circulation in the course of history, and who go to great pains to demonstrate that exchange-value was *originally* (in time) or essentially (in its adequate form) a system of freedom and equality for all, and that this system had been distorted by money, capital, etc. Or else, that previous history has failed in its attempts to execute these values in a form corresponding to their true nature. These socialists, as for example Proudhon, then believe that they have discovered a panacea by which the true history of these relations can oust their falsified form. The exchange-system, and particularly the money-system, are indeed the system of freedom and equality. But the truth is that the contradictions that appear on the deeper developmental levels are immanent contradictions, spawned by this self-same property, freedom and equality,

which, on occasion, turn into their opposite. The wish that, for example, exchange-value should not develop from the form of commodities and money into the form of capital, or that the labour that produces exchange-value should not develop into wage-labour, is as pious as it is stupid. What distinguishes these. . . .[104]

The full quotation (which Wellmer resumes at this point, having elided the entire economic argument) shows that Marx is attacking *not* the critical debate with values which have as yet only enjoyed an inadequate form, but the *uncritical* elevation of the *inadequate form itself* (in this case, commodity-production) to the revolutionary place of honour. Wellmer, in his obsession with a *differentiating* critique of ideology, reproduces that ideology *uncritically*.

It now remains to be seen whether Horkheimer really did, in the 1930s, subscribe to this distorted Wellmerian picture of Marx. Did Horkheimer regard Marx as a tendential metaphysician, a logician of history, and a crypto-positivist who reduced historical materialism to a mechanistic study of the economy, thus shirking the problem of the genesis of ideological struggle? No! Horkheimer stated explicitly, concerning the dialectic of history:

> Whereas . . . the articulation of this dialectic emerges in Hegel's case out of the logic of Absolute Spirit, out of his metaphysics, the Marxian presentation, by contrast, rejects the idea of any logically supra-historical insight providing a key to the understanding of history. Rather, the correct theory emerges from the study of real men, living under specific historical conditions and maintaining their existence with the help of specific tools. The laws that can be discovered in history are neither a priori constructs, nor a registration of facts by a supposedly independent observer, but are produced as a reflection of the dynamic structure of history, by a thought which is itself involved in historical praxis.[105]

So spoke the Director of the Institute in 1932.

The question as to the Frankfurt School's conception of class-consciousness and mass ideological struggle cannot be answered until the following chapter, where this question is viewed in its proper context of critical social praxis. But Wellmer's accusation that Marx tendentially presented the revolution as 'inevitable' can be dispensed with very quickly. Indeed, it is one of the Frankfurt School's lasting services to Marxism that they cleared up this confusion surrounding Marx's 'laws'. For example, *Reason and Revolution* explains:

> it would be a distortion of the entire significance of Marxian theory to argue from the inexorable necessity that governs the

development of capitalism to a similar necessity in the matter of transformation to socialism. . . . The revolution depends indeed on a totality of objective conditions: it requires a certain attained level of material and intellectual culture, a self-conscious and organised working class on an international scale, acute class struggle. These become revolutionary conditions, however, only if seized upon and directed by a conscious activity that has in mind the socialist goal.[106]

Marcuse was well guided when he dedicated this book to Horkheimer and the Institute: it sums up beautifully the assessment of Marxian theory by Horkheimer's team in that period which *Reason and Revolution* brings to a close.

Finally, there is the question of whether Horkheimer, and his team, subscribed to the view that the Marxian critique of political economy lost the full historical materialist force of being an ideology-critique. The answer to this question is, once again, negative; Horkheimer actually formulated his own ideology-critique in terms of the analysis in *Capital:*

In *Capital*, Marx faithfully introduces, according to their precise meaning, the basic concepts of Classical English Economics: exchange-value, price, labour-time, etc. What were, at that time, the most advanced definitions, on the basis of scientific experience, are all incorporated. However, in the process of presentation, these categories acquire new functions; they play a role in a theoretical whole which repudiates the static perspective that formed them, and which repudiates in particular their uncritical, isolated application.[107]

Horkheimer emulated Marx's method, and thus, in the 1930s and early 1940s at least, succeeded in appropriating categories and values *critically*. Unlike Wellmer, Horkheimer knew that 'the demand for a general implementation of the bourgeois notion of justice leads of necessity to a criticism and abolition of the exchange-society, which originally gave this idea its substance'.[108] Thus, the notion of justice can be transformed into an agitational weapon, whereas the concept of exchange-value, which rises and falls with the transformation of use-values into commodities, cannot. Horkheimer saw this and accepted this in his earlier days, not despite, but thanks to, Marx. If, as Wellmer suggests,[109] Horkheimer was in fact 'only pretending' to be an orthodox Marxist at this time, then so much the worse for Horkheimer, since the evaluation of Marx to which he 'deceitfully' subscribed, is the correct one.

However, having dispensed with Wellmer's incorrect account of the Frankfurt School's reading of Marxism, it should be established that his errors do have a certain basis in the work of the Frankfurt School, of which he was a latter-day member. Wellmer (born 1933) did study philosophy and sociology under Adorno, after which he held an assistant teaching-post in philosophy, Adorno's department. Surely, Wellmer's arguments must reflect some real state of affairs? The answer, not surprisingly, lies in the role that economic analysis played in 'critical theory of society'.

Horkheimer wrote in 1938 that 'an attack on ideology, if this attack is not based upon an analysis of the respective economy, is poor critique, or, rather, no critique at all'.[110] Yet this methodological imperative is one that the Frankfurt School themselves ultimately failed to satisfy; despite the numerous insights into economics, and despite Pollock's systematic work in this area, the Frankfurt School's own analyses were largely superstructural, and basically lacking in terms of economic concreteness. Horkheimer's *Origins of the Bourgeois Philosophy of History*, described by the author as his 'self-clarification', was devoid of any systematic economic basis; yet these collected essays were archetypal for the subsequent *Zeitschrift*, whereas Marx and Engels's 'self-clarification' (the *German Ideology*) was later regarded by the two colleagues with a certain critical distance, as proof 'how incomplete our knowledge of economic history was at that time'.[111] Marx proceeded to a thorough analysis of the economic base, as the only adequate framework for an attack on the latter's ideology. Horkheimer showed no such progression.

Of course, the Frankfurt School could draw on the Marxian critique of capitalist commodity-production. But the analysis of monopoly capitalism was never adequately taken up. Indeed, despite the work of Pollock, there is an implicit belief in the *Zeitschrift* as a whole that monopoly capitalism was not all that problematical after all; Marcuse, in 1964, said of his essays of the 1930s:

> In political economy, Marxian theory had traced to their
> origins the tendencies that linked the liberal past with its
> totalitarian liquidation. What I attempted was to detect and
> trace these tendencies in the cultural spheres, particularly in the
> society's representative philosophy.[112]

Unfortunately, this is a slight exaggeration: Marx had demonstrated the increasing exploitation of wage-labour, as well as the tendency of the rate of profit to fall. But Marx could not know what measures the capitalists would take, at the turn of the century, to counteract this tendency. Pollock touched on a number of aspects of monopoly capitalism, as did Horkheimer's team as a whole. But, generally speaking, the essential economic dimension of manipulation within the monopoly capitalist era remained unspecified. It is this gap that gave rise to a tendentially a-historical critique of ideology in Frankfurt School theory. That tendency is discussed in the subsequent chapter, as are the divergent developments of the original team after the war. For the present, it has to be conceded that a fundamental gap in 'critical theory of society' does exist, even in its 'manifesto' days. It is this gap, amongst other things, that has helped create so many misunderstandings in accounts such as Wellmer's.

10 The problem of contemporary metaphysics

Despite the absence of systematic economic analysis, 'critical theory of society' still has many outstanding qualities which must be discussed. One such quality is the Frankfurt School's extension of the dialectical debate with metaphysics, beyond the Hegel-Marx constellation to the problem of contemporary metaphysical tendencies. A pioneer of this new ideology-critique was Ernst Bloch, who had a profound impact on the intellectuals of the Frankfurt School. Bloch was of the same generation as Horkheimer's team, and in many ways a kindred spirit. In a crucial work of 1935, entitled *Legacy of this Time*,[113] he asked whether the bourgeois world did not, in its decline, throw up a dialectically serviceable legacy in the form of the manifold elements which its own decomposition set free. Replying in the affirmative, Bloch analysed the mystical component of fascism in a highly differentiated manner:

> Viewed in itself, that is, directly, fascism's glitter and smoke of delusion serve big capital, which uses them to distract or obscure the perspective of those social strata exposed to immiseration. But, indirectly, this distraction reveals a superficial break in a hitherto tightly sealed surface; and the irrational smoke reveals steam from abysses that can be of use not merely to capitalism. Alongside the vileness and fantastic brutality, alongside the stupidity and boundless propensity for deception, which are revealed in every hour and every word of Terror-Germany, there is also an element of an older and romantic anti-capitalism, with an awareness of the hollowness of contemporary life, and with a longing for an (as yet unclear) other.[114]

Plainly, the dialectical appropriation of this 'longing' means making the latter *clear*.

The Frankfurt School were of a similar mind. Horkheimer, for example, stressed that the turn against rationalism by impressionist art, and by the philosophies of Nietzsche and Bergson, revealed not only the insecurity of the bourgeoisie in its humanist tradition, but, in addition, a 'protest against the fettering of individual life under the increasing concentration of capital'.[115] This protest also revealed, quite correctly, the awareness of the futility of individual striving; this insight, too, must be appropriated, dialectically, via 'critical theory of society'. It thereby becomes a revolutionary insight:

> The type of man in whom a clear understanding of the present form of society really asserts itself as a force to reckon with, alters the significance this insight had in the sceptical thought of the disillusioned bourgeois individual. Now, in this new, coherently critical type, the insight becomes a progressive force, thrusting forwards.[116]

In this way, ideology-critique leads directly into ideological struggle.

Horkheimer was convinced that neo-metaphysics, for example Max Scheler's anthropology, was anti-'traditional' in that it was concerned to relate anew to a whole series of objects that had come to be regarded as 'unscientific'. Metaphysics, noted Horkheimer, could, in this form, be a 'lesser evil' than the 'neutrality' of the natural sciences and their 'traditional theory'.[117] It was for this reason, and this reason alone, that Horkheimer's very important essay, 'The Latest Attack on Metaphysics', went to the defence of the latter. The motivation for this defence was that the attack concerned came not from a historical materialist perspective, but from the camp of positivism. Far from being a sublation in the sense of the Marxian critique of Hegel, the positivist attack constituted a repudiation of the very *problems* discussed in metaphysics.[118] Horkheimer sided with the latter, just as Marx had avowed himself, in the face of the uninformed attacks on Hegel, 'the pupil of that mighty thinker'.[119]

However, Horkheimer's defence of metaphysics against positivism is, at the same time, a dialectical critique of metaphysics. As in his inaugural lecture, the Director shows that instead of transcending the 'class-based narrowness' of 'traditional theory', metaphysics had identified the latter with rationality itself and thus proceeded to repudiate analytical thought altogether, abandoning itself to 'arbitrary objects of study and a method divorced from all science'.[120] Horkheimer is particularly harsh on Mortimer Adler, who believed that 'metaphysics alone can give humanity the hold it has lost', that 'metaphysics makes true community possible'. Such uncritical notions about metaphysics, argued Horkheimer, 'misconstrue the present historical situation'.[121] Horkheimer had no compunction about conceding that 'science is largely the critique of metaphysics'.[122] The only qualification was that the critique of 'traditional theory' was itself a sublated form of metaphysics, namely, of Hegelian logic: 'The dialectical method is the key intellectual means for transforming the abstract moments, won by analytic reason, into fruitful elements in the presentation of the living object'.[123] Metaphysics and natural science are viewed by Horkheimer, as by Engels (see p. 41), as both moments of the true method of analysis and presentation. The moments are reconciled, and sublated, in 'critical theory of society'.

But the significance of this constructive debate with metaphysics is not merely academic. The 'unclear longing', as long as it remained 'unclear', could, and did, become a component of fascist ideology. This is uppermost in Horkheimer's mind when he discusses Bergson's vitalism:

> The same historical dynamic which ... forced the originally progressive elements of the bourgeoisie (before and during the war) into the camp of the economically decisive groups, also transformed the meaning of activist *Lebensphilosophie*, turning it, often against the intention of its creators, from a socially progressive force into an element of contemporary nationalist ideology.[124]

Similarly, but more to the point, Bloch wrote, in 1937, that the reason the Nazis could monopolise (and castrate) the anti-mechanistic revolt against contemporary life, was that the 'true revolutionaries' were 'not on their guard' in this sphere. The Marxist does not need to 'disavow a priori' the entire phenomenon of irrationalism; in Voltaire's day, that disavowal was progressive, but today it plays into the hands of the counter-revolution.[125] In short, the dialectical appropriation of metaphysics, including modern metaphysics, is no mere academic debate, but a serious constituent of ideological struggle.

11 The critique of logical positivism

Whereas 'critical theory of society' perceives a positive content in metaphysics, positivism regards the latter as nonsense. Thus, the sublation of philosophy comes under fire even on the theoretical level. The Frankfurt School of the 1930s was determined to keep alive the *full* dialectical force of the Marxian critique, and this gave rise to its constructive debate with metaphysics. But it also gave rise to a fundamental critique of positivism, and one of the Frankfurt School's outstanding contributions was its extension of this critique to the most recent forms of positivism. Despite the continued assertion that the Frankfurt School does not appreciate the nature of modern positivism,[126] the truth is that Horkheimer's 'The Latest Attack on Metaphysics' is nothing less than an analysis of logical positivism.

The Frankfurt School's enthusiasm for the legacy of German Idealism was, in part, due to the latter's stress on the subjective constituents of knowledge, in contrast to any crude materialist absolutisation of 'external objects'. Although Kant's presentation of the forms and categories tended towards an a-historical perspective, and although Hegel's historical perspective was idealist, none the less, the Frankfurt School, following Korsch's line, emphasised the Marxian debt to German Idealism:

> Like Hegelian Logic, materialism transcends the flaws of abstract thought by attempting to grasp the dependence of individual categories on a formative process. But in materialism, this process is no longer purely mental, and its result is not the self-reflecting infinite Idea. Rather, materialism regards the individual and his categories as dependent on the social development.[127]

Precisely this genetic relation of thought was what distinguished Marx's theory from middle-class materialism.

A major criticism of positivism was that it undermined this relation; Marcuse showed that positivism 'shifts the source of certainty from the subject of thought to the subject of perception', whereby 'the spontaneous functions of thought recede, while its receptive and passive functions gain predominance'.[128] Horkheimer, in his essay on metaphysics, traced this reduction to its logical conclusion in modern positivism: the 'subject' disappears altogether, and theoretical 'reflection' is reduced to an ordering of fixed judgments.[129] Metaphysics is correct to accuse this modern analytic method of fragmenting its object: logical positivism aims 'more at the results of abstraction than at the theoretical reconstruction of the whole'.[130] As such, it has a purely 'traditional' attitude towards that whole.

Naturally, Horkheimer accepts the structure of such statements as, for example, the definition of an anthropod; such statements are regarded, by and large, as unproblematical. By contrast, the thesis that the commodity is the unity of use-value and exchange-value, though a crucial thesis in the portrayal of capitalist society, cannot be taken so lightly:

> the 'given' is not, in this case, something that exists generally and independently of theory. Rather, it is mediated through the conceptual whole in which such statements function. This does not, however, deny that the reality aimed at by the theory is fully substantial, that is, that it exists independently of the consciousness of the theoretician.[131]

In contrast to Lenin's polemics against Hume and Berkeley, Horkheimer endeavours to show that historical materialism did draw on, though critically, the great philosophical refutation of naive materialism. On the subject of the genesis of knowledge, historical materialism and positivism, particularly logical positivism, are irreconcilable. The Frankfurt School established this fact once and for all.

12 The dialectical critique of liberalism in the era of monopoly capitalism

As demonstrated above, the sublation of philosophy is more than a *methodological* rationalisation of German Idealism; it is also the materialisation of the *values* propounded in that philosophy, values which, in a new form, will be 'actualised' in classless society. The Frankfurt School's preoccupation with this intention of Marx's critique of liberalism was more than a restatement; it was an attempt to revitalise the full dialectical intent of Marxian thought at a time when liberalism had been not sublated, but undermined, eroded. This new constellation was reflected as early as Marcuse's essay 'The Struggle Against Liberalism in the Totalitarian View of the State',[132] which was thematic for Marcuse's essays in the *Zeitschrift* as a whole. Marcuse was to write, years later:

> For if there was one matter about which the author of these
> essays and his friends were *not* uncertain, it was the
> understanding that the fascist state was fascist society, and that
> totalitarian violence and totalitarian reason came from the
> structure of existing society, which was in the act of overcoming
> its liberal past and incorporating its historical negation.[133]

This is why Marcuse described the dialectical critique of ideology, such as undertaken by 'critical theory of society', as concerned 'to a hitherto unknown extent with the past—precisely insofar as it is concerned with the future'.[134]

In the Frankfurt School's work of the 1930s, and in Marcuse's theory to this very day, the annihilation of liberalism was viewed, in line with Pollock's theory of fascism, as a problem of monopoly capitalism as a whole: 'Total mobilisation in the era of monopoly capitalism is incompatible with the progressive aspects of culture centred about the idea of personality.'[135] The 'inner' freedom of liberal capitalist society had been externalised, but not in the Marxian sense of economic freedom, but actually in the interests of capitalist domination: the 'private' sphere had been invaded by advertising and technological rationality. In Marcuse's later terminology, liberalism had been 'repressively desublimated'.

The sublation of philosophy must now resist the theoretical annihilation of those values that are to be realised in revolutionary praxis; Horkheimer expressed this clearly when he wrote, in 1933:

> Today, we hear people maintaining that the bourgeois ideas of
> freedom, equality and justice have exposed their poverty. But it

is not the ideas of the bourgeoisie that have proved untenable, but the social conditions that did not correspond to them. . . . The dialectical critique of the world cowering behind these ideas, consists precisely in showing that such ideas retain their significance, despite the development of social reality.[136]

What is needed, is the *actualisation* of these ideas.

While 'critical theory of society', as propounded in the *Zeitschrift*, did, unfortunately, reveal a lack of concreteness in its discussion of these values, thus giving rise to a tendentially a-historical defence that came to fruition in Horkheimer's later work (see Chapter 3), the *Zeitschrift* performed the invaluable methodological service of *demanding* a precise definition of, for example, 'freedom'. In this sense, the Frankfurt School pointed to a major weakness of Social Democratic revisionism. For example, Siegfried Marck, a theoretical ally of the SPD, came under fire for his abstract humanism; Horkheimer wrote:

The protestation that Classical Liberalism at least had the right ideas, and that all we need is to apply them, is not enough. Anybody who talks of 'freedom' today, must indicate clearly what he means. Freedom in abstracto goes too easily hand in hand with the edicts of French Police Prefects and the *Erlösung* of our Austrian brothers.[137]

When 'freedom' becomes social reality, Marcuse had already stressed, this real freedom will have as much, and as little, in common with its previous form, 'as the association of free men with competitive, commodity-producing society'.[138]

This sublation has two stages: first, the concept of freedom is re-defined in terms of classless society; second, the new concept ceases to exist in the hypostatised realm of 'pure theory'. Philosophy was not just a resistance to alienation, but itself a product of alienation: not only were its analyses confounded by a mystifying idealism, but its entire existence as 'higher values' reinforced the ideological defence of a society which perverted these values. This is why, for Marx, the 'actualisation' of philosophy also meant 'the negation of previous philosophy, i.e., of philosophy as philosophy'.[139] What was needed was the rational expression of society's real contradictions, along with the practical transcendence of those contradictions. The latter was effected in revolutionary class-struggle, of which Horkheimer said: 'This struggle retains the positive element of bourgeois morality —the demand for freedom and justice—while sublating the ideological hypostatisation of that element.'[140] To recall Marx's words, the dialectical appropriation of Hegelian philosophy was part of a theoretical struggle confronting 'tasks for whose solution there is only one means—praxis'. It is to the latter that the analysis must now turn.

3 The historical materialist theory-praxis nexus

'Critical theory of society', as formulated by Horkheimer and his team in the period of the *Zeitschrift*, did a great deal to clarify, revitalise and continue the full dialectical nature of Marxian theory. In particular, the various problems of ideology-critique, the genesis of knowledge, the totality-perspective, the sublation of philosophy, etc., were all presented clearly in their relation to the category of 'praxis'. This category features heavily in 'critical theory of society' and marks a positive advance beyond the conception of the role of theory as expressed in Horkheimer's inaugural lecture. The Frankfurt School came to regard their theoretical work in the following terms: the opposing forces within society must be clearly outlined and raised to the level of self-consciousness; in this way, social tension is raised to its extreme expression as revolutionary class-struggle; successful social praxis could resolve the objective contradictions within bourgeois society, but only by overthrowing that society. The role of 'critical theory of society' was, essentially, to be one of ideological enlightenment of the social forces destined to carry out this momentous act. This is the crucial link in the theory-praxis nexus.

But the theory-praxis nexus has an additional significance: not only must theory *teach* the progressive social forces; it must also *learn* from their struggles, as well as from the theories that those struggles have thrown up. Horkheimer seems to accept this when he asserts:

the picture of a better world . . . becomes specified, corrected and confirmed in the course of historical struggles. Action is thus no mere appendage that should be conceived of as 'beyond' thought, but penetrates theory at all levels and at all times. Praxis is inextricably fused with theory.[1]

For the Frankfurt School between 1930 and 1942, the full theory-praxis nexus should have meant the following problems: the Marxian and Leninist theory of class-consciousness and revolutionary organisation; the Bolshevik revolution, and socialist construction in the USSR; the struggle against fascism in Germany; the defeat of the German working class; and, of course, the lessons to be learned. Needless to say, 'lessons', for the historical materialist theory-praxis nexus, are of a practical nature, involving the evolution of a revolutionary theory adequate to the new constellation of the class-struggle. The question is: How far did 'critical theory of society' satisfy these demands?

It must be stated immediately that 'critical theory of society' was not adequate to the theory-praxis nexus in this materialist sense. Marxism-Leninism was never discussed explicitly in the *Zeitschrift*, or anywhere else; the Russian revolution and the subsequent economic construction never received any serious analysis, not even of the limited scope of Pollock's study of 1929; the defeat of the anti-fascist struggle, though a constant nightmare for these intellectuals, was never discussed in any adequate terms. The whole thrust of Frankfurt School activity, though centralising the problem of 'praxis', was ultimately academic: 'praxis' was a theoretical category, not a constituent of a concrete revolutionary struggle.

In 1937, Horkheimer revealed a clear alienation not only from fascist barbarism but from the degenerate organisations of the working class; in the face of this constellation, he formulated the role of theory as follows:

And, more than ever, at a time when the European forces of freedom are themselves disorientated and attempting to re-group, when the indifference to specific detail (an indifference resulting from defeat, despair and corrupt bureaucracy) threatens to eradicate all spontaneity, experience and insight on the part of the masses, despite the heroic courage of individuals, at a time like this, the supra-partisan and thus abstract conception of the role of the intelligentsia serves only to cloud the real issues.[2]

Unfortunately, this is merely a stated methodological imperative; the work of the Frankfurt School at this time failed to satisfy this imperative. While stressing the revolutionary role of the critical intellectual, 'critical theory of society' could not formulate itself as a practical theory of ideological struggle. Indeed, it failed to assimilate in an adequate, conscious manner the lessons of defeat of the German and Russian workers. Fascism and Stalinism remained, for the Frankfurt School (with the exception of the radicalised Marcuse of the 1960s), traumas that blocked the view of any concrete critical praxis.

However, as in the case of monopoly capitalist economy, the failure to analyse class-struggle systematically did not mean an ignorance as to this problem. On the contrary, the Frankfurt School was head and shoulders above the normal variety of the 'ivory tower', and had a great number of highly differentiated observations to make on the *general* problems of class-struggle. What is needed, is a distillation of these observations, an evaluation of their individual significance, as well as of the possibility of transforming these observations into a *practical* theory of class-struggle, and, finally, a precise judgment as to the consequences of the Frankfurt School's weaknesses for its 'critical theory of society' as a whole. Such a meta-critical intention is to be realised in this chapter.

1 Marx, Lenin and the Frankfurt School on class-consciousness and the party

The fundamental problem in the theory-praxis nexus is the relation between the revolutionary theory and the class-consciousness of the working class. Marx himself never finished *Capital*, and thus never gave a definitive account of class and class-consciousness. In the *Communist Manifesto*, the stress is essentially on the revolutionary nature of capital as the unwitting organiser of the proletariat; yet even here, the complexity of the problem is consciously grasped, by means of a dialectical use of the term 'class'. On the one hand, it denotes an objective socio-economic grouping; but, in addition, it denotes a goal of political enlightenment, as with the proletariat. Thus, the immediate aim of the Communists is 'formation of the proletariat into a class'. In this political development, the Communists have, over the great mass of the proletariat, the advantage of 'clearly understanding the line of march, the conditions, and the ultimate general results of the proletarian movement'.[3] Although the proletariat is organised by capital into a combined force, an articulate social theory is necessary for the purpose of political enlightenment; party, theory, and class form a dynamic unity.

Lenin's theory of revolutionary organisation retained this dynamic unity, along with its differentiation. In 1902, he wrote:

The history of all countries shows that the working class, exclusively by its own effort, is able to develop only trade union consciousness. . . . The theory of socialism, however, grew out of the philosophic, historical and economic theories elaborated by educated representatives of the propertied classes, by intellectuals. . . . In the very same way, in Russia, the theoretical doctrine of Social-Democracy arose altogether independently of the spontaneous growth of the working class movement. . . . Hence we had the spontaneous awakening of the working masses, their awakening to conscious life and conscious struggle, and a revolutionary youth armed with Social-Democratic theory and straining towards the workers.[4]

For Lenin, the fact that the masses are spontaneously being drawn into the movement does not make the organisation of the struggle less necessary, but *more* necessary. Organisation is not opposed to spontaneity, but a force to safeguard the latter and give it greater efficacy. In fact, Lenin asserts, only a firm organisation of the various working class struggles can transform these latter into the proletariat's *genuine* class-struggle at all.[5]

Horkheimer, without explicitly relating to Marx or Lenin, does, in his 'manifesto', seem to subscribe to this general conception of a dynamic unity of party, theory and class. Although the proletariat develops the 'interest' in the cause of its misery (and precisely *because* of this misery), none the less, even the situation of the proletariat is 'no guarantee of correct awareness'.[6] The proletariat's 'interest' must be 'formed' and 'directed' by theory.[7] And the sharpness of theory is reflected in the 'ever present possibility of a tension between the theoretician and the class his thought concerns'.[8] Horkheimer's criteria for his 'critical theory of society' are very stringent:

> The intellectual who, in amazement and reverence, can only
> sing the praise of the creative powers of the proletariat, and
> who rests content with adapting to, and transfiguring this class,
> fails to see that the passivity of his thought means a shirking of
> theoretical application, as well as an evasion of that
> temporary opposition to the masses which real active thought
> might demand. Such evasion only makes the masses blinder and
> weaker than they need be.[9]

Significantly, Walter Benjamin quoted this very passage in an article of that time, commenting: 'This insight already indicates the object of a critical theory of society.'[10]

However, Horkheimer's differentiation of class and theory goes beyond Lenin's conception: whereas the latter saw the revolutionary theoreticians and the political avant-garde as one, Horkheimer envisages a separate category of critical intellectuals over and above the theoreticians of the avant-garde:

> If . . . the theoretician and his specific activity in conjunction
> with the oppressed class is viewed as a dynamic unity, so that
> his presentation of the social contradictions appears not merely
> as an expression of the concrete historical situation, but equally
> as a stimulating, active factor within that situation, then the
> function of critical theory becomes apparent. The course of the
> debate between the advanced elements of the class and those

individuals who pronounce the truth about the former, and, further, the debate between these most advanced elements, together with their theoreticians, and the rest of the class, must be understood as a process of interaction, in which consciousness unfolds not only its liberating force, but also its inciting, disciplining and violently practical force.[11]

This formulation completes Horkheimer's conceptualisation of the theory-praxis nexus. What is needed now is to trace the development of 'critical theory of society', and to establish the extent to which this programme was realised.

2 Socialist construction and the dictatorship of the proletariat

However, by the time of Horkheimer's appointment as Director of the Institute, socialism was no longer merely a theory of revolution; the problem of socialist construction had become an objective reality, throwing up concretised theories as to the ways and means of this economic task, as well as throwing new light on the needs of revolutionary struggle itself. The development of the USSR had posed the question, and in its own way answered it, of the precise meaning of the 'dictatorship of the proletariat'.

The *Communist Manifesto* had, of course, held up a picture of a classless society: 'When, in the course of development, class distinctions have disappeared, and all production has been concentrated in the hands of a vast association of the whole nation, the public power will lose its political character.'[12] But even at this stage, Marx and Engels emphasised that the proletariat's successful revolution will necessitate a strong state, defined as 'the proletariat organised as the ruling class'.[13] This, as it was later termed, could be nothing less than '*the revolutionary dictatorship of the proletariat*'.[14]

But 'dictatorship' here does not imply the abolition of democracy; rather, it is conceived *as* democracy. The dictatorship of the proletariat is a dictatorship vis-à-vis the counter-revolutionary forces; as regards the exercise of this rule, however, democracy is the logical means, since the proletariat *is* the state. The Frankfurt School of the 1930s did not object to the *notion* of a proletarian dictatorship; indeed, they stressed its democratic nature. Marcuse wrote: 'Wherever Marx and Engels contrast the socialist state with its preceding forms, they do so in terms of the actual *subjects* who *constitute* the state. . . .'[15] However, in the Frankfurt School's return to the Marxian conception, there is an implicit and often explicit belief that this democratic vision has been lost in the USSR.

Lenin's 'The State and Revolution'[16] was essentially an assembly of Marx and Engels's writings on the subject, and the democratic perspective thus emerges clearly. But history is not made according to quotations! The chaos that confronted the new Russian state proved inimical not only to the idea of the state 'withering away', but even to the idea of the state being 'the proletariat organised as the ruling class'. The tension between party, theory and class was carried over into the new Russia: a tension arose between spontaneous demands and acts of the masses (syndicalism, division of land, etc.) and the Party's intentions for a planned socialist construction. This was exacerbated by counter-revolution and foreign intervention, which made central direction, irrespective of democratic niceties, a condition of survival.

But the economic chaos continued beyond the period of 'war-communism'. The 'New Economic Policy', a compromise attempt to revive the shattered economy, proved equally harsh for the masses, including the industrial proletariat. On top of the unemployment, low relief, and depressed wages, the proletariat experienced a political oppression in the form of the authority of the factory managers, which was upheld at the expense of workers' control.[17] Yet, all this could still be regarded as temporary deviations from the Marxian conception. Lenin, to his dying day, counted on the imminence of revolution in the advanced European countries, which would give the USSR 'timely support'.[18] Implicit in his entire theory was the awareness that one could not 'squeeze' socialism out of a backward proletariat. The reason was clear: the coercion necessary for this would destroy the political form of socialism, which was 'the proletariat organised as the ruling class'. With the enunciation, in 1924, the year of Lenin's death, of the Stalinist doctrine of 'socialism in one country', a serious and irrevocable step was made which would transform the entire USSR. Although the Union could not be guaranteed against imperialist aggression, it could, with the productive forces available, build socialism, said Stalin.[19]

3 The Frankfurt School and Stalinism

It was in the wake of the centralised, planned economy, that most of the critical intellectuals of the West turned their backs on the 'socialist fatherland'. They did so at varying stages in this development. As for Horkheimer, his disillusionment occurred some time in the early 1930s. His close friend Pollock, as late as 1929, had still been eager to show up the real problems created by the uninformed, syndicalist interventions of the Workers' Control Soviets.[20] Horkheimer, for his part, showed an enthusiasm qualified only by his own admitted ignorance, when he wrote in *Twilight*, which was published under a pseudonym:

I do not claim to know where the country is heading;
doubtless, there is much misery. But those among the educated

who feel nothing of the spirit of endeavour there, and who dismiss the entire development without a thought ... are poor companions, whose company brings no reward. Anybody who has eyes for the senseless injustice of the imperialist world (an injustice not attributable to technical backwardness), will regard the events in Russia as the continued effort to overcome this dreadful social injustice, or, at least, he will ask, anxiously, whether this attempt can survive.[21]

This is probably one of the earlier sections written (*Twilight* was a collection of short aphorisms, written between 1926 and 1931), since the evaluation of the USSR in the period of the *Zeitschrift*, and ever since, was wholly negative.

In an interview of 1970, Horkheimer explained that his essays in the *Zeitschrift* developed an idea of a 'just' and 'true' society with a critical eye not only to Nazi Germany but also to 'other totalitarian states', adding that in Russia, 'conditions obtained which came very close to those in Germany, if not being equally serious, or even worse'.[22] In another interview of the same year, he spoke of 'terroristic communism' and 'Stalin's reign of terror', a 'symbol that revolution can lead to terror'.[23] And, looking back at his essays in the *Zeitschrift*, which were to be republished, he explained, in 1968, that 'Stalin's variety of fascism' was one of the forces against which the critically appropriated values of liberalism had to be defended.[24]

Horkheimer actually outlined, in 1970, a crucial question which bourgeois education never even poses: namely, 'how did the original desire for freedom turn into dictatorship?'[25] Unfortunately, Horkheimer himself never answered this question. However, his work in the 1930s did, despite the absence of explicit relation to the USSR, articulate a number of categories which are useful for general discussion of proletarian revolution and socialist construction. For example, Horkheimer emphasised that socialism was not merely a question of planning and raising productivity, but of liberating mankind from economic enslavement; he wrote, in 1937:

This historical transformation does not leave the relation of the cultural spheres untouched, and, if in the present state of society the economy rules man (this constitutes the lever for social change), then in future, man will rule his entire relationships, if with a necessary eye to natural needs. Isolated economic data will thus not be the measure of true community. This holds even for the period of transition. ... Economism, to which critical theory is reduced in many places (despite claims of upholding it), does not consist in taking the economic factor too seriously, but in taking it too narrowly. Its original meaning, which aimed at the totality of social forms, recedes in

proportion as the theory resorts to isolated phenomena. . . .
The subjection of industrial production to a centralised state-control is a historical fact which, in critical theory, is given its precise significance only on the basis of careful scrutiny of its respective form. Whether one can speak of socialisation, in the sense of critical theory, and to what extent a higher principle can be observed, does not depend simply on the alteration of certain property-relations, nor merely on the raising of productivity in new forms of social cooperation, but, equally, on the nature and development of the society in which all this happens.[26]

This has been quoted at such length because it reveals the economic significance of so many of the Frankfurt School's 'cultural values'. While this passage reveals a major weakness in Horkheimer's application of these values (instead of a dialectical interplay of base and superstructure, both are regarded as 'significant', and the 'new forms of social cooperation' are never specified), none the less it also exemplifies the Frankfurt School's concern with the *subjects* of socialist construction. No matter how great were the threats to the USSR, the 'needs' of the economy were also the needs of the people for economic liberation; if *these* needs were not satisfied, there was no socialisation.

Horkheimer was not averse to all leadership, however. Just as he accepted the need for a revolutionary avant-garde, he accepted that there was such a thing as an 'enlightened, even revolutionary despotism'. He also accepted that the severity of such despotism could not be explained 'in itself', but only by reference to 'the general level of development of the subjected masses'.[27] But this general principle, enunciated in 1934, did not vindicate the USSR. Horkheimer did not believe that the government was doing enough to raise the general level of development of the subjected masses; the Stalinist despotism was not doing enough to prepare the conditions for its own dissolution. This assessment emerged clearly, if only implicitly, in an essay of 1935, where Horkheimer reveals the historical materialist truth hidden, and distorted, within Nietzsche's despisal of the masses:

The masses are only miserable wretches as long as the real power that rules them places a pseudo-power in their hands, in order then to hide behind this pretence. Such is indeed the distinctive feature of mass-rule in history so far. But as soon as the masses transform themselves, by really taking control, then power itself will lose its 'decadent' quality and become the result of a united, and for this reason 'super-human' social force.[28]

The assertion as to 'history so far' was repeated in the 'manifesto', where Horkheimer stressed that despite the need for self-discipline, the revolutionary class-struggle reveals 'something of the freedom and spontaneity of the future', adding: 'where the unity of discipline and spontaneity has vanished, the movement turns into a function of its own bureaucracy, a spectacle that already belongs to the repertoire of recent history'.[29] As Marcuse wrote, decades later, the anti-authoritarian movement's idea of fusing spontaneity and organisation was an attempt to reverse the anti-Marxist feeling created at the sight of 'the repressive Stalinist development of socialism'.[30]

It is to the credit of the Frankfurt School that their criticisms of Stalinist Russia were more than a horrified reaction to the 'Purge Trials'. Certainly, these trials were a terrible shock, and Marcuse's preface to his reissued essays of the 1930s remarks on their significance;[31] but the Frankfurt School regarded the trials as symptomatic of a deeper problem: namely, the bureaucratisation of the USSR, and the dissolution of the real organisations of the workers. By the early 1930s, 'socialism in one country' had placed terrible burdens on the industrial proletariat (let alone the peasants); not only did wages lag and intensity of labour rise, but, in addition, the working-class's political self-assertion was brought into question. The Trade Unions were rebuked for syndicalist tendencies, and although this was couched as an attack on union bureaucracy, it was in fact a challenge to all working-class representation.[32] Such was the USSR's version of the 'proletariat organised as the ruling class'.

Alfred Sohn-Rethel, who knew many of the Frankfurt School team, has revealed[33] that the Institute's disenchantment with the USSR did indeed take place before the 'Purge Trials'. And, according to Sohn-Rethel, their suspicions were confirmed by a biography of Stalin which appeared in the early 1930s and impressed them greatly. Sohn-Rethel cannot recall either the author or the title, but it could well have been Boris Lifšic's *Staline: Aperçu historique du Bolchévisme*.[34] What marks off this biography from all others of this period, is that it avoids both a eulogy of Stalin, as well as an undifferentiated repudiation of Marxism-Leninism. The author shows a high regard for Lenin and actually quotes the latter's disregarded demands for gradualism, contrasting this with the coercion, repression and terror which distinguish the 'post-Leninist variety of Bolshevik morality'.[35] Similarly, Horkheimer spoke, in one of his last interviews, of this period as being 'no longer in the tradition of Lenin'.[36]

4 The break in the theory-praxis nexus

Although Horkheimer defined Stalinism in terms of the dissolution of the dictatorship of the proletariat, he did not analyse this development in its proper historical context. Marcuse's *Soviet Marxism* of

1958 did much to rectify this, pinpointing the isolation of the USSR and the threat of growing fascism in Germany as the historical factors behind the transition from Leninism to Stalinism.[37] But by this time, Marcuse had split with his former colleagues from the Institute. The Frankfurt School of the 1930s failed to evolve a *practical* critique of the USSR; instead, the rise of Stalinism was a dead end for them.

The *Zeitschrift*, despite announcing its concern with political struggles, did not relate either way to the Stalin-Trotsky debate. In conjunction with this, the Institute could not relate concretely to the praxis and theory of the class-struggles in Germany. These crucial problems did not even figure in the *Zeitschrift* in the form of book reviews. 'Praxis' thus became a theoretical, methodological category rather than a concrete notion of socio-historical class-struggle. It is true that, as Ernst Mohl has stated, the Frankfurt School's return to dialectical *theory* appears, in the face of Stalinism and the pusillanimity of the SPD, 'in a totally different light'. But this 'light' is an explanation, not a vindication. Certainly, the serious discussion of dialectics was constructive, but what of the other components of historical materialism? What of materialism? What of class-struggle? The return to theory must not be a farewell to praxis. With Horkheimer's team, it was. Again, Mohl comes to the rescue:

> Was Critical Theory unpractical? Certainly, it had no
> addressee, for the working-class was tied to its two major parties,
> one of which furthered the integration of the proletariat into
> the existing order, while the other, the Communist Party,
> refused to recognise this advancing integration.[38]

But this too is no justification: Horkheimer himself actually accepted in his 'manifesto' that the workers were organised under their own avant-garde, while the critical intellectuals were autonomous. And these intellectuals were to mediate their 'truth' to the avant-garde via a 'debate'. Although a 'tension' between the theoretician and the class was possible, even necessary, the three elements of the dynamic unity were to be in a process of constant 'interaction'. Thus, only the 'debate' guaranteed the crucial link in the theory-praxis nexus, according to Horkheimer's conception. Yet this very 'debate' was singularly absent in the *Zeitschrift*. Perhaps future research will bring to light certain exchanges between the Institute and various political groupings, but such exchanges would only be abstract appendages to their theoretical publications, which were divorced from the practical realities of class-struggle.

This does not mean that the vast edifice of 'critical theory of society' can be dismissed by the Marxist. On the contrary, this theory contains a large number of highly pertinent observations on problems relating to proletarian class-struggle. These observations, and the categories within which they are framed, must be appropriated, if critically. They must be assessed according to their individual significance for praxis, and they must be dismantled and restructured, as well as supplemented, to establish whether or not they could form a conceptual whole in terms of a practical theory. If not, then the distortions involved in the abstractified use of these categories must be exposed and rectified. Needless to say, such a metacritique can only be achieved by explicitly relating the whole debate to the class-struggles of that period.

5 The Frankfurt School and Rosa Luxemburg

As the Nazi regime was crumbling, Adorno wrote the following words, revealing his despair for socialism:

> Even solidarity, the noblest mode of conduct in socialism, has fallen sick. Solidarity was once intended to make the talk of brotherhood real, by lifting it out of the generality, where it was an ideology, and reserving it for the particular, the Party, as the sole representative of generality in an antagonistic world. . . . In the course of time, however, solidarity has turned into confidence that the Party has a thousand eyes.[39]

This observation reveals something of the political implications of the Frankfurt School's *dialectical* critique of ideology: solidarity must be realised, not undermined. The same phenomenon can be detected in Horkheimer's advice to the student movement of the 1960s:

> Despite her support for the Russian Revolution, Rosa Luxemburg, whom so many students venerate, said fifty years ago that 'the remedy which Trotsky and Lenin have found, the elimination of democracy as such, is worse than the disease it is supposed to cure'.[40]

Franz Borkenau had referred to this same attack in 1938, in his scathing attack on Comintern, entitled, simply, *The Communist International*.[41] Whereas Horkheimer did not share, at that time, the latter's total repudiation of Leninism, his real sympathies did lie with Rosa Luxemburg.[42] She, more than anybody, seemed to defend and develop the Marxian notion of a democratic dictatorship of the proletariat.

As early as 1904, Luxemburg had assailed Lenin's 'ultra-centralist' conception of the party, which, she maintained, made the central committee into the 'active nucleus' and reduced all other departments to mere 'executive organs'.[43] In addition, Lenin revealed an undialectical, repulsively positive attitude towards the discipline of the factory. In an anti-authoritarian tone, she retorted:

> It is not by linking to the discipline impressed upon the workers by the capitalist state, and it is not by transferring the baton from the bourgeoisie to any social-democratic central committee, but only by breaking and uprooting this slavish spirit of discipline, that the proletariat can be prepared for the new discipline, the voluntary self-discipline of social democracy.[44]

Marcuse, in 1972, quoted this very passage as proof that 'Rosa Luxemburg knew that a radical transformation of the working class was a condition of revolutionary strategy'.[45]

This argument extended to the question of socialist construction. Like the Frankfurt School, Luxemburg operated with the notion of a dialectical fusion of spontaneity and organisation. Only this could preclude bureaucratisation. Thus, like Marcuse and Horkheimer, she emphasised the *democratic* nature of the dictatorship of the proletariat:

> Yes, dictatorship! But this dictatorship consists in the *manner of applying democracy*, not in its *elimination*. . . . This dictatorship must be the work of the class and not of a small leading minority in the name of the class—that is, it must proceed step by step out of the active participation of the masses; it must be under their direct influence, subjected to the control of the public as a whole; it must arise out of the growing political development of the mass of the people.[46]

While conceding the harsh realities of the Russian situation, she pointed to one massive danger: that the Bolsheviks 'make a virtue out of necessity', and hold up their experience as a 'model' for all.[47]

If we wish to assess the extent of the Frankfurt School's 'Luxemburgism' and to establish whether this component assumed practical significance in their theory, it is necessary to look at the objective political form of Luxemburg's 'democracy'. This is the soviet-system, or council-system: the councils, wrote Luxemburg, must 'realise their mission' and 'learn how to become the sole public authorities throughout the realm'.[48] Her criticism of Lenin and Trotsky at this time was that, while upholding the soviet principle as the sole true representation of the workers, these two leading Bolsheviks, by stifling political activity generally, actually undermined the active life of the soviets.[49] Thus, when Luxemburg defended the Bolsheviks in public, she held up, as the highest instance of the movement, not the

Party, but the soviets; this was the 'alphabet' as taught by the Russian revolution.[50]

Horkheimer, in an unpublished essay of 1940, spoke directly of the 'democracy of the councils', and explicated this as follows:

> The concept of a transitional revolutionary dictatorship was in no way intended to mean the monopoly of the means of production by some new elite. Such dangers can be countered by the energy and alertness of the people themselves. . . . The theoretical conception which, following its first trail-blazers, will show the new society its way—the system of workers' councils—grows out of praxis. The roots of the council system go back to 1871, 1905, and other events. *Revolutionary transformation has a tradition that must continue.*[51]

Similarly, in his attack on Marck, Horkheimer regarded the development in Germany from 1919 to 1933 as 'quite consistent', adding: 'Even the most extreme horrors of today have their roots not in 1933, but in 1919, in the shooting of workers and intellectuals by the feudal accomplices of the Weimar Republic.'[52] For Horkheimer, the councils held up a vision of realising the Marxian conception of 'the proletariat organised as the ruling class'. With their destruction in Germany in 1919, Horkheimer seems to have lost all orientation to concrete class-struggle. Clearly, he never saw a comparable hope in the subsequent development of socialist theory and praxis in Germany. Even the KPD, the issue of the Spartacists, must have failed to revitalise this democratic form.

6 The Frankfurt School and the KPD

The original KPD was orientated to active involvement with the masses in all aspects of their relations with capital. Rosa Luxemburg, co-founder of the Party, had said as early as 1900 that the wage-struggles and parliamentary reforms were the ground on which the revolutionary goal of overthrowing wage-labour was prepared.[53] In 1918, she said: 'The struggle for socialism has to be fought out by the masses, by the masses alone, breast to breast against capitalism; it has to be fought out by those in every occupation, by every proletarian against his employer.'[54] The struggle on the production-front was thus the schooling of the workers; the revolutionaries could only do their job in conjunction with that struggle. That is why the early KPD did not shy away from active involvement in the Trade Unions.[55]

This was also the conception of Marx, Engels and Lenin. Indeed, the Frankfurt School's respect for the latter was due in large measure to his ability to retain the dynamic unity of party, theory and class, a unity subsequently lost. Marcuse's *Soviet Marxism* is here representative of the entire Frankfurt School:

> During the Revolution, it became clear to what degree Lenin
> had succeeded in basing his strategy on the actual class
> interests and aspirations of the workers and peasants. . . . Then,
> from 1923 on, the decisions of the leadership have been
> increasingly dissociated from the class interests of the
> proletariat. The former no longer presuppose the proletariat as
> a revolutionary agent but rather are imposed upon the
> proletariat and the rest of the underlying population.[56]

What is more, this degeneration was carried over into the KPD, and constitutes one of the basic aspects in the Frankfurt School's alienation from communism by the early 1930s.

Bolshevism exercised a direct influence on the KPD via Comintern, which by 1921 had shifted the real seat of power from the full congress to the ECCI (Executive Committee of the Communist International), thus subordinating the various CPs to a central authority dominated by the RCP.[57] This subjection was subsequently made increasingly effective, particularly when in the mid-1920s the parties were given a draft for their reorganisation, for their 'Bolshevisation'.[58] As for the KPD, this interference began to be a serious problem in 1923, and it proved to undermine the Luxemburgian tradition of this party. The failure of the expected revolution to materialise was explained by Heinrich Brandler, leader of the party, in terms of a dissolution of the objective revolutionary potential: the Cuno government, against which the masses had been mobilised, had resigned, and the army's assumption of power had strengthened the bourgeois state. An uprising under these conditions would have been no revolution by the masses, but a putsch by the KPD.[59] Zinoviev, the Chairman of Comintern, saw things differently: Brandler had 'betrayed the revolution'.[60]

The KPD's new theory was that of a united front 'from below'. In fact, it was no united front at all:

> The substance of this change of tactics amounted to replacing
> the tactic of the united front with the direct propagandistic
> appeal to the Social Democratic workers, abstracting from the
> fact of their being organised in the SPD, and with a
> corresponding renunciation of dealing with representatives of
> this party. This was the so-called 'united front from below,'
> which, even then, found its logical complement in the
> discrimination of the leadership of this party as a 'faction of
> German fascism with a socialist mask'.[61]

The subsequent precept of 'main blow against the Social Democracy'[62] cemented this development, splitting the labour movement, and assisting the Nazis in bringing down the Republic.

The Frankfurt School's alienation from the KPD was inevitable, given their alienation from Stalinism. They traced the degeneration of this party, as of the USSR itself, to 1923, when Luxemburg's theory and praxis were discredited. Karl Korsch wrote, in 1941, that after 1923 the KPD became 'a mere technical instrument in the hands of a secret leadership, paid and controlled exclusively by the Russian State, entirely independent of any control by its membership or by the working class at large'.[63] In a letter from Korsch to Mattick, dated 6 May 1941,[64] Korsch related that the exiled team of Horkheimer's Institute had 'received me well' on a recent visit, and, in particular, 'praised my review of Valtin' (where Korsch had made these charges against the KPD). On this point, the Frankfurt School and Korsch were in agreement.

But the Frankfurt School objected to the KPD not only because of its undemocratic nature; in addition, these dialectical intellectuals were horrified by the notion of 'social fascism'. Adorno wrote, in *Minima Moralia*, the following (concerning certain misguided Marxists):

> Cured of the Social Democratic belief in cultural progress, and confronted with growing barbarism, they are under constant temptation to advocate the latter in the interests of the 'objective tendency,' and, in an act of desperation, to await salvation by their mortal enemy who, as the 'antithesis,' is supposed to help prepare the good end, blindly and mysteriously.[65]

Here, in abstract terms, is the rejection of the Stalinist notion of 'social fascism'. The veiled political pronouncement springs directly from the Frankfurt School's entire conception of a *dialectical* critique of ideology. The undialectical nature of 'orthodox Marxism-Leninism', along with the Stalinist manipulation of the KPD, helped bring Hitler to power. Horkheimer later wrote that the possibility of 'the united workers and intellectuals' preventing the Nazis' rise to power, was 'no mere wishful thinking'.[66] The united front was sabotaged.

7 The Frankfurt School and Trotsky

Looking round for a possible *practical* exponent of these views of the Frankfurt School, one immediately encounters the figure of Trotsky. Being himself a victim of Stalinism, he violently denounced the bureaucratism of the USSR, which, he maintained, completely disregarded Lenin's conception of the dialectical interaction of party and class.[67] Similarly, Trotsky regarded the idea of 'social fascism' as complete nonsense; the Social Democratic workers *would* fight against fascism, but only together with their own organisations, for the moment. The Communists should support them in this fight, since this fight would expose the bankruptcy of reformism far more effectively than could demagogy. Significantly, it is in this sense that Trotsky propounds the role of the councils, which as yet only exist in the form of factory councils. These latter must be used by the Communists to involve all trade unionists in increasing encroachments into the life of the factory, the city, and, ultimately, the state:

> By extending their function, setting for themselves ever bolder tasks, and creating their own federal organs, the factory councils can grow into soviets, having closely united the Social Democratic and Communist workers; and they can serve as the organizational base for the insurrection.[68]

Only such a strategy would guarantee the emergence of a self-activated, class-conscious united front of workers.

However, it should be kept in mind that Luxemburg's accusation of the 'elimination of democracy as such' was directed against Lenin *and* Trotsky; and Horkheimer quotes it as such. In the same way, Marcuse's assertion that Lenin, despite his success in relating to working-class needs and aspirations, did establish 'the priority of the Soviet State over Soviet workers', is coupled with the observation that Lenin's position was 'then fully endorsed by Trotsky'.[69] Similarly, Trotsky continued to affirm the need for a strong party lead of the councils: 'to avow that the soviets "by themselves" are capable of leading the struggle of the proletariat for power—is only to sow abroad vulgar soviet fetishism. Everything depends upon the party that leads the soviets'.[70] Horkheimer, in the face of the degenerate RCP and KPD, seemed unable to envisage *any* party lead. True, he accepted that 'no patented system worked out in advance can preclude regressions', and this held for the council-system too,[71] but Horkheimer did not proceed to affirm the role of the revolutionary party; instead, he specified one sine qua non for democratic socialism, and sat back, hoping it might come to pass.

'Critical theory of society' reveals here a fundamental difference not only from Trotsky but from all *practical* theoreticians. The Frankfurt School emphasise the council-system as a democratic form, but fail to feature this form within a concrete theoretical whole in the sense of revolutionary theory. As Trotsky wrote, after the depressing defeat of the German working class (in which the SPD and KPD had played a fatal role), the Marxist theoretician must still retain the concrete historical perspective of class-struggle:

> It is not a question of counterposing abstract principles, but rather of the struggle of living social forces, with its

inevitable ups and downs, with the degeneration of organisations, with the passing of entire generations into discard, and with the necessity which therefore arises of mobilising fresh forces on a new historical stage. No one has bothered to pave in advance the road of revolutionary upsurge for the proletariat. . . . Those who are frightened by this had better step aside.[72]

The Frankfurt School, while upholding a number of principles (which became 'abstract' in their passivity and isolation), did indeed, in this sense, step aside.

8 The Frankfurt School and Brandlerism

Trotskyism never generated a significant political movement in Germany at this time, and it is thus difficult to assess fully the practical significance of this theory. The Frankfurt School's failure to enter into any 'debate' with Trotsky is thus not altogether inexcusable. However, this is not true for another anti-Stalinist Communist grouping, which did constitute a practical movement to be reckoned with: namely, the KPO (short for KPD-O, where 'O' signified Opposition). This party emerged out of the theory and praxis of the early KPD, and was headed by Brandler. The latter, along with his sympathisers, had been rehabilitated in 1925 (at the time of the Stalinist broadside against the 'ultra-left'), but with the second left turn, in the late 1920s, the right wing of the KPD was denounced and expelled.[73] This development was regarded by Korsch, in his review praised so highly by the Institute, as the second major stage in the KPD's degeneration; so one is justified in expecting to find in the KPO a concretised form of some of the Frankfurt School's principles.

Indeed, the KPO denounced the degeneration of the KPD into a self-satisfied bureaucracy on the one hand, and a passive membership on the other, saying that such a party can 'neither prepare, nor carry out the revolution'.[74] Simultaneously, like Trotsky, the Brandlerites repudiated the Stalinist version of the united front, which for them was no united front at all. In particular, the practice of setting up 'red trade unions' was denounced for exacerbating the hostility between the Social Democratic workers and their Communist counterparts; far from isolating the SPD and trade-union bureaucracy, it led to the application of 'cudgel-tactics' towards the reformist rank and file.[75] Horkheimer, in his *Twilight*, said something very similar: the Communists were scarcely concerned with individual problems, and, being concerned only with the *one* 'truth' (revolution), 'enlightened' the Social Democrats with 'moral, and, if necessary, physical force'.[76]

However, despite its serious concern to preserve the concrete dialectical unity of theory, party and class, the KPO cannot be regarded as any real embodiment of the Frankfurt School's ideas about democratic socialism. First, like Trotsky, the Brandlerites came down firmly on the side of the party, rejecting any fetishisation of the soviet form. Whereas Horkheimer simply bemoaned the smashing of the German soviets, the KPO's analysis stressed the responsibility of the soviets in their own downfall: the First Soviet Congress, of December 1918, was too irresolute, and too inexperienced, to take the necessary draconian measures against the bourgeois state. The bloody suppression of the Spartacists in early 1919 only 'sealed the decision' that had been made (by default) by the Soviet Congress itself.[77] For the KPO, any acknowledgment of the dictatorship of the proletariat, without a simultaneous recognition of the soviet organisation, *as well as* of the CP's leading role in this organisation, was 'worthless'.[78] Unlike Horkheimer, the KPO's awareness of the vicissitudes of revolutionary struggle led not to an abstract hope, but to an affirmation of strict Marxism-Leninism.

But what really demarcated the Frankfurt School from the KPO was the latter's approval of the Stalinist regime. While attacking the 'bureaucratic centralism' of Comintern in the 1920s (of which they were the victims),[79] the Brandlerites refused, until the mid-1930s, to extend this critique to the Stalinist regime itself.[80] Meanwhile, they propounded a thoroughly obnoxious theory as to the relation between party, theory and masses: only industrialisation and collectivisation could prepare the ground for the reduction of the bureaucratic elements and for the active involvement of the masses in political life. During the Five Year Plan, nobody could be allowed to argue against the general line behind this policy. It could only be a question of 'party members and workers being involved in the carrying-out of the Five Year Plan'.[81] Presumably, if Brandlerism had been victorious in Germany, the restored 'democracy' of the KPD would have been used to silence all who were opposed to a German 'socialisation' modelled on Stalin's Russia!

Yet, strangely enough, the KPO had one theoretician who came very close indeed to the Frankfurt School's conception of the dictatorship of the proletariat: namely, Paul Frölich. Frölich, together with two similar-minded comrades, took exception to many of the KPO's policies, and found the above pronouncement on the Five Year Plan particularly repulsive. Their proposed amendment reads like a page from the *Zeitschrift*, with the one exception that it referred explicitly to the USSR:

We must never abandon the principle that the realisation of socialism is no mere socio-economic and technical problem.

The goal of socialism can only be achieved as the conscious work of the working-class, which itself can only mature to its task through its own conscious action. That means not merely the cooperation in the execution of state tasks (which has already been achieved in large measure), but, in addition, the involvement in political decision-making, as well as the assumption of responsibility, and the increase in initiative. The highest authority in the Communist Party of the Soviet Union is, today, not furthering this process of educating the masses to take the responsibility of self-activation; on the contrary, the CPSU is stifling this process.[82]

Indicatively, Frölich and his sympathisers were soon unwelcome in the KPO, and ended up in the SAP (Socialist Workers' Party).[83] This only confirms the KPO's distance from the Frankfurt School's notions as to socialism. But, in addition, it means that the search for a practical embodiment of Frankfurt School theory must eventually turn to the reformist camp, of which the SAP was an issue, if a highly critical one.

9 The Frankfurt School and 'Council Communism'

Before turning to the Social Democratic groupings, there remains one final legacy of Luxemburgism to be discussed: namely, 'Council Communism' (*Rätekommunismus*). In Germany, in the early years of the Weimar Republic, a party calling itself the KAPD (Communist Workers' Party of Germany) emerged out of the KPD, *not in response to any abandonment* of Leninism, but in *defiance* of Leninism;[84] as early as 1920, Lenin recognised and denounced it as such, '*Left-Wing*' *Communism* being largely a polemic against this very political current.[85] The KAPD repudiated what it called 'pre-revolutionary organisational forms' and concentrated almost exclusively on the soviet form, which would arise spontaneously as the ultimate expression of the needs and goals of the masses in a revolutionary situation. The 'Red Fighters' (*Roten Kämpfer*), a later exponent of Council Communism, produced the following document in 1932:

At the present time, the revolutionary party must argue, over and against bourgeois democracy, for the higher form of proletarian democracy, i.e., soviet dictatorship. . . . Only revolutionary consciousness on the part of the workers can lead to the formation of soviets. Thus, everything depends on advancing this revolutionising of consciousness. In parliament, 'leaders' think and act for the masses. But what is needed is for the masses to think for themselves and act through their own organisations, the soviets. . . .[86]

Unlike the KPO, but similar to Horkheimer, the Council Communists did not point out the soviets' own responsibility for the collapse of the revolutionary wave of 1918–19. They did not affirm the Leninist conception of the party. Dedicated to the principle of the dictatorship of the proletariat *by* the proletariat, they absolutised the soviet-system, and waited for a new revolutionary upsurge. One is not without some justification in asking whether Council Communism could perhaps be a concrete embodiment of many of the principles of the Frankfurt School.

Karl Korsch, who had such an influence on 'critical theory of society', had been expelled from the KPD as an 'ultra-left' in the mid-1920s, since which time he had become increasingly sympathetic to Council Communism. In New York, Korsch did a number of reviews for the *Zeitschrift*, or *Studies in Philosophy and Social Science*, as it was now entitled. But Korsch's real interests lay with Paul Mattick's *Living Marxism: International Council Correspondence*. He did try to coax Horkheimer's team into some form of practical commitment in their theoretical work, but this came to nothing. This marks the limits of Korsch's influence on the Frankfurt School, and further illustrates the latter's failure to maintain the theory-praxis nexus.

The whole issue turned on the figure of Anton Pannekoek, the Dutch Council Communist. In 1919, Pannekoek had been positive in his evaluation of the new Russian state, equating Marx's dictatorship of the proletariat, and Communism, with Bolshevism.[87] But the evaluation was subsequently revised; in the 1938 study, *Lenin as Philosopher*,[88] the bureaucratisation of the USSR was traced back to the crude materialism of Lenin's *Materialism and Empirio-Criticism*. Like Korsch and the Frankfurt School, Pannekoek emphasises that historical materialism regards the source of knowledge as the dialectical interaction of social labour and creative mental activity, whereas Lenin 'takes the contradistinction materialism-idealism in the sense of middle-class materialism, with physical matter as its basis'.[89]

For Pannekoek, this had a direct significance for the fatal development of the new Russian State after 1917:

Hereafter the revolution, under the new system of state
capitalism—a combination of middle-class materialism and the
marxian doctrine of social development, adorned with some
dialectic terminology—was, under the name 'Leninism',
proclaimed the official State-philosophy. It was the right
doctrine for the Russian intellectuals who, now that natural
science and technics formed the basis of a rapidly developing
production system under their direction, saw the future open
up before them as the ruling class of an immense empire.[90]

Pannekoek's vision of a true dictatorship of the proletariat shows an unmistakable Luxemburgian influence, as well as a proximity to the Frankfurt School. For example, he says of the proletariat:

> Its object is to be itself master of production and itself to regulate labour, the basis of life. Only then is capitalism really destroyed. Such an aim cannot be attained by an ignorant mass, confident followers of a party presenting itself as an expert leadership. It can be attained only if the workers themselves, the entire class, understand the conditions, ways and means of their fight; when every man knows from his own judgment what to do. . . . Only in this way will a real class organisation be built up from below, having the form of something like workers' councils.[91]

Significantly, Pannekoek's pencilled alterations to his copy of the English translation delete the words 'something like'.

Korsch was highly enthusiastic about the book, apart from one or two minor differences, and described it as 'extraordinarily good in every regard'. This was in a letter of 24 August 1938 to Mattick, where Korsch said he intended to try and interest Horkheimer and the Institute in Pannekoek's book; either he, Korsch, would write a review for the *Zeitschrift*, or else, at the Director's request, he would leave this to Horkheimer himself.[92] Surely Korsch was justified in expecting some response from the Frankfurt School, if only for Pannekoek's philosophical reckoning with Lenin! Yet, no such review appeared, by Korsch or anybody else, in the *Zeitschrift*. And this failure reveals, more than anything else, the break in the theory-praxis nexus: Horkheimer's team steered clear of any debate which had direct political implications. The concrete reality of their otherwise abstract theory was something they actually resisted.

A subsequent letter of 23 December 1938 from Korsch to Mattick[93] reveals the former's total disillusionment with the Institute and their 'impotent philosophy'. Korsch is particularly bitter about 'the metaphysician Horkheimer'. To substantiate this accusation, Korsch refers Mattick to the Director's 'The Latest Attack on Metaphysics'. This is a typical Korschian exaggeration, and when he adds that, 'on the other hand, I am, of course, as a Marxist and *social-scientific* materialist, opposed even to the best form of natural-scientific materialism', Korsch is not doing Horkheimer justice: Horkheimer's entire motivation in this essay was to show the limitations of naive materialism, as well as to show that metaphysics's reflection of these limits was ultimately itself a distortion (see Chapter 2). Yet Korsch had a valid point: the renewed debate with metaphysics was not, in the case of the Frankfurt School, the sublation of philosophy in the true Marxian sense of a *practical* theory of revolutionary struggle.

Korsch must have suspected that dialectics, in a state of suspension, could easily tip over into idealism. As history proved, Horkheimer did indeed go this path (see p. 87). This raises the question of reformism.

10 The Frankfurt School and reformism

All the theories and movements discussed so far have one thing in common: the belief in the need for the revolutionary overthrow of the bourgeois state. The Frankfurt School, in a general sense, subscribed to this view as well. Unfortunately, they could not accept any of the above theories as an adequate embodiment of their views. If one wishes to continue scanning the class-struggles of this period, in the hope of finding such an embodiment, one will eventually have to turn to the reformist camp. Even if the Frankfurt School cannot be located here, a discussion of reformism will prepare the ground for an analysis of left-wing Social Democracy. With the discussion of the latter, which arose as a negation of reformist theory, the outline of the class-struggle will be complete.

The basic characteristic of reformism is the absolutisation, to all intents and purposes, of reforms. Reform and revolution, a dialectical unity in Marxian theory, are separated; the former is elevated to the means of achieving socialism, thus making the latter not only unnecessary, but an undesirable disturbance. Eduard Bernstein, father of reformism, formulated his theory not as a renunciation, but as a 'rationalisation' of Marx. He also substantiated his theory with frequent and positive recourse to Marx and Engels's emphasis on the value of democratic struggles for the vote, freedom of assembly, etc.; but in fact, Bernstein alters the entire significance of these struggles, which now become an aspect in an *evolutionary* development:

> universal suffrage is only a part of democracy, although a part
> which in time must draw the other parts after it, as the magnet
> attracts to itself the scattered iron filings. This certainly
> proceeds more slowly than many would wish, but in spite of that
> it is at work. And Social Democracy cannot further this work
> better than by taking its stand unreservedly, in theory too, on
> the principle of universal suffrage, with all the tactical
> consequences resulting therefrom.[94]

And just to emphasise his reformism, Bernstein fingers out a number of programmatic demands which have become 'dead weight', including the Marxian doctrine of the dictatorship of the proletariat. Such a notion must be thrown overboard, says Bernstein, since the entire SPD is involved in a democratic process which is totally opposed to violent upheavals, and to all dictatorship.[95]

A mark of Bernstein's integrity is that he admits to challenging a basic element in the Marxian method: dialectics. For Bernstein, the 'real' value of Marx's analysis is the emphasis on economic development and democratic advance; the 'weakness' in Marx's work is the stress on revolution. The latter bears witness to a 'residue of utopianism in the Marxian system'.[96] It also reveals a residue of Hegelian dialectics, which constitutes 'the treacherous aspect in the Marxian doctrine, the snare laid in the path of all logical analysis'.[97] Marx's own deviation from reformism is regarded as due exclusively to the unmastered influence of Hegel: 'Every time we see the theory of the economy, as the basis of social development, capitulate to the theory that elevates the cult of force to the pinnacle, then we encounter a Hegelian formulation'.[98] Though Bernstein does speak of the rational application of a 'dialectic disrobed of its mystical character',[99] none the less, dialectic really remains, for the reformist, tantamount to arbitrary construction.[100]

To the Frankfurt School, by contrast, the Hegelian legacy, fully rationalised by Marx, was precisely what marked off historical materialism from crude determinism. Thus, in *Reason and Revolution*, Marcuse attacks Bernsteinian revisionism for ditching the dialectic:

> revisionism replaced the critical dialectic conception with the conformist attitudes of naturalism. Bowing to the authority of the facts, which indeed justified the hopes of a legal parliamentary opposition, revisionism diverted revolutionary action into the channel of a faith in the 'necessary natural evolution' to socialism.[101]

Since theory and praxis were intimately bound up with each other, Marcuse continues, the transformation of theory was bound to result in a 'neutral or positivist attitude to the existing societal form'.[102] Thereby, Marcuse rejects the entire, fatal history of the SPD in the Weimar Republic.

The SPD's faith in evolutionary socialism via parliamentary democracy knew no bounds. With the dissolution of the Great Coalition in 1930, the SPD's share in government had come to an end as far as Weimar Germany was concerned. Parliament itself increasingly lost in importance, yet the SPD's commitment to the parliamentary road to socialism was unshaken. In October 1930, it formulated these priorities: 'In the light of the recent election results, the Social Democratic Reichstag faction sees its primary task as the defence of democracy, the security of the constitution and the protection of parliamentarism. . . .'[103] The logic of this is somewhat absurd: the election concerned was that of 14 September 1930, where the SPD, who had appealed to the masses to reaffirm and strengthen the Social Democratic parliamentary party,[104] had lost support. In fact, the SPD lost more seats than the KPD gained; the victors were the Nazis, multiplying their support sevenfold.[105] But the SPD's conclusion was to reaffirm the very strategy which had alienated so many staunch working-class supporters! Reformism became parliamentary cretinism. Meanwhile, Hitler was appointed Chancellor.

Bernstein had actually considered this possibility, and affirmed that if the reactionaries tried to undermine the efficacy of the SPD's growing parliamentary strength, then revolutionary means would be necessary, and in no way diminished by the reformist strategy practised so far. The recourse to revolution was an unwritten right, guaranteed as securely as a 'natural law'.[106] Similarly, the SPD remained confident that the working-class energy it encompassed could 'go revolutionary' if the worst came to the worst. The reformist media spoke of 'one million members! The might of German Social Democracy'.[107] But the fetishisation of numerical strength, lacking any concrete theory of armed action, even in self-defence, proved its bankruptcy as Weimar democracy crumbled: the SPD lost working-class support increasingly fast, while the many militant trade-unionists and socialists who remained loyal to the party looked in vain for the necessary leadership against the class enemy. 'Utopianism' proved to lie not in the Marxian unity of reform and revolution, but in the abandonment of it; this was no abandonment of the 'speculative' method, but of the reality of class-struggle itself.

Horkheimer, in 1938, saw the demise of the SPD as a lesson to all reformists:

> The history of German Social Democracy should warn against any 'love of culture.' A critical attitude to the dominant culture would have been the only chance for the preservation of the latter's elements. Instead, the picture was largely of a concern to don the bourgeois wisdom of yesterday. . . .[108]

Marcuse's 'The Struggle Against Liberalism in the Totalitarian View of the State' showed clearly how the economic contradictions of capitalism had undermined liberal ideology, and stressed that the monopoly form of capitalist production could not tolerate even liberal democracy indefinitely and uninterruptedly. Reformism wanted to win the masses to the culture of the capitalist social order; this conception misses 'the main point: the abolition of this culture'.[109] As Horkheimer observed, 'freedom' had to be transformed from a 'political philosophy' into 'political praxis'.[110]

11 The Frankfurt School and left-wing Social Democracy

The Frankfurt School thus repudiate the theory and praxis of reformism. However, Horkheimer's team did not proceed to adopt the theory of 'social fascism', which was regarded as undialectical and fatal. But nor did the Institute affirm the anti-Stalinist theories of Trotsky or the KPO. And Council Communism, though it seemed to embody many of the critical concepts of Horkheimer's team, was passed over in silence. The suspicion is engendered that the Frankfurt School, while critical of reformism, did not themselves conceptualise any concrete strategy for transforming 'freedom' into 'political praxis'. However, one final political current has to be reviewed before that suspicion can be confirmed: that is the political current known as left-wing Social Democracy.

The outstanding theoretician of this movement was Max Adler, the Austro-Marxist who exerted tremendous influence on the left-wing of the SPD. Adler's work as a whole covers a vast range of problems, both philosophical and practical. In the former, he was hardly inferior to the Frankfurt School; for example, Adler, in an essay for the *Grünberg Archive*, had anticipated Horkheimer's discussion of Giambattista Vico in *Origins of the Bourgeois Philosophy of History*. Just as the later Director of the Institute sought to learn something 'of practical value' from an analysis of Vico, so Adler had viewed the Italian as 'instructive and stimulating'.[111] And not only did Adler focus on those aspects of Vico's work which had anticipated many of the dialectical insights of Hegel and Marx, but Adler actually anticipated a major concern of Horkheimer's 'critical theory of society': namely, the metacritical evaluation of the attack on natural science:

> In an age that had received the strongest impulses for its view of the world from Descartes, Gassendi and Galilei, seeking to liberate thought from the shackles of theology and replace divine providence with the rule of natural law, it was inevitable that Vico's opposition to this new thought should exclude him from the contemporary scientific current. It had not yet been realised that this opposition to natural science was not a repudiation of science in toto, but simply an objection to naturalism and mechanism, which Vico refused to acknowledge as the governing forces of intellectual and historical processes too.[112]

But this dialectical method of analysis was, for Adler, more than a philosophical weapon: it was also a revolutionary weapon for clarifying and developing correct strategies of class-struggle. In this regard, Adler parts company with the Frankfurt School.

As early as 1919, Adler had broached the question of the council-sytem in all its problematicity. While affirming the soviet form, Adler did not (as Horkheimer did, years later) rest content with any abstract hope that all would go well, but actually spelled out the organisational realities of building socialism. Adler came out openly against syndicalism, referring the reader to Lenin's and Trotsky's qualification of the soviets' role.[113] The spontaneous character of the soviets must be complemented and balanced by a clear commitment to socialism; thus only socialists would be eligible for election to the soviets of the proletarian dictatorship. In fact, the franchise itself could be made dependent on an explicit commitment to socialism.[114]

In the first year of Horkheimer's Directorship in Frankfurt, Adler argued that although the so-called 'dictatorship of the proletariat' in the USSR was, in fact, the 'terrorism of the Communist Party', none the less, terrorism had to be assessed according to its specific socio-historical role; as for the USSR, this terrorism 'carried' the goals of the proletarian dictatorship and found its 'historic class-revolutionary justification' therein.[115] Adler was not blind to the bureaucratic tendencies; on the contrary, he admitted these freely, but he did so by relating directly to the political currents that were actively criticising and attacking such tendencies. In particular, the Stalin-Trotsky debate is regarded as pivotal, and Adler comes down clearly on the side of Trotsky.[116]

Adler did subsequently become so disillusioned with the USSR, that he too, like Horkheimer, made increasingly abstract propaganda for the council-system, without serious discussion of the latter's problematicity,[117] but in Adler's case, unlike Horkheimer, this disillusionment did not break the theory-praxis nexus altogether. Adler's theory was still geared to the concrete realities of class-struggle. In 1932, the year of the *Zeitschrift's* first appearance, Adler attacked the SPD's 'uncritical and deluded *cult of democracy*', which prevented the proletariat from 'using this democracy as a revolutionary weapon of class-struggle'. Horkheimer's later talk of 'a critical attitude to the dominant culture', assumed, in Adler's theory, a much more concrete form:

> the development towards socialism is not that mechanical, economic process which many Marxists still regard it as. Rather, the process is effected only by the conscious, purposive action of men and classes. . . . The class-antagonism of capitalist society creates a situation where, the more the economic conditions prepare the downfall of capitalist society, the more resolute becomes the will of the ruling classes to oppose this economic development and to suppress its effect, as long as possible, by force.[118]

Class-war is thus a need, a duty, and an irresistible fact of life for the labour movement. Left-wing Social Democracy rejected Bernstein's evolutionary economism and reinstated the dialectic of class-struggle.

In Germany, the Frankfurt School's country of origin, left-wing Social Democracy began, in the late 1920s, as a critical faction within the SPD, and was inspired not least of all by Max Adler. The left-wing of the SPD maintained that a sine qua non for success was an unconditional commitment to defend the rights and living standards of the working class, irrespective of the balance of parliament. While lacking any articulate theoretical base, the left-wing dissidents rejected Hilferding's notion of 'organised capitalism', according to which a strong SPD government would be sufficient to realise the full socialist character residing in the development of capitalist planning.[119]

With the financial crash of 1929, the SPD's reformism became even more absurd: in the simile of a leading Social Democrat, capitalism became the 'poorly patient', while the SPD itself became not so much the anxious heir, as the 'doctor'. According to this conception, the worst crises of capitalism were not opportunities to develop a revolutionary class-consciousness, but unfortunate disturbances in an economy that, for the SPD, was within reach of being transformed into a socialist paradise. The SPD's left-wing saw things differently: capitalism could only be 'restored to health' by grinding the 'medicine' out of the workers' bones. Reformism, at a time such as this, turned into an accomplice of the exploitation of the proletariat.[120]

Max Seydewitz, a leading SPD leftwinger, claimed that the pusillanimity of the party was actually weakening the potential force that the labour movement would be able, and obliged, to muster against the coming fascist onslaught; sooner or later, the unrelenting demands by the capitalists for cuts in the standard of living of the workers would force the SPD to stand firm and shout: Thus far, and no further!

> At this juncture, the reigning monopoly capitalism, *in order to pursue its purpose further, will deploy its ultimate weapon, fascism, directly*. And in this situation, the possibility of defence against capitalism's reactionary demands *will depend solely on the military strength that the working-class can muster against its class-enemy*. The more concessions Social Democracy continues to make, and the further the line of 'thus far, and no further' is extended, the more precarious becomes the ultimately decisive military strength of the proletariat.[121]

The influence of Max Adler was unmistakable. But what of the organisation of this military strength?

In the same year as this challenging thesis of Seydewitz, the SPD expelled the left-wing opposition, which now organised as the SAP.[122] The history of this party, and of the practical fight to achieve the principles of left-wing Social Democracy, proved to be a disappointment. The evaluation of the USSR was ambivalent, revealing an unmastered contradiction;[123] and, like Horkheimer, the SAP made the council form into a 'great historical lesson', without considering the *practical* lessons emerging from the Russian experience since 1917.[124] And in terms of class-struggle, the SAP remained a splinter-group; in fact, despite being the largest splinter-group of Weimar Germany's last years, its efficacy was far inferior to the relatively smaller KPO.[125] Even as critics within the SPD, the left wing had lacked any articulate theory of monopoly capitalism, socialism, or bureaucratic degeneration: this weakness was carried over into the SAP.[126] Despite the gaining of the KPO's right wing, including Frölich, left-wing Social Democracy did not generate any significant revolutionary praxis. In late 1932, the party's real Marxists, aware that they were at a dead end, denounced their colleagues bitterly for their wishy-washy politics and their sacrifice of socialism to abstract democratic form.[127]

Like the Frankfurt School, left-wing Social Democracy rejected the undialectical and fatal reformism of the SPD, while simultaneously rejecting the Stalinist notion of 'social fascism'. In addition, again like the Frankfurt School, the SAP kept a clear distance from Trotsky and the KPO, whose militant Leninism seemed to encroach upon the finer democratic principles. But, last, and still in line with 'critical theory of society', the SAP was incapable of structuring its various theoretical elements into an articulate theory of mass political praxis.

12 The practical-theoretical metacritique of the Frankfurt School

But the Frankfurt School, unlike even the SAP, seem to have been convinced in the early 1930s that political praxis, given the conditions obtaining, was already doomed. The 'truth' of 'critical theory of society' became, of necessity, increasingly isolated from the organised oppositional groupings; the only hope was that, at some future date, 'the truth' would once more be taken up in earnest by a significant political movement. Horkheimer wrote in the *Zeitschrift*, in a tone indicative of the period:

> Prior to the vital historical transformation, the truth can be the preserve of numerically small groups. History teaches that such groups, ignored and proscribed even by the oppositional elements of society, are, nonetheless, steadfast and can, on the basis of their deeper insight, take the lead at the decisive moment.[128]

Thus, even in the 'manifesto', the concept of an 'interaction' of critical intellectuals, political avant-garde, and masses, turns from a continued 'debate' into the possibility of a spontaneous transformation of theory into praxis.

Naturally, a spontaneity-theory is conveniently freed from the necessity of formulating organisational categories, but any such theory can hardly claim to be the revolutionary 'truth'. In fact, while stating the possibility of some critical praxis, it says nothing whatever about that praxis. While 'critical theory of society' does demonstrate the theoretical significance of the concept of praxis, it does not itself develop into a practical theory. Thus, when Frankfurt School theory did, in the 1960s, assume a practical significance, in the form of the student anti-authoritarian movement, that very same movement was immediately and unavoidably involved in a fundamental meta-critique of 'critical theory of society'. For example, Hans-Jürgen Krahl, Adorno's most brilliant, and most critical, student, wrote:

> Critical Theory benefited from the tradition of the German Idealists in that its intellectual activity was fitted out against positivism with the mediating reason of dialectics. Critical Theory was able to recognise a concept of totality—and, in reflection upon the critique of political economy, this was an anti-metaphysical concept of totality—but Critical Theory was none the less unable to grasp this totality in its concrete expression as class-antagonism. . . . The practical class standpoint, to put it crudely, did not enter into the theory as an active constituent of that theory.[129]

This is more than an observation as to the limits of Frankfurt School theory: it is a refutation of the claims made by the Frankfurt School regarding their theoretical activity. Krahl says of Adorno: 'his critical option that a theory which is to be vindicated as true must transcend itself and aim at the practical transformation of social reality, loses its binding force if this theory is not able to constitute itself in organisational categories.'[130] Similarly, Horkheimer was a 'revolutionary moralist' of proletarian revolution, and a 'critical theoretician' of bourgeois ideology; 'he was not able to bridge this gap'.[131]

Horkheimer's claim that 'critical theory of society' serves to increase social tension by enlightening the contradictory forces as to their revolutionary significance, now appears in a different light. As Manfred Clemenz, another latter-day critic of the Frankfurt School, has pointed out, the conceptualisation of the theory-praxis nexus by Horkheimer's team regards the relation between ideology-critique and practical theory as unproblematical, assuming 'the direct transition of the one into the other'.[132] This criticism is not the radicalist accusation that 'the Frankfurt School failed to lead a revolution'. Rather, the student anti-authoritarian movement felt that 'critical theory of society' had evaded the problem of evolving a concrete, practical-critical reflection upon class-struggle, past or present.

The student movement of the 1960s in Germany did not delude itself that the revolution was imminent; on the contrary, the most outstanding theoreticians stressed that it was not a question of an 'immediate struggle for political power', but of 'initiating what will certainly be a very long process of enlightenment'.[133] Yet, even here, 'critical theory of society' had little to offer: while it exposed many of the mechanisms of psychic and cultural manipulation, Frankfurt School theory was isolated from the practical categories evolved by other Marxist intellectuals at this time. As a result, the critique of ideology offered no concrete guide even to ideological struggle (see Chapters 4 and 5).

The student movement's appropriation of 'critical theory of society' was metacritical not in a purely theoretical sense, but in a *practical* manner. For example, the critique of 'traditional theory' became an awareness of the need for organised ideological struggle. Krahl maintained:

> technologisation adequate to the needs of capital destroys the time essential for real education, for scientific reflection, and sacrifices it to the de-historicised, purely formalistic capitalist time: labour time. An intellectual cannot afford to let himself be robbed of this qualitative time of conscious scientific reflection. . . .[134]

Thus, the German form of the student anti-authoritarian movement organised to criticise the social significance of the content and method of university courses. They demanded, and themselves instituted, new courses, encouraging reflection upon society and upon education in particular; and they exposed the ultimate capitalist dictatorship in education.

13 Alfred Sohn-Rethel

It is not possible here to give an adequate history of the theoretical and practical activity of the student anti-authoritarian movement. Rather, the point is to thematise the inadequacies of 'critical theory of society'. The same point can be made by reference to Alfred Sohn-Rethel, a theoretician of the same generation as Horkheimer's team, but who went a path very different to that of the Frankfurt School. Sohn-Rethel was in personal contact with Benjamin and Adorno, and, on his own admission, was greatly influenced by Horkheimer and Marcuse.[135] He has also stated that 'in a certain sense' he considers himself a part of the Frankfurt School.[136] But, in a decisive sense, he is not; on the contrary, his theoretical work took him in a direction that helped him to transcend the fundamental weaknesses in 'critical theory of society' as outlined above. Sohn-Rethel's theory, appearing in mature form in the 1970s, includes a serious attempt to provide a historical materialist analysis of the specific nature of capitalist exploitation in its *monopoly* phase, together with a Marxist critique of the USSR, and finally, a concept of complete emancipation.

Sohn-Rethel's work began as a fairly obscure analysis of the commodity form, which he regarded as the key to the transcendental subject. As early as 1937, Sohn-Rethel wrote:

> *The constitutive synthesis* at the base of all theoretical knowledge, both *logically* and *genetically, is reification and the reified societation effected by exploitation.* The proof of this thesis contains the critical liquidation of idealism in the form of a liquidation of the antinomies in which men's own reason entangles them via the fetishism of reification.[137]

Benjamin, looking at this manuscript on behalf of Horkheimer's Institute, wrote a marginal note to this point, saying: 'it would be tremendous if he were right.'[138] And in a letter of 28 March 1937, Benjamin told the Director that the attempt to derive pure theoretical thought from commodity-production, though incredibly difficult, was highly 'significant'.[139]

Sohn-Rethel felt that the Institute, more than anybody, would be receptive to his work. He wrote an expository letter to Adorno in 1936,[140] and decades later, in *Negative Dialectics*, Adorno referred to Sohn-Rethel as the first to point out that 'hidden in the transcendental principle, in the general and necessary activity of the mind, lies labour of an inalienably social nature'.[141] Sohn-Rethel, for his part, admits that nobody was more sympathetic than Adorno, 'who, in his own theoretical work, and in his own peculiar way, was on the track of the same insight'.[142] But Sohn-Rethel's subsequent development led him beyond the methodological premises of Adorno's metacritique of epistemology; thus, Sohn-Rethel says of his work in the 1930s:

> At this stage, it was still not clear to me that my concern with ideology-critique did not aim at ideology itself, but, through it, at the critique of being, that is, at a better understanding of the hidden economic developments of the present. In fact, ideology-critique was inadequate to the task of a 'metacritique of knowledge'. . . .[143]

This has critical significance for the entire Frankfurt School, and, in particular, for their critique of ideology.

One of the crucial phenomena Sohn-Rethel re-examined was the division of labour, especially the split of mental and manual labour.

For Marx, the latter was the first *true* division of labour.[144] Thus, when he stressed, as a sine qua non of the 'higher phase of communist society', the disappearance of 'the enslaving subordination of the individual to the division of labour', he added that 'therewith also the antithesis between mental and physical labour' would have 'vanished'.[145] This is why production in a classless society, though remaining a necessity, will involve a new freedom: 'Freedom in this field can only consist in socialised man, the associated producers, rationally regulating their interchange with Nature, bringing it under their common control, instead of being ruled by it as by the blind forces of Nature.'[146] Thus, freedom is not merely the transcendence of the labour-process, but an aspect of the latter. The mental control over the labour-process must be reappropriated by the labourers: this is the economic base of classless society.

Analysing contemporary society in this light, Sohn-Rethel evolves a theory of economic manipulation in *monopoly* capitalism. Taking Frederick Winslow Taylor as an ideal-type, as the 'signature of an entire epoch', Sohn-Rethel explains 'scientific management' (time-and-motion studies, or industrial engineering) in terms of the absolutisation of the split of mental and manual labour; indeed, Taylor himself conceived of it as such. But what Taylor did not see was that the new science of industrial engineering was 'the alienated societation of the workers' own labour'.[147] This, for Sohn-Rethel, is the fundamental aspect of manipulation in monopoly capitalism.

The Frankfurt School, though lacking an articulate economic theory, are not blind to the problem. Marcuse came very close to Sohn-Rethel's insight, in the *Zeitschrift* article entitled 'Some Social Implications of Modern Technology', where he actually focused on the significance of Taylorism.[148] Marcuse is discussed at a later stage in the chapter, because he constitutes a more advanced position than his colleagues. But Adorno and Horkheimer too came close to the problem; in an outstanding passage, which qualifies the usual absolutisation of superstructural manipulation, they focus on economic manipulation in contemporary society; the occasion is a discussion of Odysseus and the Sirens:

> Through the mediation of the total society, which embodies all relations and emotions, men are once again made to be . . . mere species beings, exactly like one another through isolation in the forcibly united collectivity. The oarsmen, who cannot speak to one another, are each of them yoked in the same rhythm as the modern worker in the factory, movie theatre, and collective. The actual working conditions in society compel conformism— not the conscious influences which also made the suppressed men dumb and separated them from truth.[149]

Unfortunately, the primacy of *economic* manipulation was not reflected in the overall direction of Horkheimer's and Adorno's research.

Sohn-Rethel's economic theory enabled not only an understanding of economic manipulation, but equally, a theory of the emancipation of labour. Horkheimer, it will be remembered, stressed, quite correctly, that socialism meant more than a transfer of property rights, and more than just the 'raising of productivity in new forms of social cooperation'. Unfortunately, Horkheimer concentrated on 'the nature and development of the society in which all this happens', and failed to ask after the precise nature of the 'new forms of social cooperation'. Thus, he reiterated Marx's idea of 'the true realm of freedom' as being beyond the working day, but failed to specify the freedom *within* the classless production-process, a freedom that formed the essential base of any other freedom. Nor was this economic freedom ever specified by the Institute's economists; on the contrary, their concrete economic theories often fell behind the abstract, but well-informed, observations of the Director. For example, Kurt Mandelbaum and Gerhard Meyer wrote that 'with the socialisation of the means of production, the basis for class-rule would have been eradicated'. Yet they conceive of classless society in terms of a 'planned control of the economy', without emphasising that socialisation means control *by the producers*.[150]

Clearly, the most advanced concepts and categories of the Frankfurt School were not complemented by an adequate economic theory. What is needed today is a redress of this balance; and Sohn-Rethel's work is a clear indication of how to sublate 'critical theory of society'. For example, the degeneration of the USSR can be grasped fully only by recourse to a theory of economic alienation. Sohn-Rethel is not blind to the hardships forced on the Bolshevik state by the chaotic state of the war-ravaged economy, but he criticises the Bolsheviks for canonising the early expedients of economic direction. The theory of reconciling mental and manual labour has been lost in the USSR, says Sohn-Rethel:

> Certainly, democratising tendencies have made themselves felt, but, as in the West, these tendencies do not in the least aim at replacing the authority of the factory-directors with a socialist authority of the workers. Rather, it is a question of a gradual involvement of the workers in the former.[151]

In Luxemburg's terms, the Russian Communists have made a 'virtue' of necessity. They have lost the true Marxian vision of the 'proletariat organised as the ruling class'.

Sohn-Rethel's economic theory means that he can take up a critical position vis-à-vis the USSR, without relinquishing the concrete relation to class-struggle. As Sohn-Rethel rightly claims, the Frankfurt School's distance from Stalinist Russia resulted, due to the absence of an economic theory, in an 'inability to form any concept of communist politics or workers' praxis'. In this sense, the Frankfurt School 'turned their backs on the political praxis of class-struggle'.[152] This is not to deny that the Frankfurt School made a large number of highly incisive observations; for example, Horkheimer stressed, in true Luxemburgian terms, that 'in the struggle for classless society, the masses must first organise themselves, and transform themselves from a mere object into the active subject of history, thereby throwing off their character of being masses once and for all'.[153] But no indication is given as to the practicalities of this struggle; a spontaneity-theory takes the place of an embarrassed silence. Sohn-Rethel's theory, by contrast, has developed into a general theory of the class-struggle for control of the factories; it is the theory of 'a praxis which, without such theoretical consciousness, will get lost in the frustration of mere pseudo-revolutionary work-struggles within a capitalist framework'.[154] Sohn-Rethel's theory as to the real revolutionary struggle is far from complete; in particular, the prospects of a deskilled proletariat evolving an adequate class-consciousness and a radical offensive against capital are totally unclear. But these are questions which the Frankfurt School, due to a lack of economic analysis, never even approached.

14 The degeneration of 'critical theory of society' in Horkheimer

The lack of economic theory in the work of the Frankfurt School means, ultimately, not only the abandonment of class-struggle, but, equally, a tendential idealisation of the values that 'critical theory of society' drew from liberal ideology. Horkheimer himself stressed that when the concepts of freedom and equality are employed without 'clear reference to the historical present and to praxis', then these concepts 'degenerate into pure ideals'.[155] Unfortunately, this accusation, levelled against Social Democratic theory, also strikes Horkheimer himself. Even in the 1930s, his 'critical theory of society' had lost the theory-praxis nexus (in its materialist dimension). As time went on, the tendential idealism was progressively realised.

Dialectic of Enlightenment, written jointly with Adorno, and published in the mid-1940s, marks a stage in this degeneration. Despite the brilliant attack on 'culture industry' (see Chapter 5), the lack of economic analysis produces a hypostatisation of many of the central concepts. Thus, the cause of the regression of Enlightenment into a new, repressive mythology is to be found 'in the Enlightenment itself when paralysed by fear of the truth'. Despite the authors' stress that 'Enlightenment' and 'truth' must be understood not just as cultural values, but in their 'real', materialist dimension 'in actual life',[156] none the less, this dimension is never delineated in any adequate manner. Any relation to critical praxis is thus precluded, and the assertion that 'the Enlightenment *must examine itself*, if men are not to be wholly betrayed',[157] remains a sad but impotent precept. Not surprisingly, Wellmer, who wrongly depicts the early Frankfurt School as fundamental critics of Marx (see Chapter 2), regards *Dialectic of Enlightenment* as a positive advance by 'critical theory of society'.[158]

The student anti-authoritarian movement, which drew so much of its theoretical armament from 'critical theory of society', failed to provoke Horkheimer and Adorno (who had returned to Europe) to reconsider their work. On the contrary, the student movement was met either by a silence, or actual hostility. As Krahl relates, the organised struggle was repudiated as 'actionist' and lacking in any conceptual coherence.[159] Horkheimer, in prefacing the reissue of his *Zeitschrift* essays, was predominantly concerned to distance himself from any practical expression of his ideas in the German students' revolt:

> To protect, preserve, and, where possible, extend the limited and ephemeral freedom of the individual in the face of the growing threat to this freedom, is far more urgent a task than the abstract negation of it, or the endangering of this freedom by actions that have no hope of success.[160]

This is not merely the repudiation of the notion of 'social fascism', but, ultimately, the abdication of all critical praxis. Instead of a 'critical attitude to the dominant culture', which Horkheimer had demanded as a *practical* strategy in the 1930s, Horkheimer now himself reverts to a reformist acceptance of the 'lesser evil', and leaves the next move to his most hated enemy.

This marked the beginning of Horkheimer's total theoretical collapse, a collapse that vindicated Korsch's accusation against 'the metaphysician Horkheimer' (see p. 74). For example, the former Director of the Institute came to an abstract defence of liberal capitalism:

> the development of man is tied up with competition, the most important element in liberal economy. Competition in the economic field also furthered man's mind. . . . Marx projected the all-round development of the personality, as a goal, into the future. Yet this very development was to a large extent a consequence of the liberal era, and, as such, tends to vanish along with liberalism itself.[161]

In this way, liberalism is vindicated retrospectively, and the critical praxis that might realise all-round development in a classless society disappears from view.

Horkheimer's conception of 'critical theory of society' had actually turned full circle by the time of his death. In his inaugural lecture, and in his preface to the *Zeitschrift*, Horkheimer viewed society as subject to change, a change that was to be registered in 'critical theory of society', but without this theory assuming an active agitational role in directing this change. The subsequent conception of the role of the critical intellectual went far beyond this, but the actual analyses failed to achieve the full theory-praxis nexus of *practical-critical* theory. In his dotage, Horkheimer returned to his earlier conception: 'Critical Theory always had a dual task: to specify what must be changed, and to retain certain cultural moments. In addition, it must describe the process of change that our world is subject to.'[162] What Horkheimer has forgotten completely is that a theory which does not relate to the active subjects of change cannot even identify 'what must be changed' to begin with.

15 The radicalisation of 'critical theory of society' in Marcuse

To Marcuse, Horkheimer's last interviews are 'beneath criticism'.[163] The harshness of this judgment, even though directed at a former colleague, is fully justified: to a man of Marcuse's calibre and unswerving integrity, Horkheimer's last years were not only a betrayal of the Institute's early work on a 'critical theory of society', but, in addition, a betrayal of those very values that Horkheimer claimed, within a new-found metaphysical framework, to uphold still. But Horkheimer's betrayal was not a complete shock; after all, Korsch had anticipated it in the late 1930s. The fact is that the contradiction within 'critical theory of society', the contradiction between the appropriation of liberal values and the lack of revolutionary materialism in this appropriation, was bound to be resolved, one way or the other, in the face of the emerging student anti-authoritarian movement. Horkheimer's uncritical absolutisation of liberal ideology was one resolution of the contradiction. Fortunately, the other possible resolution, the materialisation and radicalisation of 'critical theory of society', found direct expression in Marcuse.[164]

Marcuse has recently admitted that he had differences with Horkheimer even in the 1930s; for example, Marcuse felt that the Institute's work and publications were 'too psychological' and lacked an adequate economic and political dimension.[165] Marcuse's claim can be substantiated by an examination of his personal contributions at this time. In the *Studies*, Marcuse, unlike the Director, reaffirms the Marxian notion of a freedom *in* the production-process, and not just beyond it. Marcuse quotes the relevant passage from *Capital* (see p. 85) and explains that here, for the first time, freedom is recognised as a task of 'the organisation of the social labour process'.[166] Marcuse touches on Sohn-Rethel's ideas when he says of classless society: 'The features of the authority structure determined by class society will disappear, in particular the function of exploitation and the political appropriation of "management" in the capitalist system of domination.'[167] In 'Some Social Implications of Modern Technology', Marcuse actually denounced Taylorism as 'streamlined autocracy'.[168] And in *Soviet Marxism*, he pointed out that in the so-called 'dictatorship of the proletariat' of the USSR, 'domination remains a specialised function in the division of labour and is as such the monopoly of a political, economic, and military bureaucracy'.[169]

This materialist insight led directly to Marcuse's solidarity with the emerging critical praxis of the 1960s. Unlike Horkheimer's alienation from the seemingly incoherent revolt, Marcuse justified it:

> At its most advanced stage, domination functions as administration, and in the overdeveloped areas of mass consumption, the administered life becomes the good life of the whole, in the defence of which the opposites are united. This is the pure form of domination. Conversely, its negation appears to be the pure form of negation. All content seems reduced to the one abstract demand for the end of domination—the only true revolutionary exigency. . . .[170]

But Marcuse is more than an ally: he is a relentless, though fraternal critic. He describes the total negation as an 'abstract' demand, and he stresses its 'politically impotent form'.[171] In line with his emphasis on the production front, Marcuse asserts: 'The radical transformation of a social system still depends on the class which constitutes the human base of the process of production. In the advanced capitalist countries, this is the industrial working class.'[172] Contrary to popular belief, Marcuse has *never* shifted from this basic position.

However, this did not exclude a serious discussion of the critical significance of student unrest. Marcuse, unlike his former colleagues, defended the seemingly 'extraneous' politicisation of the university by 'disrupting radicals' as the legitimate expression of the internal dynamic of education: 'translation of knowledge into reality, of humanistic values into humane conditions of existence'. Radical consciousness may indeed arise within society's institutions of learning and Marcuse, like Krahl, stresses that this sphere must be defended against total instrumentalisation: 'the struggle for a free and critical education becomes a vital part in the larger struggle for change.'[173]

However, despite the talk of the proletariat's radicalisation being dependent on 'catalysts outside its ranks',[174] Marcuse does not subscribe to any Leninist conception of an avant-garde of intellectuals. As early as *Soviet Marxism*, Marcuse wrote of Lenin:

His struggle against 'economism' and the doctrine of spontaneous mass action, his dictum that class consciousness has to be brought upon the proletariat 'from without,' anticipate the later factual transformation of the proletariat from the subject to an object of the revolutionary process.[175]

Thus, Marcuse's most recent conception of revolutionary organisation carefully precludes any notion of students and intellectuals 'taking the truth to the workers'. Rather, the two groups, workers and intellectuals, must 'act each *from its own base* and in terms of its own consciousness, grievances, and goals'. Students and intellectuals can, and indeed are obliged to, furnish the workers with agitational material relevant to their respective struggles, but there is no question of intellectuals *leading* these struggles. As Marcuse himself admits, this is 'very different' from the 'development of class consciousness from without'.[176]

For Marcuse, there is a 'chance' that 'the most advanced consciousness of humanity', and 'its most exploited force' may meet again; it is 'nothing but a chance'.[177] But this is not the spontaneity-theory as implied by Horkheimer's passive concern with the pure 'truth'. Rather, Marcuse's spontaneity links up to the anti-Leninist movement of Council Communism. Significantly, Paul Mattick's *Critique of Marcuse*[178] is not, ultimately, a total repudiation. Mattick, a former Spartacist, and ex-member of the KAPD, criticises Marcuse for his lack of precise analysis of world economics, but Mattick, too, conceives of revolution as a 'chance', not as an ever-present potential which can be realised by a Leninist avant-garde: 'The readiness to take revolutionary steps does not necessitate a consistent oppositional behaviour prior to the first independent act; an apathetic working class under certain conditions can become an aroused working class under different conditions'.[179] Thus, the revolutionary theoretician waits for such conditions to crystallise. As Marcuse recently revealed, he recognised as the real heir to Rosa Luxemburg's Spartacus not right-wing, but left-wing communism.[180] Hence, Marcuse's latest work discusses the possibility of the re-emergence of the soviets, 'organisations of self-determination, self-government (or rather preparation for self-government)'. Although he adds that such a theory and strategy must not succumb to any fetishism of 'below',[181] Marcuse does not envisage an intellectual avant-garde leading the soviets in the Leninist tradition.

Marcuse's radicalised theoretical activity has not produced any 'definitive' revolutionary strategy, since his theory is a dialectical response to an emerging new praxis, a praxis which is still in its early stages and which has itself not yet evolved any definitive theoretical or practical armament. Thus, Marcuse's work since the mid-1960s is an attempt to revitalise, radicalise and sublate the revolutionary intention of 'critical theory of society', linking it, in critical solidarity, to the incipient practical movement. In this sense, Marcuse is the 'sublation' of the Frankfurt School's work of the *Zeitschrift* period.

16 'Critical theory of society' and the analysis of manipulation

Having traced two divergent developments in the Frankfurt School, and having established Marcuse's role as the living 'sublation' of 'critical theory of society', it still remains to examine the significance of the theoretical productions of the *Zeitschrift* period. Why were these taken up, reissued and distributed in such earnest by the student anti-authoritarian movement? The answer has already been given, in part, by Krahl: the Frankfurt School helped students and intellectuals to realise the critical significance of German Idealism and dialectics in general. But 'critical theory of society' also focused on the problem of manipulation; Krahl states:

> Critical Theory provided a political movement of intellectuals, which was an offshoot of a past bourgeois class, with concepts of emancipation. Critical Theory demonstrated how the bourgeois individual and the domination-free ideology of the liberal market are irrevocably lost. Critical Theory also demonstrated how this society as a whole develops a tendency towards a technological class-society which reduces individuals to the reaction-patterns of Pavlovian dogs, robbing these individuals of all those critical ego factors that the bourgeois family had still tolerated, although one has, at the same time, to recognise that what Horkheimer apologetically observed in liberal society, only really holds for the families of the bourgeoisie.[182]

Krahl does not mean, by 'concepts of emancipation', that the Frankfurt School evolved a practical vision of ideological struggle; what he means is that the general notions, contained within what is largely a critique of manipulation, have a critical, and *potentially practical* significance. At the same time, the lack of economic and socio-political specificity in 'critical theory of society' means a distortion of these notions.

In 1965, Horkheimer wrote the following words, relating his *Zeitschrift* essays to his present position: 'The faith which at that time, on the basis of an analysis of society, I had in progressive activity, now turns into fear of new evil, fear of totalitarian administration.'[183] However, even in the 1930s, the faith in praxis was qualified by an awareness, highly acute, of the modern-day machinery of manipulation. The 'manifesto' said that the critical theoretician could not count on the support of any social group, since each and every such group could 'under present conditions be ideologically restricted and corrupted, no matter how much its social position should destine it for truth'.[184] Thus, even in the *Zeitschrift* period, the concern was largely with an analysis of manipulation. But, in addition, any 'faith' Horkheimer entertained in praxis was not based on any adequate 'analysis of society'. In fact, the lack of economic and political theory turned any optimism into an abstract, purely subjective preoccupation.

Having outlined, in Chapter 2, the methodological contributions of 'critical theory of society', and having pinpointed, in this chapter, the ultimate break in the theory-praxis nexus, it remains to examine in detail the Frankfurt School's analysis of manipulation. The metacritical perspective, however, demands a stringent procedure in this examination: the critical categories must be appropriated in such a way as to qualify the theoretical distortions, and relate the contradictions within the manipulative machinery to the needs, possibilities and goals of critical praxis. The intention is not to demolish, but rationalise the Frankfurt School's work in the period concerned (1930–42).

4 Historical materialist psychology: the psychic dimension of manipulation and revolt

The analysis of manipulation, which was predominantly super-structural manipulation, began as a psychological undertaking. This was announced in Horkheimer's inaugural lecture, as well as his editorial preface to the first issue of the *Zeitschrift*. One of the central questions outlined by the Director was that of the 'psychic connecting links' between the economic base and the superstructural expression of ideology. An essay by Horkheimer in the first issue of the *Zeitschrift* continued to point out the problematicity of this question:

> As long as theory has not recognised how structural changes in economic life are transformed, via the psychic constitution of the various social groups at a given moment in time, into changes in the expression of their life as a whole, then the theory of the dependence of the one on the other contains a dogmatic element which seriously restricts this theory's hypothetical value in the explanation of the present.[1]

The question of a historical materialist psychology is thus not merely academic, but a crucial need of 'critical theory of society' in the face of modern history (the rise of monopoly capitalism and fascism).

Horkheimer's inaugural lecture mentioned the need for a methodical study of the relevant scientific writings on the subject.[2] Hence, the *Zeitschrift*, in contrast to the *Archive*, undertook to review the writings of Freud, Jung and other psychologists. But before analysing the Frankfurt School's work in this field, it is essential to establish the fundamental question to be answered in this analysis: namely, is *any* psychological component compatible with historical materialism? This raises the problem of 'orthodox Marxism'. It is not a problem to be resolved easily. For example, Lukács stressed in 1923 that 'orthodoxy refers exclusively to *method*'. Marxist 'orthodoxy' was the belief that dialectical materialism is the 'road to truth', and that 'its methods can be developed, expanded and deepened only along the lines laid down by its founders', whereas 'all attempts to surpass or "improve" it have led and must lead to over simplification, triviality and eclecticism'.[3]

Despite Engels's admission (see Chapter 1) that he and Marx had, in their theory of ideology, 'stressed the content and neglected the form, i.e. the ways and means by which these notions come about', the general consensus among 'orthodox Marxists' (who are usually 'orthodox Marxist-Leninists') is that psychology cannot deepen historical materialism; psychology is not encompassed within the lines laid down by the founders of historical materialism, and must thus lead to 'eclecticism'. Walter Jopke, for example, maintains that even where the Frankfurt School does employ the basic concepts of Marxism, they are stripped of their real significance and replaced by 'an eclectic mixture of Hegelian, Marxian and Freudian categories'.[4] Robert Steigerwald speaks of a 'biological, drive-structural revision of historical materialism',[5] and Gert Meixner states that 'the attempt-to transfer psychoanalysis to human society is doomed from the start'.[6] Any combination of Marx and Freud is *necessarily* eclectic, at least according to Marxist 'orthodoxy'.

While it has already been established that the economic categories of 'critical theory of society' were not integrated into a coherent conceptual whole, and that this gap created a tendential idealisation and hypostatisation in the *Zeitschrift* period, it has also been established that the Frankfurt School's work on manipulation did make a considerable contribution to the theoretical armament of the student anti-authoritarian movement. What is thus called for is a careful appropriation of the Institute's progressive analyses, in such a way as to establish whether the eclecticism of 'critical theory of society' is in fact not due to the *attempt* to reconcile depth-psychology and historical materialism, but to the failure to *integrate* the former without undermining the latter.

1 Fromm and the significance of depth-psychology

The only adequate psychology that could be of use to 'critical theory of society', was, for the Frankfurt School, Freud's.[7] The member of Horkheimer's team designated the task of propounding and realising the task of integrating Freud's work into 'critical theory of society' was Fromm. The first major statement on this problem by Fromm was *The Development of the Dogma of Christ*.[8] Written before joining the Institute, Fromm's study had exposed both the historical materialist implications, as well as the a-historical distortions, of

Freudianism. The analysis was reviewed favourably by Borkenau, in the *Zeitschrift*, as 'the first attempt to illustrate, on the basis of a concrete example, the methodological synthesis of Marxism and Freudian psycho-analysis'.[9] Fromm subsequently joined Horkheimer's team, undertaking to give an exhaustive exposé, and a concrete application of this synthesis.

Fromm's programmatic first essay bore the obvious title 'The Method and Function of an Analytic Social Psychology'.[10] It did not fail to quote the relevant admission by Engels of a gap in historical materialism.[11] Fromm then proceeded to show how the attempts to fill this gap had, due to the complete ignorance as to the mechanisms of the psyche, produced a 'purely idealistic psychology', smuggling in a disguised 'innate moral principle'.[12] Therefore, a depth-psychological component was not only *compatible* with Marxism, but *necessary* to it, if idealist appendages to concrete analyses were to be forestalled.

Fromm maintained that a largely acceptable psychology had been developed by Freud: psychoanalysis was a materialist, historical and social science.[13] The drive theory was compatible with Marxism, Fromm argued, since the 'drive-constitution' only manifests itself in a dialectical interaction with the socio-historically specific 'life experiences'.[14] Marx, in his early writings, had referred to man's 'drives' or 'instincts' (*Triebe*),[15] and in *Capital* he accepted the primary nature of certain drives, referring to 'human nature in general' and 'human nature as modified in each historical epoch'.[16] For Marx, the satisfaction of basic needs 'leads to new needs',[17] while at the same time producing 'the object of consumption, the manner of consumption and the motive of consumption'.[18] Man thus produces himself by satisfying his needs, creating new forms of these needs, and creating new needs.

For Marx, production also involves intellectual production; this, in turn, involves the problem of ideology, a crucial concern of the Frankfurt School. Marx, it should be recalled, precluded any crude economic determinism:

Men are the producers of their conceptions, ideas, etc. . . . .
Consciousness can never be anything else than conscious
existence, and the existence of men is their actual life-process.
If in all ideology men and their circumstances appear
upside-down as in a camera obscura, this phenomenon
arises just as much from their historical life-process as the
inversion of objects on the retina does from their physical life-
process.[19]

But this process, by which the alienated social world is then further distorted in an alienated form of intellectual activity, is a process which can be attested, but not explained, unless recourse is made to depth-psychology. This is the precise point at which the Frankfurt School intend to make an original contribution to the historical materialist analysis of ideological manipulation.

Fromm argues that Freudian psychology and Marxian materialism coincide in regarding consciousness not as the ultimate motor of history, but as the reflection of 'other, hidden forces'.[20] To Marx, these forces were precisely man's instincts, needs and productive capacities; they had become 'hidden' because these human forces had, within class-society, taken on a reified, alienated aspect. Man's own creative powers had turned into an alien force that dominated him. Fromm endeavours to reveal the psychic effect of this alienation; the key factor is the peculiarity of the sex-drive. Whereas hunger, though modifiable, is not so modifiable as to be capable of satisfaction by anything but food, the sexual urge is capable of extreme modification: it can be postponed, repressed, sublimated, transformed: 'A man's hunger can only be satisfied by food; his desire to be loved, however, can be satisfied by fantasies about a good and loving God. . . .'[21] The vicissitudes of the sexual drive mark off this instinct as capable of the greatest 'adaptations to the real possibilities for satisfaction that exist'.[22] It thus actually has an accommodating, even justificatory, function; and this, for Fromm, is the key to ideology: 'Psychoanalysis can show that man's ideologies are the products of certain wishes, instinctual drives, interests, and needs, which themselves, in large measure, unconsciously find expression as rationalisations, i.e., as ideologies.'[23]

2 Freud versus Jung

In the *Studies*, Fromm explained that the only psychologist to whom 'critical theory of society' could link was Freud, first because Freud's psychological categories, due to their 'dynamic character', were the 'only ones of any use', and, second, because Freud had applied these categories to the problem of authority (a central concern of the Institute), producing 'many important and fruitful insights'.[24] Freud's work passed through several quite distinct phases, of course, but it is essentially the post-1920 period of Freud's theoretical production which is of greatest significance for the Frankfurt School. It is this period of Freud's work from which Horkheimer's team draw most of their ideas and direct quotations. And this is because 1920 was a major turning-point in Freud's work, introducing the controversial thesis of a death-instinct, which in turn paved the way for the concept of the super-ego. It was this latter which, for the Frankfurt School, provided the key to the problem of ideology.

The attitude to Jung, by contrast, was wholly negative. Leo

Löwenthal, as early as 1932, rejected the entire Jungian perspective, particularly its propensity for mythical doctrines of race.[25] This evaluation in the *Zeitschrift* was echoed by Marcuse in later years: Jung was an example of the 'right wing' of 'neo-Freudian revisionism'.[26] It is significant that Jung, in turning his back on Freud, criticised the latter for precisely those qualities which Fromm regards as the historical materialist component of psychoanalysis. Whereas Freud, like Marx, accepted that even the primary needs of man were historically modified, Jung emphasised the a-historicality of both the drives and consciousness: 'From the unconscious there emanate determining influences which, independently of tradition, guarantee in every single individual a similarity and even a sameness of experience, and also of the way it is represented imaginatively.'[27] This not only repudiates the dialectical interaction of man with his sociohistorical context ('an exlusive reduction to causes', according to Jung),[28] but also, in conjunction with the 'archetypes', produces an idealist distortion of the genesis of religions, which, says Jung, 'contain a revealed knowledge that was originally hidden', and now 'set forth the secrets of the soul in glorious images'.[29]

To Freud, religion was a culturally induced 'illusion', a 'universal neurosis', a 'wish', a 'delusion', a 'mass-delusion'.[30] This was, of course, the position of the Frankfurt School. Adorno, for example, wrote the following about Wagner's use of myth:

> On the one hand, his mythological intention aims at the conscious illumination of the individual psychology and views the seemingly autonomous individual in his dependence on the totality. On the other hand, the myths themselves serve the regression to the primeval and would-be immutable. The antithesis of Freud and Jung is virtually contained in Wagner's work.[31]

To Marcuse, Jung's psychology was not even a mythology, but an 'obscurantist pseudo-mythology'.[32] What was needed was not a revision of Freud's tendential historical materialism, but the realisation of the latter.

3 Strengths and weaknesses of Freud's depth-psychology

Freud's fundamental achievement was to evolve a critical methodological and categorial apparatus for illuminating the interaction of experience, response and 'human nature'. This is Fromm's judgment as to analytic psychology: 'It locates man's instinctual apparatus among the natural factors that modify the social process, although there are limits to this modifiability. . . . The human psyche always remains a psyche that has been modified by the social process.'[33]

Unfortunately, Freud himself was no consistent historical materialist. On the contrary, his incisive analyses of the family are often complemented by a retrospective absolutisation of the psychic structures of modern society.

An example of this is Freud's thesis of the slaying of the 'primal father'. Meixner relates this thesis, though somewhat inaccurately,[34] in order to reveal the absurd a-historicality of Freudian theory and thus vindicate his assertion that psychoanalysis is incompatible with the Marxian analysis of society. This particular anecdote is indeed an example of all that is bad in Freud. Although he tried to justify and qualify the thesis by calling it a 'hypothesis', a 'Just-So-Story' that endeavours to 'lighten the darkness of prehistoric times',[35] the fact remains that the myth of the primal father's murder is lacking precisely in historical detail.

At best, this anecdote may cast light on the mechanisms of guilt within contemporary society. But, unfortunately, Freud's analysis of contemporary man (or rather middle-class men) is presented by Freud himself as the depiction of 'man'. Consequently, there is no room for a conscious differentiation between class-society and class-less society, let alone between classes themselves. Alienation becomes, as with Hegel, an integral aspect of material life: thus, 'the great majority of people only work under the stress of necessity', proof for Freud of a 'natural human aversion to work'.[36] However, the historical materialist does not have to reject such a view out of hand; rather, by qualifying it, he can turn it into a valid indictment. Marx said, of Adam Smith's view of work as sacrifice: 'He is right, of course, that, in its historic forms as slave-labour, serf-labour, and wage-labour, labour always appears as repulsive, always as *external forced labour;* and not-labour, by contrast, as "freedom, and happiness".'[37] This is the same perspective as Horkheimer advocates in his essay on philosophical anthropology.[38] And it is a method that the Frankfurt School applied, in large measure, to Freud's psychology.

But if the a-historical tendencies outlined above can be surmounted, there remains one major component of Freud's metapsychology which the Frankfurt School did not resolve: namely, the so-called 'death-drive'. The latter, paradoxically, gave rise to some of Freud's most critical social insights, including the operation of the super-ego; but the entire thesis of a 'death-instinct' in the sense of a primary, immutable psychic force, reveals a fundamentally a-historical and socially uncritical character. The Frankfurt School of the *Zeitschrift* period did reject this particular Freudian thesis, but they never resolved the problematic which had prompted Freud to it. And they appropriate, as the most telling of Freud's concepts, precisely those ones which were derived from the death-drive theory. The Frankfurt

School fail to reconstitute these concepts, and fail to free them from the metapsychological thesis out of which, sadly, they grew. Thus, the contradictions of Freud's theory are, in this crucial case, reproduced in the Frankfurt School's otherwise critical appropriation. This being the case, the question of fusing Marx and Freud can only be answered by taking the death-drive theory, laying bare its contradictions, and resolving them.

4 The pitfall of the death-drive theory

The Frankfurt School's rejection, in the figure of Fromm, of the death-drive theory does not fail to concede that Freud's argument for this thesis is 'significant'.[39] Going out from the problem of the 'repetition compulsion', Freud came to the conclusion that the human organism is essentially conservative, even retrogressive; the goal of the drives is 'an *old* state of things, an initial state from which the living entity has at one time or other departed and to which it is striving to return by the circuitous paths along which its development leads'.[40] In the face of a human psyche which appears passive rather than active, retiring rather than forward, Freud concluded that the human organism longed for death, and peace.

But, paradoxically, the 'repetition compulsion' has the opposite significance for the sex-drive, which now, under the noble name of Eros, becomes 'the true life instincts',[41] combining organic substances into ever-larger units, and thus socially progressive. In this way, the earlier dualism of sex and self-preservation is replaced by the dualism of death-drive and Eros. Fromm rejects this, stating, on behalf of the Institute, that Freud's overall position of an 'adaptation to life's processes and necessities' implies that 'the instincts as such are contrary to the biological death principle'. As a general point, Fromm criticises Freud's post-1920 writings for being 'far more speculative and less empirical than his original position'.[42]

Horkheimer, for his part, criticised the tendency to declare all psychic manifestations a 'drive',[43] and felt that this applied to the otherwise discerning Freud. Horkheimer maintained that Freud had succumbed to the temptation to explain history in the metaphysical terms of a struggle between life and death, good and evil, thus losing the originally 'dialectical' quality his categories had possessed. All in all, Freud's positing of a 'death-drive' is socially uncritical.[44] For this reason, Fromm explains, 'we take off from Freud's original position'.[45] However, the thesis of the death-drive is not refuted by being ignored: and, what makes matters worse, the Frankfurt School's work in psychology is based on concepts which were formulated by Freud in direct, inextricable conjunction with this very thesis. Thus, what is needed is not a preference for the earlier dualism, but an articulate refutation, or rather qualification, of the post-1920 position. Otherwise, the appropriation of Freud's method and categories will reproduce and exacerbate the latter's contradictions.

Freud's most critical contribution to the historical materialist theory of ideology and manipulation is the notion of the super-ego. This notion depends, logically and genetically, on the problem of aggression, sadism and masochism, which all in turn rest on the mysterious 'death-drive'. The latter thesis prompted Freud to revise the idea of a 'natural aggressive component' in sexuality, and he proceeded to explain aggression in terms of 'a death instinct, which, under the influence of the narcissistic libido, has been forced away from the ego and has consequently only emerged in relation to the object'.[46]

This aggression assumes the significance of an autonomous 'instinct' in Freud's later writings. As Horkheimer pointed out, this meant both an abstract cultural pessimism and an undialectical social conformism:

> Freud explains the cruelty manifested in war (and elsewhere) not in terms of a transformation of drives that are basically orientated to material goods, nor in terms of the compulsion to bear misery passively. Rather, he tends to regard the 'pressure of civilisation,' in as far as this affects sexuality, as a pressure on the inherent destruction-drive, rather than a pressure on the overall needs which the masses, despite the social potential for gratification, have to repress.[47]

Freud, forgetting that Eros was 'the true life instincts', came to the point where he conceded, totally uncritically, a 'disinclination to give up an old position for a new one' on the part of Eros.[48] This does not of itself preclude co-operative labour for the necessities of life, but taken in conjunction with man's 'natural aggression', the conservative nature of Eros makes social disintegration inevitable, unless sexuality is subjected to systematic repression.

Manipulation becomes a sine qua non of social life, for Freud, and this is all due to the destruction-drive:

> Civilisation has to use its utmost efforts in order to set limits to man's aggressive instincts and to hold the manifestations of them in check by psychical reaction-formations. Hence, therefore, the use of methods intended to incite people into identifications and aim-inhibited relationships of love, hence the restrictions upon sexual life.[49]

Indeed, Freud doubts whether even this repression can ever be fully effective, and he uses this argument to 'refute' the Marxian doctrine that with the abolition of private property social hostilities would cease. No matter what man does to curb aggression, 'this indestructible feature of human nature will follow it there'.[50] It is thus apparent that Freud's cultural pessimism and social conformism are not an accident but the logical outcome of the theory of a 'destruction-drive'. And this latter, it must be remembered, is itself only a manifestation of the 'death-drive'. The historical materialist appropriation of Freud's work must, ultimately, refute the latter thesis.

5 The super-ego and psychic manipulation

Fromm's expository first essay in the *Zeitschrift* stressed the significance of Freud's depth-psychology for the understanding of ideology; this is essentially the theory of the super-ego. Freud, in his major study of 1923, entitled 'The Ego and the Id',[51] came to recognise within the ego a component which, while itself actively repressing and rendering unconscious, was also itself repressed and unconscious. Freud discerned an antithesis 'between the coherent ego and the repressed which is split off from it'.[52] Unlike Jung, who was concerned with a would-be a-historical 'collective unconscious', Freud now turned this 'dynamically unconscious' into a socially critical category. He did this by locating the genesis of the super-ego in the family; and while Freud does absolutise the nuclear family as *the* family, what he says about the latter is an incisive critique of the former.

Freud expounds the following model of the child's development: the boy (Freud concentrates on the male child, whose pattern of development is then superimposed on the girl) identifies with his father and develops an object-cathexis for his mother. As time passes, the boy requires, and receives, less attention and less physical contact. The father now appears to be monopolising the mother's attention, and the boy thus resents this competitor. But rebellion is useless, owing to physical inferiority; the object-cathexis is doomed. At this stage, the flexibility of Eros comes into play: the original psychic impulse gives way either to an identification with the mother or an intensification of the identification with the father. The latter is the usual outcome of the Oedipus Complex, and this is the key to the super-ego, which, by giving permanent expression to the influence of the parents, 'perpetuates the existence of the factors to which it owes its origins'.[53]

Freud uses this theory to repudiate the notion of a 'herd instinct', reducing the latter to an extension of the concrete experience within the family: groups of individuals, all having gone through a similar Oedipal conflict, can easily *'put one and the same object in the place of their ego ideal*'.[54] Society, as shown above, actively manipulates the sex-drive so as to effect such identifications. But what is most important of all is that (as in the resolution of the Oedipal situation) the ego ideal, or super-ego, can be precisely that person, or group, who most deserves one's hatred and active hostility; thus, despite justified resentment, 'the suppressed classes can be emotionally attached to their masters'.[55] This is Freud's central contribution to the theory of ideology.

The problem with the Freudian theory of the super-ego is that it is directly dependent on the thesis of the death-drive. Although Freud speaks of the super-ego's genesis in terms of the sublimated libido of the first object-cathexis,[56] the vicissitudes of the death-drive play a crucial role in the perpetuation of this repressive instance. Freud views the consolidation of man's super-ego as follows:

> His aggressiveness is introjected, internalised; it is, in point of fact, sent back to where it came from—that is, it is directed towards his own ego. There it is taken over by a portion of the ego, which sets itself over against the rest of the ego as super-ego, and which now, in the form of 'conscience,' is ready to put into action against the ego the same harsh aggressiveness that the ego would have liked to satisfy upon other, extraneous individuals.[57]

As long as this aggressiveness is attributed to an irreducible 'death-drive', then Freud's insight into ideological deflection of consciousness is complemented by an uncritical defence of this process: repression and manipulation appear as the sine qua non of human society. Any historical materialist appropriation of the super-ego theory must, clearly, free it from its dependence on the death-drive.

Freud himself was never happy with the hypothesis of a death-drive; he could not identify any energy-source for it, as he had been able to do for Eros (libido). Prophetically, he wrote, concerning the polarities of love and hate, affection and aggression: 'If only we could succeed in relating these two polarities to each other and in deriving one from the other.'[58] Freud himself never achieved this reduction. Nor did Fromm, who simply ignored the problematic and returned to the earlier position which Freud had been obliged, out of intellectual integrity, to abandon. But the reduction outlined was achieved by another Marxist critic of Freud: Wilhelm Reich.

Reich had never operated with any concept of a 'death-drive'. In fact, even his use of 'destruction-drive' was implicitly critical of Freud; Reich defined this phenomenon not in terms of an externalised 'death-drive', but as the biologically necessary process of breaking up and digesting. As for the irrational manifestation of such an urge, this was a 'product of civilisation': 'Man's destruction-drive is distinguished, above all, by the fact that its goals are not biologically necessary. In this regard, it corresponds exactly to the savagery of many animals who are deprived of sexual gratification.'[59] Even here, in 1927, Reich sees irrational aggression as the response to a frustrating environment, not as a primary drive. Implicitly, the 'destruction-drive' is reduced to Eros, within an overall historical materialist framework. Reich's final breakthrough came in 1933, a year after the programmatic essays by Fromm in the *Zeitschrift*. But long before that, Reich's serious re-examination of Freudian metapsychology had put him on a path that made him not only an important forerunner of the Frankfurt School, but their decided superior.

6 The Frankfurt School and Wilhelm Reich

Fromm's evaluation of Reich's work in 1932 is mixed. On the one hand, Reich has produced some 'outstanding empirical investigations' into social psychology, as well as doing 'extensive research into the social conditioning and the social function of sexual morality'.[60] But Fromm does not recognise the profound implications of the latter for the refutation of the 'death-drive' theory. And otherwise, the evaluation of Reich is largely negative; Fromm, concentrating on methodological considerations, reveals that the Institute considers it erroneous 'if one—as Wilhelm Reich, for example—restricts psychoanalysis to the sphere of individual psychology and argues against its applicability to social phenomena (politics, class consciousness, etc.)'. Although Fromm adds that 'in his latest works Reich seems to have modified this standpoint in a very fruitful way',[61] the fact is that Fromm does not fully understand Reich's method, either now or later.

Reich's original position, to which Fromm refers by quoting quite extensively, was as follows:

> The real object of psychoanalysis is the psychic life of
> societised man. The masses come in for consideration only in so
> far as individual-based phenomena crop up in them (e.g., the
> problem of the leader), and only in so far as traits of the
> 'mass psyche'—anxiety, panic, obedience, etc.—can be
> clarified from our knowledge of individuals. It would seem
> that the phenomenon of class consciousness is hardly accessible
> to psychoanalysis, and that sociological problems (mass
> movements, politics, etc.) cannot be the object of the
> psychoanalytic method.[62]

Thus, for Reich, a historical materialist psychology cannot say anything positive about the genesis and nature of class-consciousness, but, at most, only explain the latter's absence. Presumably, Fromm intends to show that psychoanalysis *can* explain the *presence* of class-consciousness. Whether he succeeds, however, remains to be seen.

But apart from anything else, Fromm's general criticism seems remarkably misguided. First, Reich did not wish to 'restrict psychoanalysis to the sphere of individual psychology'; on the contrary, his object was, from beginning to end, 'societised man'. Second, the polemical, ironical rejection of the 'mass psyche' is obviously a deliberate distantiation from Jung's 'collective unconscious'. And, third, Reich's controlled extension of 'individual-based phenomena' to social manifestations is the method that Horkheimer subscribes to in the essay 'History and Psychology',[63] and which Fromm himself applies in his essay 'Concerning the Sense of Impotence'.[64]

Indicatively, Fromm himself only manages to give a socially orientated analysis of one of the *negative* manifestations of the masses: namely, the sense of impotence. Nowhere did Fromm provide any meaningful illumination of the *positive* emergence and operation of class-consciousness. Reich, by contrast, developed his theory in this very regard. And he did so because of his active involvement in ideological struggle. In 1934, Reich wrote that class-consciousness was 'present in every nook and cranny of everyday life'.[65] He did not thereby reduce class-consciousness to the subjective state of the proletariat, which *still* needed the resolute ideological leadership of the political avant-garde. But Reich emphasised that the elements of a mass class-consciousness *existed*, in 'the awareness of one's own needs in all spheres'; in 'the awareness of the means and possibilities of satisfying them'; and in 'the awareness of the hindrances placed in their path by a society based on private ownership of the means of production'.[66] These 'concrete elements', if seized upon, enlightened, and drawn together, would form a revolutionary consciousness.[67] Thus, Reich's version of a historical materialist psychology involved a Leninist conception of revolutionary organisation and leadership. It remains to be seen how the Frankfurt School responded to *this* stage of Reich's work.

7 The Institute's analysis of authority

Horkheimer's 'General Section' of the *Studies in Authority and Family* introduces a method which is historical materialist in the differentiated sense of 'critical theory of society':

> The production-process influences men not only in the
> immediate and contemporary form in which they themselves
> encounter it in their work, but also in the form it has assumed

in the relatively stable, slow-changing institutions such as family, school, church, and art.[68]

As for the first form, it has already been shown (see Chapters 2 and 3) that the specific *economic* dimension of contemporary social determination is not analysed adequately by the Frankfurt School. The corresponding contributions to the *Studies* are fragmentary, and do not provide the hoped-for economic back-up of the superstructural analyses by Horkheimer, Fromm and Marcuse. But the latter still constitute a significant contribution to the analysis of manipulation; the merits, and ultimate limits, of this contribution must now be established.

Horkheimer's preface to the *Studies* introduces a categorial distinction that would seem to be programmatic: 'authoritarian' (*autoritär*) means authority-affirming, that is, on the part of the *object* of authority, the *ruled;* 'authoritative' (*autoritativ*) means authority-demanding, that is, on the part of the *subject* of authority, the *ruler*.[69] In point of fact, this distinction is not adhered to with any stringency in the *Studies* themselves. This is not proof of laxity, however, but indicates the omnipresence and complexity of the authoritarian pattern within contemporary society. The fundamental authority is capital; economic conditions themselves are 'authoritative'.[70] Thus, the authoritarian experience dominates the lives of all men, of all classes, in the sense that they are the *objects*, not the *subjects*, of social determination. Horkheimer and his team can therefore speak of 'the authoritarian state',[71] and, within this constellation, of an 'authoritarian intervention by parents'.[72]

In exposing the network of mediations in this authoritarian society, 'critical theory of society' goes beyond Freud's horizon, which focused almost exclusively on the child's treatment at the hands of its parents, thereby ignoring the continued authoritarian experience of the father in the socio-economic sphere. This is particularly significant for the class of wage-labourers, for, in the 'free' selling and buying of labour-power, the 'constraint to enter into the contract is not the same for both parties'.[73] Thus, ultimately, the solution to the problem of authoritarian subjection is not 'personal liberation' but revolution. This is a reiteration of *Capital*.

The Frankfurt School's concept of revolution, though lacking in concrete specificity, clarifies the psychological difference between the petit-bourgeois rebel and the true revolutionary. Although the Frankfurt School themselves failed to accept any sort of party discipline (Adorno holds up Lukács as an example of the misguided submission of intellectual to party organisation),[74] Horkheimer's team did subscribe to the theoretical *principle* of revolutionary discipline; Marcuse wrote: 'Revolutionary subordination in one's own ranks and revolutionary authority towards the class enemy are necessary prerequisites, in the struggle for the future organisation of society.'[75] Horkheimer stressed, as had Lenin, that anarchism was a product of the petite-bourgeoisie, stretching the ideology of 'individual freedom' to absurd limits, instead of transpiercing it.[76] Fromm backed this up by showing that the 'rebellious' type feels the oppressive weight of society but fails to perceive its true nature, thus revolting against all authority, and, in his disillusionment, often reinforcing authoritarianism by turning fascist. The 'revolutionary' type, by contrast, wants to eradicate the blind economic authority of class-society and realise in the socio-political sphere what he is already attempting to achieve in his personal relations with others: namely, the end of authoritarian character-formations.[77] However, the Frankfurt School felt that revolutionary theory and strategy so far had failed to identify the *full* mediations of the blind economic authority as it determined the institutional and personal relations within society. Thus, the Institute's analysis tried to rectify this imbalance by tracing the authoritarianism within the family.

8 The Institute's analysis of the family and its dialectics

The active authoritarian figure of the nuclear family is clearly the father. Freud regarded this as the 'natural' outcome of the father's physical and intellectual superiority; in this way, all society, for Freud, was viewed in patriarchal terms. Horkheimer points out that the father is the master in the home because he is usually the wage-earner.[78] And as to the father's *need* to dominate, Horkheimer stresses that the father's experience in the work-process is the most direct exposure to the authority of capital.[79] Horkheimer's depiction of the repercussion of this authority on the home-life is a continuation of Kracauer's simile of 'cycling' (see Chapter 1).

But if the father's authority is based on his wage, then this authority must be subject to all the vicissitudes of the labour-market. The first contradiction outlined by the Frankfurt School is the wage-earning capacity of the youths. The questionnaires distributed by the Institute reveal that adolescents, particularly boys, become 'more independent of paternal authority' and actually 'an economic force to reckon with'.[80] Certainly, this new-found authority does not survive its economic undermining in periods of unemployment,[81] but the same applies to the father himself. This is the second contradiction discussed in the *Studies:* society inculcates the values of 'work and discipline', yet capitalist production cannot guarantee the availability of gainful employment; Horkheimer says of the father: 'If he ceases to earn, or at least possess, money, he thereby loses his social standing, and that threatens his prestige in the family too.

The law of bourgeois society then takes its toll of him'.[82] Not even unemployment benefit and social security payment can completely compensate for the shattering of the normal authority-structure, as the questionnaires demonstrate.[83]

But the Frankfurt School's attitude to the dissolution of the family is dialectical, and not without a note of sadness. While they do not entertain any illusions that 'the family' ever *did* exist in any real meaningful sense for the masses (Marcuse relates Marx and Engels's dreadful picture of proletarian existence and of prostitution),[84] none the less, Horkheimer's team regard the family as more than a lie, more than just one more reification. In fact, the family is a sphere where reification is halted, if only slightly: here, man can be not just a 'function' but a *man*.[85] Although authority-patterns are carried over into family life, and although sexual enjoyment is debased (as the *Studies* show so well), the family is regarded as *more* than this. The Frankfurt School are sorry to see it undermined by advertising, social engineering and fascism. The most poignant expression of this is Adorno's *Minima Moralia:* 'The rising collectivist order is the mockery of a classless one. While liquidating the bourgeois individual, it also liquidates the Utopia that once drew sustenance from motherly love'.[86] The family is being not sublated but annihilated. In the tradition of their general ideology-critique, the Frankfurt School thus jump to the rescue, at least of the *idea* of the family.

But the dialectical evaluation of the family goes beyond this note of sadness; Horkheimer actually perceives a new, constructive force emerging from the hollow shell of the nuclear family:

> on this basis, where the original interest in the family has largely vanished, perhaps it may generate that same feeling of community as unites these people with their kind outside the family. . . . The children will then be raised not as future heirs, and will thus no longer be regarded in the specific sense as 'one's own.' In as much as work, if to be found at all, is no longer just a case of providing them with bread, then it will become geared to the realisation of the historic task of creating a better world for themselves, their children, and for others.[87]

This would seem to be something approaching class-consciousness and revolutionary praxis. Indeed, Horkheimer's contribution to the *Studies* ends on the enthusiastic, animated note that 'the explosive aspect of culture gains ascendance over the conservative element'.[88]

9 The refutation of the 'death-drive'

Horkheimer's vision of liberation is in no way related to the theory and praxis of ideological struggle, and, instead, rests on an abstract spontaneity-theory. This deficiency will be discussed below. But before that, an even more fundamental problem emerges: on what theoretical grounds does Horkheimer believe that liberation is possible at all? As a Marxist, of course, he can base his belief on the vision of a society where the control over the means of production has been socialised in the full sense of the word. But is Freud's depth-psychology compatible with this vision? After all, Freud uses the theory of a death-drive, upon which his explanation of ideology is based, to vindicate the repressive society and refute the doctrine of a classless society.

It is not enough simply to ignore Freud's cultural pessimism and social conformism, for the psychoanalytic analysis of ideology is bound up far too tightly with them. Horkheimer, for example, is right to deny the primacy of any 'submission-drive' and to reduce it instead to the authoritarian family. He is also correct to imply that this submissiveness draws on energies which could otherwise be progressive: 'The bad conscience developed in the family absorbs innumerable impulses which might otherwise direct themselves against the respective social conditions involved in the individual's disappointment'.[89] Certainly, one can assert, as do Fromm and Horkheimer, that these 'impulses' do not presuppose any 'death-drive', but the fact remains that Freud was only able to explain the super-ego adequately by recourse to this pessimistic thesis. In addition, the positing of the 'death-drive' was based, as Fromm admits, on a 'significant' argument.

What is needed is the systematic refutation of the 'death-drive' and the reduction of all its seeming manifestations to a psychic force which would allow of, and actively require, liberation. This was the method employed by Reich in his appropriation of Freud. Reich's metacritique, beginning in the 1920s, first re-examined the notion of Eros. Anticipating Marcuse's later differentiation of 'repressive' and 'non-repressive' sublimation, Reich maintained that 'true' sub-limation was not only *not based on* repression, but actually *precluded* by the latter: 'A sine qua non of sublimation is that the respective drive-forces are not exposed to the crippling effects of repression, which blocks not only direct gratification, but *all* constructive activity on the part of the drives.'[90] Repression turned the re-maining direct sexual activity into an unsatisfactory, neurotic experience that then called forth all the perversions and reifications normally attributed to 'free sex'; and, in this way, sexuality did indeed become anti-social.

The only answer to Freud's dilemma was to uphold the pro-gressive interpretation of Eros, which alone made true sublimation possible; thus, Reich demanded the establishment of the 'ability to work and love'.[91] Fromm, by contrast, while repudiating the thesis of a death-drive, returns to the earlier polarity of sex and ego instincts. Thus, Eros is no basis for a non-repressive society; on the contrary, some sort of control over it would seem to be called for. In addition, Fromm is uncritical as to what constitutes sexual gratification; he says that 'the drives towards self-preservation must be satisfied by real, concrete means, while the sex drives can often be satisfied by pure fantasies'. He does add that 'there is not only a physical but also a psychic minimum existence, and the sex instincts must be satisfied to some minimal extent'.[92] But there is no indication as to the concrete limit of this minimum, nor as to the nature of non-repressive satisfaction.

However, the final resolution of the contradictions within Freud's metapsychology demands not only the progressive evaluation of Eros, but the eradication of the death-drive thesis. This was achieved by Reich in 1933, in *Character Analysis*,[93] which is nothing less than a total restatement of the psychoanalytic theory of masochism, repetition-compulsion and the pleasure principle. The phenomenon of a repetition-compulsion only prompted the positing of a death-drive because this compulsion seemed to operate 'beyond the pleasure principle'.[94] Thus, Reich re-examines this repetition-compulsion in the light of his theory of sexuality and repression. Reich differentiates two kinds of fear: 'real fear' (*Realangst*), which is the normal response to a genuine threat, and which prompts either flight or aggression, depending on the prospect of victory; and 'storage fear' (*Stauungsangst*), which is the permanent, dynamic state of the neurotic character, who internalises what would otherwise be a rational aggression, directing this at himself.[95] This is the key to masochism.

While the repetition-drive operates *within* the pleasure principle, there is no question of a 'death-drive'. So Reich endeavours to refute the interpretation of those cases where the compulsion seems to operate *beyond* the pleasure principle. This is essentially the phenomenon of masochism, which Freud viewed as follows:

> I have been led to distinguish a primary or *erotogenic* masochism, out of which two later forms, *feminine* and *moral* masochism, have developed. Sadism which cannot find employment in actual life is turned round upon the subject's own self and so produces a *secondary* masochism, which is superadded to the primary kind.[96]

But, in fact, what Freud had really done was to observe certain manifestations of 'secondary' masochism, and, owing to his uncritical acceptance of the 'need' for sexual repression, project this masochism backwards, inventing a 'primary' masochism as a theoretical expedient. And, in addition, Freud had actually misinterpreted masochism.

Reich took the most extreme manifestation of the 'death-drive', namely suicide, and reduced this to the mutilated sexual instinct, which had been chanelled into an intolerable 'storage fear'. A human being commits suicide not because he 'wants to', nor because he is 'biologically motivated to', but simply because the social reality has produced 'tensions that have become too much to bear, and that can only be released by self-annihilation'.[97] Less extreme forms of masochism reveal the same principle: they are not a reinstated form of 'primary masochism' or 'death-drive', but the perverted release of a tension that is sexual in origin. In fact, Freud's whole interpretation of masochism as 'pleasure in pain'[98] is incorrect: masochism is simply the endurance of pain by a neurotic personality as the only means of releasing 'storage fear'.[99] There is no 'beyond the pleasure principle':

> In as far as repetition-compulsion was taken to mean, firstly,
> that every drive strives for the establishment of a state of
> peace and quiet, and, secondly, that there is a compulsion to
> experience ever anew such pleasures as have already been
> experienced, there was no objection to the notion of a
> repetition-compulsion. . . . But, understood in this sense, the
> repetition-compulsion remains *within* the framework of the
> pleasure principle. Indeed, it is the pleasure principle itself which
> alone can explain the compulsion to repeat.[100]

In this way, the entire foundation upon which the 'death-drive' rested crumbles, and the ultimate contradiction of Freud's metapsychology is resolved.

In his next major work, *Mass Psychology of Fascism*, Reich extends the clinical findings of *Character Analysis* to the problem of political impotence:

> The repressive moral restraints on the natural sexuality of the
> child, culminating in the severe restriction of *genital* sexuality,
> produces people who are anxious, shy, reverent, obedient, and,
> in the bourgeois sense, 'good' and responsive to education.
> Henceforth, every aggressive impulse is beset by extreme fear,
> thus crippling the rebellious powers within man. Similarly,
> the repressive precept of 'clean in mind' creates a general
> inhibition on all active thought and criticism.[101]

Reich clearly shows that the Freudian thesis of the 'death-drive' can be demolished without relinquishing the critical concept of the super-ego. Indeed, the latter only assumes its full critical value *through* a systematic refutation of the 'death-drive'.

Fromm's position, by comparison, is much weaker: he never frees the super-ego from its fatal involvement with Freud's pessimistic

111

metapsychology. At one point, Fromm actually holds up Freud's 'The Economic Problem of Masochism' as the authoritative work on masochism.[102] This is no less than astounding, since Freud here bases his entire theory on the hypothesis of the 'death-drive', explaining the super-ego in terms precisely of the vicissitudes of 'primary' masochism.[103] (When Fromm later[104] details the *Studies* themselves as the authoritative text, he only perpetuates an unresolved contradiction.) Fromm does acknowledge that Reich has made some progress on the question of masochism, and that, in particular, Reich has demonstrated the fallacy of any 'beyond the pleasure principle'. But Fromm fails to see, or, at least, to admit, that Reich has thereby demolished the 'death-drive'. Instead of applauding Reich's reduction of this 'drive' to Eros, Fromm actually states that the fecundity of Reich's work on masochism is 'seriously limited by his usual physiologistic overestimation of the sexual factor'.[105] Clearly, Fromm understands nothing of Reich's theory.

10 Contemplative psychology and the loss of praxis

The Frankfurt School, in their appropriation of Freud's work, fail to satisfy their own criterion of systematically exposing and eradicating the ideological distortions within otherwise critical works of contemporary theoreticians. But Horkheimer's team, in their discussion of Freud, also fail to live up to their other methodological imperative: namely, that such critical studies as Nietzsche's, Bergson's and Freud's should, in a new theoretical form, be constituted as components of a *practically* critical movement. How do the Frankfurt School envisage raising the contradictions of authoritarianism to the point of a 'conscious contradiction', so that consciousness unfolds 'not only its liberating force, but also its inciting, disciplining and violently practical force', thus 'sharpening' the 'struggle' with which the critical intellectual was 'linked', at least according to the Institute's 'manifesto' of this period? In fact, none of these questions is answered.

The Frankfurt School of the *Zeitschrift* period lack not only all relation to concrete praxis, but, in addition, all notion of ideological struggle, even anti-authoritarian struggle. This is not due to the objective collapse of revolutionary potential within Germany, but, as in the case of class-struggle (see Chapter 3), reveals the Frankfurt School's failure to even *pose* the question of organised struggle. This is why Horkheimer's section in the *Studies* ends on such an enthusiastic, but contemplative note. Organised revolutionary praxis is regarded as spontaneous, and, consequently, the emergence of revolutionary consciousness does not have to be broached in terms of mass ideological struggle. Fromm implied, in his critique of

Reich's work, that a historical materialist psychology would illuminate the emergence of class-consciousness. But the Institute never
fulfilled this promise.

In as far as the Frankfurt School have any conception at all of
political organisation, there seems to be some room for an intellectual
avant-garde: thus, 'world-historic transformations' (presumably
revolutions!) are usually precipitated by 'groups who are free of any
deep-rooted psychic patterns, and who base their actions on knowledge (*Erkenntnis*)'.[106] These groups are not specified as to their
socio-political character; indeed, they seem to be destined to lead by
virtue of some fortunate anti-authoritarian education. But even apart
from this weakness, Horkheimer makes the theoretical transition
from 'knowledge' to political leadership far too immediately,
speaking of those moments when:

> the economic decline of a specific mode of production has
> loosened the corresponding cultural life-forms to such an
> extent that the suffering of the majority of society can easily
> turn into revolt, and it only requires the resolute will of
> progressive groups to effect a victory over the mere force of
> weapons, which by now is all that is propping up the entire
> system.[107]

For the Institute, the 'dialectics' of the authority-structures are
simply registered by 'critical theory of society' as something that *may*
happen to materialise into revolution. The psychological theory of
the Frankfurt School is not structured according to the needs of
any ideological struggle of the present. Nowhere are there indica-
tions as to a theory and strategy of anti-authoritarian struggle.

Reich's position was significantly different; although 'only a
socialist economy can provide a basis for the free development of
intellect and sexuality', none the less, psychoanalysis can and must
play a revolutionary role in the sphere of child education 'as a
psychological basis for socialist education'.[108] The strategy for the
latter was outlined in Reich's *Sexual Maturity, Abstinence and
Repressive Matrimonial Morality*,[109] as well as being pursued
actively, under the auspices of the KPD, as 'sexual politics towards
a conscious social goal (*zielbewusste Sexualpolitik*)'.[110] Reich
actually criticised the KPD for its failure to appreciate fully the
revolutionary significance of anti-authoritarian education. The party
leadership made a fetish of 'Politics' and rested content with exposing
Hitler as the agent of the most reactionary monopoly capitalism.
They did not link positively to the 'petty, banal, primitive, simple
everyday life' of the masses. Only such a link could 'unify the
objective sociological process and the subjective consciousness of
men'. Reich stresses that it is not enough to *note* contradictions in

113

the socio-economic totality; these contradictions must be *exploited* to the full.[111] Only the reconciliation of economic necessity and proletarian consciousness could produce the unifying deed of revolution.

Reich had been active in this work during the crucial, and fatal, class-struggles of the last years of Weimar Germany. The Frankfurt School, by contrast, held no hopes for changing the world; so they set about explaining it. That explanation, though dialectical, did not throw up any concepts for an anti-authoritarian strategy, and even failed to emphasise the *need* for such a strategy. Despite the Institute's repudiation of the SPD's reformism and abstract evolutionism, and despite the Institute's emphasis on the role of class-struggle, the Frankfurt School's psychological theory did not develop any *practical* concepts to further this struggle. The one exception, Marcuse's work since the mid-1960s, is discussed below.

11 The absolutisation of psychology

The lack of concrete praxis in the Frankfurt School's psychological theory is no mere slip, but is in fact the logical outcome of 'critical theory of society' as a whole. The materialist dimension of praxis can only be grasped by a theory which relates directly to what Horkheimer regards, in a generalised way, as the motor of history: namely, class-struggle. And that relation presupposes an economically founded class analysis, which the Frankfurt School, despite criticising Freud for failing to differentiate his categories according to the class-constellation,[112] never provided.

But in the absence of a sound economic theory, the role of psychology becomes distorted. Originally, Horkheimer conceived of it as an 'auxiliary science' in the elucidation of history, which was to be founded upon categories that were essentially economic.[113] As Adorno stressed, quite rightly, the recourse to psychology was not without its dangers; speaking of Marx, he wrote:

> The latter did not have a 'superficial psychology.' He had no psychology at all, and for good theoretical reasons. The world Marx scrutinised is ruled by the law of value, not by men's souls. Today men are still the objects or the functionaries of the societal process. To explain the world by means of the psychology of its victims already presupposes an abstraction from the basic and objective mechanisms to which men are subject.[114]

While the Frankfurt School were head and shoulders above any crude psychologism themselves, their appropriation of psychology did, due to the lack of economic theory, tend towards precisely the 'abstraction' that Adorno points to above.

Ultimately, the Frankfurt School is unclear as to precisely what psychology *can* reveal about manipulation. Can it reveal anything about the failure of the united front in Weimar Germany? Can it reveal anything about fascism? One answer is that a historical materialist psychology might help to illuminate the psychic aspect of the petit-bourgeoisie's propensity for fascism. In this regard, Horkheimer was correct to announce that the Institute would concentrate its analysis on the white-collar workers (see Chapter 1). But as time went on, the psychological concern freed itself from the overall historical materialist intention, and the study of the so-called 'middle classes' was extended, as some 'ideal-type', to the urban proletariat. Thus, Horkheimer wrote in 1933, the year of Hitler's appointment as Chancellor, that the proletariat, too, shows 'bourgeois traits'; and Horkheimer is talking here largely in psychological terms.[115]

This thesis, simplistic and, to this day, unsubstantiated, of the 'embourgeoisement' (*Verbürgerlichung*) of the proletariat, militates against any real class-analysis. In particular, it hazes over the theoretical need for an analysis of *economic* manipulation, the sort of analysis Alfred Sohn-Rethel worked on and which is not encompassed by the method and categories of 'critical theory of society'. Martin Jay, in a chapter on the Institute's first studies on authority, wrote: 'As to be expected, Critical Theory was applied to the most pressing problem of the time, the rise of fascism.'[116] Unfortunately, the problem of fascism encompasses far more aspects than the Frankfurt School of the *Zeitschrift* period undertook to examine. It should never be forgotten that in the last pre-terroristic election of Weimar Germany (November 1932), the 'combined' vote for the two workers' parties was greater than the Nazi vote. Clearly, any attempt to explain the rise of fascism in terms of a characterological 'embourgeoisement' of the proletariat *is* an eclectic mixture of Marx and Freud.

12 The role of psychology in Marcuse's radicalised 'critical theory of society'

Marcuse has recently revealed that one of his many disagreements with Horkheimer in the 1930s was that the Institute's work was 'too psychological'.[117] Thus, it is interesting to see how Marcuse's own use of psychological categories in his radicalised theory since the 1960s differs from that of his colleagues in the *Zeitschrift* period. This is not the place for a thorough analysis of Marcuse's re-examination of Freud's entire metapsychology. Suffice it to say that *Eros and Civilisation*, in contrast to Fromm's work, recognised the need to appropriate the problematic of Freud's post-1920 work, as well as to free Eros from Freud's ideologically limited theoretical horizon. Although Marcuse does defend the 'death-drive' (against 'neo-Freudian revisionism'), this thesis is systematically disentangled from Freud's ultimate pessimism.[118]

But in Marcuse's recent work, psychology has an entirely different significance than it had in the early Institute. *Eros and Civilisation* was both a protest and a vision. In the 1960s, Marcuse's theoretical activity became a response to an actual *movement*, the student anti-authoritarian movement, which was putting forth the demand for total liberation and tentatively evolving a theory and strategy for this liberation. While Horkheimer turned reactionary, renouncing his earlier work and actually defending the Pope's pronouncements on the birth-pill,[119] Marcuse allied himself to the new movement, drawing fresh inspiration from it for 'critical theory of society'.

In the face of monopoly capitalism and the degenerate, bureaucratic mass workers' parties, Marcuse affirmed the significance of the struggle against reification within oneself and between friends; this is the meaning of the commonly misunderstood 'biological' revolution:

> But while the image of the libertarian potential of advanced industrial society is repressed (and hated) by the managers of repression and their consumers, it motivates the radical opposition and gives it its strange unorthodox character. Very different from the revolution at previous stages in history, this opposition is directed against the totality of a well-functioning, prosperous society—a protest against its Form—the commodity form of men and things, against the imposition of false values and a false morality.[120]

But Marcuse is a *critical* ally, intent on pushing the new movement ever forward. He thus affirms the transition from anti-authoritarianism to the so-called 'Organisational Phase'. Although, as already shown (Chapter 3), Marcuse's position tends towards the spontaneity-theory of Council Communism, he does not fail to make some incisive judgments as to the legacy of the earlier phase. Anti-authoritarianism must be saved from the pitfall of petit-bourgeois anarchism: 'individual liberation means transcendence beyond the *bourgeois* individual', which presupposes the 'liberation of society'.[121] And that presupposes revolutionary organisation.

Whereas the *Studies* spoke of the masses being led by 'groups who are free of any deep-rooted psychic patterns, and who base their actions on knowledge', Marcuse abandons the Frankfurt School's tendency to hypostatise any 'pure' knowledge; instead, he views critical knowledge as knowledge of one's *own* deformation by society:

> In the formulation of one of the young German radicals, 'each of us (radicals) is somehow infested, moronised, saturated,

distorted' by the contradictions of the established society.
Since the resolution of these contradictions can be the work
of only the revolution itself, they have to be borne by the
movement, but as *comprehended* contradictions, entering the
development of strategy.[122]

Thus, Marcuse's theory responded not only to the anti-authoritarian
movement but also to the theoretical and strategic development
beyond it. In conclusion, no matter how one evaluates Marcuse's
precise political significance, it is clear that his work since the 1960s
marks an advance on the part of 'critical theory of society' beyond
the Institute of the *Zeitschrift* period and beyond Marcuse's erstwhile
colleagues.

13 Manipulation: the transition from psychology to 'culture industry'

Returning to the 1930s, it can be said that whereas Marcuse's later
work was the theoretical expression of an actual movement demanding liberation, the Institute's psychological studies in the
Zeitschrift period were essentially a theory of *manipulation*. The
various distortions arising out of this extension of historical materialism have been outlined above. However, even during the
1930s, the analysis of manipulation underwent a transformation, and
the role of Freudian psychology was qualified. On the surface, this
was reflected in the fact that the *Studies* were published in an un-
finished state, as well as in the departure of Fromm from the Institute,
amidst an atmosphere of mutual resentment, the reasons for which
are still not fully clear.[123] But, in any case, the deeper reasons
behind this change lie in the shift in the Frankfurt School's object of
study.

In the USA, the Frankfurt School were confronted with an advanced monopoly capitalist state, with an equally advanced network
of non-fascist, but none the less manipulative, popular culture. They
no longer saw the family as the decisive agent of socialisation; on
the contrary, they perceived a dissolution of the family, and thus a
drastic qualification of the significance of Freud's model of id, ego,
super-ego. The psychological component as a whole gradually
became subsumed under a broader socio-political analysis of the
production, distribution and consumption of popular culture. The
notion of 'culture industry' will be discussed at length in Chapter 5;
for the present, it is enough to understand the shift in the Frankfurt
School's attention from the analysis of the family to the more
complex study of the mass media. Marcuse's *One-Dimensional Man*
is representative as an account of this shift and its reasons:

Introjection . . . implies the existence of an inner dimension
distinguished from and even antagonistic to the external

117

exigencies—an individual consciousness and an individual unconscious *apart from* public opinion and public behaviour. . . . Today this private space has been invaded and whittled down by technological reality. Mass production and mass distribution claim the *entire* individual, and industrial psychology has long since ceased to be confined to the factory. The manifold processes of introjection seem to be ossified in almost mechanical reactions.[124]

Marcuse adds that the family's role as an agent of socialisation has been increasingly taken over by 'outside groups and media'.[125] The specifically cultural media formed the focal point of the last issue of the *Zeitschrift* (by then entitled *Studies in Philosophy and Social Science*) and have become infamous under the Frankfurt School's label of 'Culture Industry: Enlightenment as Mass Deception'.[126]

Psychological categories still played a role, of course, but the overall frame of reference was now that of popular mass culture.[127] The Frankfurt School's critical work in this field goes back to the 1930s, particularly to the essays by Adorno, and constitutes one of the Frankfurt School's outstanding contributions to a critical theory of contemporary society. It is to this aspect of their work that this metacritical study must now turn. And, as before, the intention will be both to appropriate the critical categories and analyses, as well as to pinpoint the limits and distortions arising from their failure to evolve an adequate theory of economic manipulation and political emancipation.

5 Historical materialist aesthetics: art as 'affirmation', 'culture industry', and 'negation'

Horkheimer's inaugural lecture had focused on the question of 'the relationship between the economic life of society, the psychic development of the individuals, and the changes in the cultural spheres (in the narrower sense)'. Specifically included in the latter was art.[1] Thus, the first issue of the *Zeitschrift* carried Löwenthal's article 'Concerning the Social Position of Literature'. Not surprisingly, Löwenthal (born 1900) here emphasises the need for an overall theoretical frame of reference: 'an articulate theory of history and of society'.[2] And, significantly, Löwenthal adds:

> In the social illumination of the superstructure . . . the concept of ideology assumes a decisive position. For ideology is an element in consciousness which has the function of concealing social antagonisms and replacing an understanding of these antagonisms with the illusion of harmony. The task of literary history is largely the analysis of ideologies.[3]

This theory, which anticipates the subsequent critique of 'affirmative' art, pinpoints two major questions: first, what aspects of the respective social structures find their expression in the individual work of literature? Second, what are the effects of that work within its society?[4] In his actual analyses, however, Löwenthal concentrates exclusively on the former question; the latter question is not seriously taken up, and the question of an agitational art, reflecting society *critically*, aiming at a specific audience and at furthering revolutionary social praxis, is not even posed.

However, before proceeding to a metacritique, it must be appreciated that not only did the relative role of aesthetics change during the 1930s (see Chapter 4) but, in addition, the object itself of this aesthetics was a historically determined, and therefore changing, quantity. As Adorno later wrote: 'The definition of what is art is initially guided by what it once was, but legitimates itself only by relating to what it has become, and by keeping itself open to what it is trying to become and perhaps can become.'[5] Frankfurt School aesthetics is the analysis of art in its dynamic tension with the socio-historical totality: of its revolutionary struggle against, and victory over, feudal ideology; its heyday and subsequent decline; its denigration in 'culture industry'; as well as the question of art's continued, precarious existence as a critical social force. Any adequate analysis of the Frankfurt School must appropriate, if critically, this entire theoretical constellation.

1 Art as affirmation

Apart from the work of Walter Benjamin (a marginal figure of the Frankfurt School whose theories will be discussed later), the most advanced position on art ever assumed by the Frankfurt School is the critical notion of 'affirmation'. This notion was given its clearest expression by Marcuse in 1937:

> By affirmative culture is meant that culture of the bourgeois epoch which led in the course of its development to the segregation from civilization of the mental and spiritual world as an independent realm of value that is also considered superior to civilization. Its decisive characteristic is the assertion of a universally obligatory, eternally better and more valuable world that must be unconditionally affirmed, a world essentially different from the factual world of the daily struggle for existence, yet realizable by every individual for himself 'from within,' without any transformation of the social reality.[6]

Since this judgment is, in fact, the Marxian critique of dialectical idealism, transposed into the sphere of aesthetics, it is not surprising that this critique is no mere denunciation: Marcuse stresses that this very culture, despite, or, perhaps, because of, its idealism, was an expression of the dissatisfaction with a world pervaded by blind economic determinism. Art of the liberal bourgeois era strove to reveal the human nature and human relationships behind the reified screen of commodity-production, thereby indicting economic fetishism. However, the materialist criticism of 'affirmative culture' still stands:

> Affirmative culture uses the soul as a protest against reification, only to succumb to it in the end. . . . In the form of existence to which affirmative culture belongs, 'happiness at being alive . . . is possible only as happiness in illusion.' But this illusion has a real effect, producing satisfaction. The latter's meaning,

though, is decisively altered; it enters the service of the status quo.[7]

Thus, 'affirmative culture' is doomed to impotence, argues Marcuse, by its very medium of existence. This, in the context of aesthetics, is a forceful demand for the theoretical and practical supersession of idealism.

This raises the question of a sublation of this culture: that means, not merely a critical reflection upon it, but also, and above all, the commitment to rescue the oppositional forces expressed in art, and to rescue art itself from the distortions of idealism. The task presents itself of evolving a critical aesthetic theory and praxis which, aware of the materialist dimension of 'happiness' and 'freedom', and free of any absolutisation of 'Spirit' or 'Art', can constitute itself as a coherent oppositional force within society, linking concretely to the needs, goals and perspectives of critical social praxis as a whole. Significantly, it is precisely at this juncture that Frankfurt School aesthetics retreats in a maze of unmastered contradictions.

But before examining the precise nature of the Frankfurt School's inability, in aesthetics, as in their social theory as a whole, to assume what Krahl terms 'the practical class stand-point', it must be clearly understood that the ambivalence in the critique of 'affirmation' is not without some justification. In the face of the new socio-political constellation of monopoly capitalism, fascism and 'culture industry', the evaluation of liberal culture has to be modified. The 'affirmative' culture of laissez-faire capitalism assumes the retrospective significance of a subversive force, by virtue of being non-one-dimensional. This theory is well known from *One-Dimensional Man*, but it also figures in Marcuse's 1937 essay on 'affirmation':

> The critical and revolutionary force of the ideal, which in its
> very unreality keeps alive the best desires of men amidst a bad
> reality, becomes clearest in those times when the satiated
> social strata have accomplished the betrayal of their own
> ideals.[8]

The weakness of this evaluation is that the 'critical and revolutionary force of the ideal' is merely reinstated, not sublated into a commitment to the task of a critical aesthetic praxis geared to the needs of mass ideological struggle in the new socio-historical context. The 'critical and revolutionary force' does no more than 'become clear'. The passivity of this stance is further evidenced in the assurance that 'even keeping alive the desire for fulfilment is dangerous in the present situation'.[9] The transition from this 'danger' to critical praxis is not conceptualised.

But any discussion of such a praxis will remain necessarily abstract until the nature of 'culture industry', of ideological manipulation through popular culture, has been grasped. This task faces the critical intellectual today, no less than it faced the Frankfurt School of the 1930s. And, be it stated once and for all, the task is today well in hand, thanks in large measure to the work of Horkheimer's team in this field during the *Zeitschrift* period.

2 Art as manipulation: 'culture industry'

The Frankfurt School framed their critique of cultural manipulation as an attack not simply on fascism (as if on some 'thing in itself'), but, essentially, as an attack on monopoly capitalism as a whole. Thus, Marcuse's essay on 'affirmation', having outlined the *inner* 'freedom' of liberal society, speaks of the repressive resolution of this dichotomy in the form of the 'total mobilisation in the era of monopoly capitalism' (see Chapter 2). This, the most radical position of the Frankfurt School, gives rise to a concept of totalitarianism that cannot be used for the ideological defence of non-fascist contemporary capitalism.

It is this notion of totalitarianism that informs the Institute's evaluation of popular culture as a manipulative force. In one of his last essays in the *Zeitscrhift*, Horkheimer juxtaposes the categories of 'popular entertainment' and 'cultural industries', the mediating category being precisely 'manipulation'.[10] In *Dialectic of Enlightenment*, which synthesises and further articulates the analysis of the *Zeitschrift* period, Horkheimer and Adorno outline what they see as the repressive features of modern popular culture:

> Light art has been the shadow of autonomous art. It is the bad social conscience of serious art. . . . The division itself is the truth: it does at least express the negativity of the culture which the different spheres constitute. Least of all can the antithesis be reconciled by absorbing light into serious art, or vice versa. But that is what the culture industry attempts. . . . The abolition of educational privilege by the device of clearance sales does not open for the masses the spheres from which they were formerly excluded, but, given existing social conditions, contributes directly to the decay of education and the progress of barbaric meaninglessness.[11]

Thus, what is attacked by the Frankfurt School is not the development of mass culture qua *mass* culture, but the specific repressive form assumed by, or forced upon, mass culture under the auspices of monopoly capital.

The application of 'critical theory of society' to popular culture owes most to Adorno, who only moved to America in 1938 (significantly later than his colleagues), to work on the Princeton Radio

Research Project. Not surprisingly, Adorno's critical analysis of popular culture was simultaneously a critique of the positivistic method employed in orthodox 'media research'. Decades later, Adorno revealed the tensions between himself and his main-stream colleagues on this research project: Adorno refused to measure and classify the reaction-patterns of the consumers as if these patterns were the irreducibly 'given'. Instead, he was concerned to relate these patterns to the 'objective reality' of what the consumers were reacting to.[12]

To clarify his own position, and to begin to articulate an adequate categorial apparatus, Adorno produced what is undoubtedly his most crucial *Zeitschrift* essay, 'Concerning Musical Fetishism and the Regression of Listening'.[13] This intellectually demanding essay attempted to situate the critique of popular culture within the context of Marx's critique of commodity fetishism; Adorno wrote:

> Marx designates the fetishistic character of the commodity as
> the veneration of what one has oneself produced but which, as
> exchange-value, is alienated from both producer and consumer
> ('man'). . . . This secret is the true secret of success and fame.
> It is the mere reflection of what one has paid for the product
> on the market: the consumer really does worship the money
> that he has paid out for his ticket to the Toscanini concert. He
> has, quite literally, 'made' that success, which he reifies and
> accepts as an objective criterion without recognising himself
> therein.[14]

And, just as Marx's concept of fetishism was based on an analysis of commodity *production*, so Adorno's extension of this concept to the consumption of popular culture involved a systematic critique of the latter's *production*. This critique appeared in the Institute's journal as 'On Popular Music'.[15]

Adorno's outline of the production of popular culture begins with the phenomenon of 'standardisation', a process whereby successful hits, types and 'mixes' are enforced by the culture industry's monopolies on material to be promoted. Standardisation has as its complement the technique of 'pseudo-individualism', which provides an 'alibi' for the material's monotony by allowing, even encouraging, 'stimulating' deviations from the norm:

> By pseudo-individualisation we mean endowing cultural mass
> production with the halo of free choice or open market on
> the basis of standardisation itself. Standardisation of song hits
> keeps the customers in line by doing their listening for them,
> as it were. Pseudo-individualism, for its part, keeps them in line

by making them forget that what they listen to is already
listened to for them, or 'pre-digested.'[16]

And the distribution of this pseudo-individualised commodity finds
its adequate technique of enforcement in plugging, which breaks
down any resistance to the ever-equal by 'closing the avenues of
escape'.[17] In this way, listening habits are themselves standardised.

In this case, the claim of 'giving the masses what they want' is not
accepted (positivistically) as an irreducible fact, but is itself subjected to the charge of 'manipulation'. It is to Adorno's credit that
this manipulation *is* related, if only programmatically, to the question
of the manipulation of the masses on the production-front:

> The customers of musical entertainment are themselves objects
> or, indeed, products of the same mechanisms which determine
> the production of popular music. Their spare time serves only
> to reproduce their working capacity. It is a means instead of
> an end. . . . They want standardised goods and pseudo-
> individualisation, because their leisure is an escape from work
> and at the same time is molded after those psychological
> attitudes to which their workaday world exclusively habituates
> them.[18]

Although the picture of *economic* manipulation does not, in 'critical
theory of society', provide an adequate concept of the 'real subsumption of labour under capital', none the less, the methodological
intention is totally correct.

Equally well guided is the Frankfurt School's emphasis that the
manipulation on the superstructural level is not part of any 'fascist
conspiracy'. On the contrary, the entire production and consumption
of popular culture is guided essentially by the same kind of unconscious determining force as the 'blind' economic determinism of
capitalist society as a whole. Adorno stresses that in plugging, for
example, people behave in a manner one would expect of them only
if they were bribed; bribing does occur, but this harmonises with
the 'normal' manner of presentation.[19] The significant point is that
the manipulations involved in the production of 'culture commodities', though aiming primarily at profitable consumability
rather than ideological effect, can, in specific situations, readily be
combined with deliberate political manipulation. Hence, the role of
radio in the transition to fascism is emphasised by Horkheimer and
Adorno in terms of culture industry evolving a seemingly dis-
interested authority which 'suits Fascism perfectly'. Radio finally
becomes the 'universal mouthpiece of the Führer'.[20]

Ultimately, the analysis of the manipulated employment of the
developing means of communication raises the question of the non-
manipulative, even critical employment of the latter. However,

before this question can be examined, it is necessary first to establish the *general* notion of a 'critical' art. In its materialist expression, critical art is inextricably tied up with the overall struggle for radical social change. It is the question, to borrow Adorno's phrase (from a different context), as to what art is striving to become and 'perhaps can become'. Yet it is this very question which pinpoints the ultimate limits of the materialism of Frankfurt School aesthetics. This will be substantiated fully in what follows. However, for the sake of clarity, the concept of art as 'struggle' will be broached, in the first instance, via a brief discussion of the historical materialist conceptualisation of a critical aesthetic praxis. The discussion of Lenin, Lukács and Brecht is not an exhaustive exposé, and certainly not intended as the 'orthodox line', but is simply a convenient way of thematising a perspective to which the Frankfurt School's aesthetic theory was a critical, distorted, and ultimately deficient response. Finally, the presentation of the Frankfurt School's position draws predominantly on Adorno's *Aesthetic Theory* of 1970; this is because the latter work is the clearest expression of the relevant ideas worked out in the *Zeitschrift* period. However, at the same time, the specific articulation of these ideas in the 1930s will be related with all necessary precision.

3 Lenin and Trotsky on revolutionary art

Lenin asserted in 1905 that 'freedom' in literature was at best a delusion, at worst a hypocritical rationalisation for the artist's lack of commitment to the cause of humanity. To this he counterposed a literature that consciously allied itself to the proletariat, 'enriching the last word in the revolutionary thought of mankind with the experience and living work of the socialist proletariat'.[21] Lenin even subjected this partisan art to the demands of organisation; although he could, in 1905, only make plans for party literature, he later, in the period of socialist construction, insisted that all art be 'imbued with the spirit of the class-struggle being waged by the proletariat for the successful achievement of the aims of its dictatorship', announcing that the Communist Party would guide this work.[22]

However, two factors are crucial to any understanding of how Lenin conceptualised the evolution of such an art. First in 1905, he emphatically stated that proletarian partisanship would not block, but actually encourage, greater scope for 'personal initiative, individual inclination, thought and fantasy, form and content'. He concluded thus: 'Far be it from us to advocate any kind of standardised system, or a solution by means of a few decrees. Cut-and-dried schemes are least of all applicable here.'[23] Second, in the 1920 text, he significantly criticised the abstract notion of evolving a

125

'directly' proletarian culture without recourse to the cultural history of mankind:

> Marxism has won its historic significance as the ideology of the revolutionary proletariat because, far from rejecting the most valuable achievements of the bourgeois epoch, it has, on the contrary, assimilated and refashioned everything of value in the more than two thousand years of the development of human thought and culture.[24]

Lenin concluded that socialist construction, including the struggle for socialist culture, could only mean 'further work on this basis'.[25]

This precept is, of course, identical to the Frankfurt School's general perspective on ideology-critique. To what extent Lenin's own analyses of artistic movements lived up to his stated methodology cannot be discussed in any detail here. Suffice it to say that he was in fact completely incapable of any differentiated evaluation of the avant-garde. Adequate evidence of 'orthodox Marxist-Leninist' hostility to the latter will be found in the subsequent discussion of Lukács. The real question is: how far did the dialectical concern with art manifest itself in the case of the Frankfurt School?

As for the debates on art in the Russian Communist Party after Lenin's death, these cannot be discussed at any length here. However, one aspect of the controversy must be mentioned, since it is explicitly raised by Adorno. It concerns Trotsky's contention that bourgeois art can only be superseded by a socialist art; such, Adorno relates,[26] was the nature of Trotsky's polemic against the notion of 'proletarian culture'. Trotsky's argument may be recalled:

> as the new regime will be more and more protected from political and military surprises and as the conditions for cultural creation will become more favourable, the proletariat will be more and more dissolved into a socialist community and will free itself from its class characteristics and thus cease to be a proletariat.[27]

However, Adorno nowhere relates that this repudiation of an autonomous 'proletarian culture' does not imply a rejection of the Leninist notion of partisan art. Trotsky is speaking here of the function of culture in the dictatorship of the proletariat; he is not speaking about art's role as a weapon in the class-struggles of capitalist countries. Where Trotsky does deal with the latter, he affirms the Leninist position, stating unequivocally:

> Socialism will abolish class antagonisms, as well as classes, but the revolution carries the class struggle to its highest tension. During the period of revolution, only that literature which promotes the consolidation of the workers in their

struggle against the exploiters is necessary and progressive. Revolutionary literature cannot but be imbued with a spirit of social hatred. . . .[28]

This stance, while bearing most upon the constellation within which Adorno was operating, is completely beyond the bounds of Frankfurt School aesthetics.

4 Georg Lukács and socialist realism

At the time when Horkheimer was gathering together his team, the official Communist line on art was represented, in Germany, by Georg Lukács. Lukács, too, was concerned with the critical appropriation of bourgeois culture but, in his case, this took a very narrow form. His main argument was that a would-be oppositional novel (the genre appropriate to that era) which presented only a voluntaristic 'message' or 'tendency' fell behind the achievements of such great realists as Balzac and Tolstoy, in whose works the power of realism had countered their subjective, even reactionary, 'tendency'. Explicitly quoting Engels's letter to Miss Harkness of April 1888 (where Engels discusses the question of a novel with a 'tendency'), and in conjunction with Lenin's epistemology, Lukács develops the theory of a reconciliation, through historical materialism, of personal interest and the partisanship of reality, thereby erasing all traces of an abstract, subjective 'tendency'. Of the revolutionary, historical materialist novelist, Lukács says:

He does not bring to bear upon his forming of reality any demands 'from without,' for the simple reason that his forming of reality must itself contain the fate of those demands which grow, concretely and physically, out of the class-struggle, and he must present these demands as integrating moments of the objective reality, in their genesis, evolution and effect upon that reality; otherwise he will not portray it correctly—dialectically.[29]

This concept of realism already contains the second major element of Lukács's theory, namely 'forming', or 'fashioning' (*Gestaltung*). Although reality itself is partisan, the fetishism of economic life hides this partisanship; and fetishism can only be overcome, in art, as in political economy, via the critical force of abstraction. Quoting once more from Engels's letter, Lukács proceeds to distil the essence of socialist realism:

In the forming of reality, the individual and his fate must appear as a type, i.e. must contain the respective class-characteristics of that individual. The concrete totality of the formed world of art can only accommodate such individuals

127

who, acting and reacting upon one another in the dynamic
reality of social intercourse, serve to illuminate and fill out
both their own character and each other's, so that, firstly, those
individuals become intelligible, and, secondly, their individual
relations among themselves make the overall picture typical.[30]

Only thus can society appear in its essential nature, as relations
between human beings in a class-society.

Adorno certainly concurred on the need for forming the respective
object of the artistic work. He wrote in the early 1930s that 'content-
aesthetics turns formalistic in the light of the "magnitude" of the
objects'.[31] But, ultimately, he levelled this criticism at Lukács himself, attacking the latter's 'pre-aesthetic parti pris for the material
(*Stoff*) and communicandum (*Mitgeteiltes*) of works of art'. To
Adorno, Lukács's parti pris reflected a mistaken notion of art's
'objectivity'.[32] Thus, quite logically, the concept of socialist realism
was anathema to Adorno, who accused Lukács's entire theory as to
a critical art of being 'culturally conservative',[33] particularly in its
predilection for the bourgeois novel. And as for Lukács's claim that
the work of art was the given unity of the particular and the general,
this was nothing but a 'dogma repeated parrot-fashion from
Idealism'. Lukács, in upholding 'normal' works of art against a-
typical works, was thinking, wrote Adorno, in a manner 'alien to the
nature of art'.[34]

Adorno touches here upon one of Lukács's greatest weaknesses:
his inability to grasp the contradictions within the artistic avant-
garde. This weakness is exemplified in the critique of expressionism;
Lukács maintains that, even in their would-be oppositional efforts,
the social problems thematised in the works of the expressionists
were raised to the level of a mystical idealism that blurred the materialist essence of the problems concerned. But Lukács goes further
and accuses expressionism of being 'one of the bourgeois ideological
currents that later flow into fascism', and thus of having a 'role in
the ideological preparation for fascism'. The argument is summed up
as follows:

> Fascism, as the composite ideology of the most reactionary
> bourgeoisie of the post-war period, inherits all those currents
> of the imperialist epoch which manifest decadent-parasitic
> traits; that includes all pseudo-revolutionary and pseudo-
> oppositional movements.[35]

Lukács fails to question whether these 'pseudo-oppositional' and
'pseudo-revolutionary' movements have any practical significance,
and, in particular, whether they have evolved any artistic productive
forces capable of sublation into a *coherently* oppositional and

revolutionary aesthetic praxis. Instead, for Lukács, the label 'decadent-parasitic' says it all.

The Frankfurt School's position, by contrast, involves a highly differentiated evaluation of the artistic avant-garde. But, at the same time, this dialectical analysis goes to the opposite extreme and eulogises the anti-discursive tendencies of modern art, rather than considering the potential for a revolutionary sublation; thus, Adorno writes:

> Closed aesthetic images criticise the status quo far more
> determinedly than do those works which, for the sake of
> intelligible social criticism, go to great pains to achieve a
> formal conceptual coherence and thus tacitly recognise and
> acknowledge the all-pervasive and flourishing machinery of
> communication.[36]

Critical art, according to this conception, is critical not despite, but precisely by virtue of, its refusal to frame itself as articulate agitational communication, or as coherent conceptual communication of any sort.

This theory relates to the Marxian critique of commodity production and exchange (as presented in volume 1 of *Capital*), but this relation is a highly idiosyncratic one: Adorno stresses that art restores what functionalist cognition excludes,[37] that is, the 'nonidentical'. Thus, art restores that which repudiates the identity based on abstract labour and exchange-value; but Adorno's theory actually rejects *all* identity in the aesthetic sphere. Art cannot 'represent' classless society, the struggle for that society, nor any aspect of that struggle; art's critical force resides precisely in its repudiation of any 'standing for something else'. Instead, the work of art is *itself*: 'We have reached a point where the work of art can only suspend empirical reality (the abstract function-nexus) any longer by not taking anything specific as its content.'[38] Thus, art's critical consciousness of its social context results in an 'oppositional' stance synonymous with its own autonomy:

> Art's social character is its immanent movement against
> society, not any manifest pronouncement on that society. Its
> historical gesture repels the empirical reality, even though works
> of art are, as things, part of that reality. In so far as one can
> predicate a social function of the work of art, it is its
> functionlessness.[39]

This theory, while aiming at the abolition of economic enslavement, cannot mediate that aim to the needs and goals of actual social praxis. The 'practical class stand-point', to use Krahl's phrase, is, necessarily (at least, according to the Frankfurt School), missing.

Adorno is, of course, correct to repudiate the overestimation of the significance of art's 'manifest pronouncement', which would obscure the question of the dialectical relationship of form and content. But given the practical sterility of his conclusions as regards the critical role of art, it is crucial to consider whether an art can be envisaged which, first, like Lukács and Adorno, rejects any forced 'tendency', which, second, like Adorno but unlike Lukács, succeeds in observing the oppositional productive forces (hitherto mystified) in the avant-garde, but which also, finally, avoids Adorno's absolutisation of these forces in their 'natural' state. This question demands a more precise analysis of the avant-garde. And the dialectical question of the practical significance of the latter leads directly to the figure of Bertolt Brecht. It is the Brecht-Adorno polarity, more than anything else, which reveals the ultimate failing of Frankfurt School aesthetics.

5 Brecht's theatre

Brecht, while accepting the epistemological notion of 'objectivity as partisanship' and rejecting any abstract 'tendency', and while, further, accepting the precept of a critical realism which showed up the essential class-constellation,[40] remained highly critical of Lukács's conception of how this was to be achieved. Brecht repeatedly stated that writing a realistic novel did not mean writing in the style of Balzac or Tolstoy, but giving the reader a clear picture of the nature of his specific social reality. Since this reality was itself constantly changing, any 'norms' of realism, established by reference to specific realists, resulted in formalism. Brecht maintained that whereas the bourgeois revolution could, in accordance with its specific character, be represented through 'great' individuals, proletarian class-struggle was, by contrast, the self-activation of the majority of society. Any realistic portrayal would have to do justice to this difference:

> it is a waste of time for the author to so simplify his problem that the massive, complicated life-process of men in the era of the final struggle between the bourgeoisie and the proletariat can be 'used' as a 'plot', a landscape, a backcloth for the formation of great individuals. The individuals can scarcely be accorded more space, and certainly no other space, in books than is accorded them in reality.[41]

And it is precisely this concept of realism, and of the changing needs of critical art, that provided Brecht with the key to the artistic avant-garde.

Bloch's *Legacy of this Time* had used the dialectical analysis of bourgeois decadence to polemicise against Lukács's conception of realism, branding the latter as idealist and objectivist.[42] Brecht, for his part, upheld the maxim of 'not linking to the good old traditions, but to the bad new ones',[43] and, in a fragment written in the late 1930s, revealed a strong Blochian influence in his hostility to Lukács's isolation of the collapse of bourgeois literature from the rise of a proletarian literature:

> In reality, the decline of the bourgeoisie reveals itself in the miserable hollowness of its literature (which remains formally realistic), while the works of people like Dos Passos, despite, or, rather, precisely by, shattering the realistic forms, show the break-through of a new realism, made possible by the rise of the proletariat. This is not merely a process whereby one tendency relieves the other of its duties, but a constellation of active and dialectical struggles.[44]

Brecht conceded that expressionism did not reveal the essential nature of monopoly capitalism, but he emphasised that the same applied to the 'realistic' works of Thomas Mann. Equally, the opposition contained in expressionism was not an adequate liberation from capitalist ideology, but Brecht refused to put an undialectical and static stamp on this movement. Instead, he focused on the relation of the new productive forces and the needs of a dynamic realism; for example, Brecht wrote the following about Georg Kaiser:

> Certainly, Kaiser is . . . an individualist. And yet there is something in his technique which doesn't suit his individualism, and which, therefore, does suit us. . . . For example, Kaiser's technique foregoes the great Shakespearean device of suggestion. . . . Kaiser directs himself to man's reason. . . . For a time, he made possible in the theatres that revolutionary new stance on the part of the public, that cool, analytic, interested stance which is the stance of the audience in the scientific age.[45]

Thus, Brecht's theatre attempted to continue the development outlined and realise the full critical potential of this anti-empathising dramatic communication.

This is the key to the Brechtian 'alienation'. This alienation (*Verfremdung*, as distinct from *Entfremdung*, which is the Marxian term expressing economic alienation) divests the world of its appearance as something natural, normal, self-evident, and, instead, arouses surprise and curiosity about it. Unlike Adorno's 'total' repudiation of reified society, Brecht's alienation-technique is the dialectical representation of the latter: all relations, all values are historicised and de-fetishised. And the result is a coherent discursive

131

cognition: 'What was formerly taken for granted is, in a certain sense, made incomprehensible, but this happens only in order to make it, subsequently, all the more comprehensible'.[46] What was formerly just 'known' (*bekannt*) now becomes 'recognised' (*erkannt*). This discursive communication has a direct agitational value: the theatre lays the world bare before the audience, so that 'they, in turn, can lay hands upon the world'.[47] Brecht's theatre provides a *concrete* negation of capitalist society, thus mediating critical art to ideological struggle.

The Frankfurt School, while sympathetic to the anti-Lukácsian significance of this artistic theory and praxis, were otherwise almost totally negative. Horkheimer's *Twilight* made the following sweeping generalisation:

> The reason why a continuing revolutionary effect of the theatre is out of the question today, lies in the fact that this theatre turns the problems of class-struggle into objects of communal contemplation and discussion, thereby creating in the sphere of aesthetics that very harmony which, as it manifests itself in the consciousness of the proletarian, must be smashed; this is one of the foremost tasks of political work.[48]

Horkheimer is totally correct as regards the goals of revolutionary struggle, but he distorts the actual aesthetic praxis of the Weimar Republic when he implies that these problems had not been recognised. In particular, Horkheimer fails to reflect on Brecht's development in this period. In the early 1930s, Brecht explicitly formulated his intention to split his audience and unite only the proletarian component.[49] Indeed, he went further and, while a mass working-class audience was there to address, actually wrote and produced his plays for an exclusively proletarian audience. Yet, the Frankfurt School's major aesthetic figure, Adorno, held to the accusation of a neutralising harmony in engagé literature. For example, Adorno wrote in the 1960s:

> Literary realism, no matter of what variety, whether it calls itself critical or socialist, is much more readily reconciled to the attitude of hostility towards all that is new and strange, than are those images which, without swearing an oath to any political watch-words, suspend, by their mere appearance, the rigid coordination-system of those people who submit themselves to authoritarian rule.[50]

Brecht's aesthetic praxis was, in a word, 'positivistic'.[51]

Indicatively, Adorno's use of the concept of alienation (and he uses *Entfremdung*, not *Verfremdung*) is far less specific than Brecht's. For example, Adorno writes: 'Form acts as a magnet, so arranging the elements of empirical reality as to alienate them from the relationship of their extra-aesthetic existence, thus, and only thus, enabling them to master that existence.'[52] This is why Adorno's aesthetic theory features Kafka among the privileged, and tiny, elite of 'critical artists', not proceeding beyond a passive eulogy, whereas Brecht's admiration for Kafka (as an exponent of alienation in art) was a dynamic concern to sublate that productive force into mass ideological struggle.

The Adorno-Brecht polarity is further illustrated by their attitude to the technique of montage. Brecht claimed that Lukács rejected montage as 'decadent' because it tore asunder the supposed 'organic unity' of the work;[53] this argument against Lukács's realism was identical to Bloch's, which, in turn, seemed to be in agreement with the Frankfurt School's general position vis-à-vis culture. But Bloch explicated the technique of montage with specific reference to Brecht's dramaturgy, where montage meant 'extracting a man from his previous situation and re-programming him, casting him into a new situation', or, alternatively, 'taking a code of behaviour that is the product of a certain set of conditions and trying out this code in a radically different context'.[54] Adorno, by contrast, explicated his own conception of montage with reference to Mahler; in the essay on musical fetishism, he wrote this about the composer:

> Everything he operates with is already there. He takes it up in its depraved state of existence; his themes have been dis-appropriated. Yet not one sounds as we are accustomed to hearing it; each one is as if deflected by a magnet. And precisely those chords which have been worn out and played to death yield to the hand of improvisation, thus gaining a second life, as variants.[55]

Thus, montage is explicated not in terms of class-agitation, but in terms of a general de-ideologising 'negation'. In fact, 'negation' takes the place, in Frankfurt School aesthetics, of 'struggle'. This notion of 'negation' can now be summarised.

6 Art as negation

The concept of art as negation reproduces all the weaknesses of 'critical theory of society'. When Adorno concedes that art is 'partisan' (although he uses *parteiisch*, rather than the recognised *parteilich*), it is evident that he means this only in terms of a bringing to consciousness, rather than in terms of an agitational *class-consciousness*:

> Partisanship, the virtue of works of art no less than of people, resides in the depth in which social antinomies become the

dialectic of artistic forms: artists, in helping these contradictions to the level of speech via the synthesis of the image, are doing their bit socially.[56]

For Adorno, this process, which is the 'communication of the incommunicable', constitutes the 'smashing of reified consciousness'.[57] But, in reality, the repudiation of discursive communication breaks the theory-praxis nexus by precluding any concrete agitational struggle for mass class-consciousness. Indicatively, this latter concern is reduced by Adorno to the vulgar question of 'cui bono?' and this question is then easily dismissed as 'instrumentalist'.[58]

At times, the materialist awareness of art's isolation does break through, but the problem is expressed (by hypostatised terms) in such a way as to vindicate art's elitism: 'The only spirit (*Geist*) that respects man is the spirit which, instead of pandering to him as society has fashioned him, immerses itself in the cause which, unbeknown to him, is his own'.[59] The scurrilous reverse of this perspective (according to which, art's non-comprehensibility is due to its faithfulness to its very nature, which is negation—a theory running through Adorno's aesthetics from beginning to end)[60] is the claim that the masses do, in fact, know full well why they reject the avant-garde: because it challenges their security in their manipulated existence. Horkheimer claimed in the *Zeitschrift*:

> Yet every new work of art makes the masses draw back in horror. Unlike the Führers, it does not appeal to their psychology, nor, like psychoanalysis, does it contain a promise to guide this psychology towards 'adjustment.' In giving downtrodden humans a shocking awareness of their own despair, the work of art professes a freedom which makes them foam at the mouth.[61]

The masses are viewed as totally manipulated and as one with the alienated world that art 'negates'. Although art is not all that it would wish to be, it can do no more than defy and 'negate' the one-dimensional society of which it is a part; Adorno explains:

> It is true that art remains tied up with what **Hegel** calls the World Spirit, and thus art too carries some responsibility for this world; however, it could only escape this complicity by abolishing itself, and, if it did that, it would really be aiding and abetting actively the alien and speechless domination of man, and thus yielding to barbarism.[62]

While the critical notion of art as 'affirmation' has not been totally lost, the question of a sublation into practical-critical struggle has.

This throws a good deal of light on 'critical theory of society'.

Horkheimer's 'manifesto' spoke of a 'dynamic unity' of proletariat and intelligentsia: despite the 'tension' between the critical theoretician and the class his theory 'concerned', none the less, that theory always remained 'linked' to the class-struggles underway. But in the evolution of 'critical theory of society', this programme gave way to a view of the masses as corrupted and manipulated, thus isolating 'truth' as the preserve of the critical intellectual. Thus, the experience of fascism was, in a sense, traumatic for the Frankfurt School. Their theory was not developed with any concept of a continuing confrontation of wage-labour and capital; anything less than total revolution, with a perfect mass class-consciousness, was viewed as hopelessly caught up in the contradictions of that very world which was to be smashed. This weakness is reproduced in the Frankfurt School's aesthetics. The analysis of manipulation is highly incisive, whereas the concept of 'negation' is tendentially idealist.

In the absence of revolutionary praxis on the socio-political level, attention is diverted to the 'radical' praxis of art. To complete the vicious circle, however, art's 'negation' is passive and waits impotently for the real negation in revolutionary praxis. Adorno's theory of art is both elitist and pessimistic:

> art is more than praxis because, turning its back even on
> praxis, art equally denounces the limitations and falsity of the
> practical world. Praxis can perhaps have no direct cognisance of
> that fact as long as the practical rearrangement of the world has
> not yet succeeded.[63]

Critical even of the concrete struggle to achieve a non-alienated society, Frankfurt School aesthetics none the less waits tensely, passively and impotently for that struggle to succeed and realise concretely the negation which at present 'necessarily' resides in art alone.

However, as in the case of the psychological studies, the Frankfurt School's analysis of art does seem at times to sound an optimistic note; in particular, the analysis of culture industry stresses, if only in isolated passages, that 'something dialectical' is happening. Adorno's essays in the *Zeitschrift* often end on such a note. Thus, Martin Jay (who correctly states that Adorno never abandoned his 'cultural elitism',[64] but who fails to concretise this notion) relates that 'as in the case of jazz, Adorno felt there might still be an isolated element of negation in popular music'.[65] This, again, is true, but Jay does not ask after the materialist dimension of this 'negation'. If one does pose this question, the usual Frankfurt School weaknesses emerge once more. This is Adorno's argument:

> Enthusiasm for popular music requires wilful resolution by
> listeners, who must transform the external order to which they
> are subservient into an internal order. The endowment of musical

135

commodities with libido energy is manipulated by the ego. This manipulation is not entirely unconscious therefore. . . . But the closer the will decision, the histrionics, and the imminence of self-denunciation in the jitterbug are to the surface of consciousness, the greater is the possibility that these tendencies will break through in the mass, and, once and for all, dispense with controlled pleasure.[66]

This 'possibility', which gives no real guide as to an active heightening of ideological struggle, serves to justify once again the elitism and esotericism of the avant-garde in art; Horkheimer, for example, wrote, in conclusion to his penultimate essay in the *Zeitschrift:*

One day we may learn that in the depths of their hearts, the masses, even in fascist countries, secretly knew the truth and disbelieved the lie, like katatonic patients who make known only at the end of their trance that nothing has escaped them. Therefore it may not be entirely senseless to continue speaking a language that is not easily understood.[67]

Here is the suggestion that the masses are *not* totally manipulable. Yet the conceptualisation of any concrete relation of critical art to the weaknesses of 'culture industry' is not only vague, but non-existent. It is thus crucial to now put the question of the possibility of critical work in popular culture; this is the question of the progressive employment of the advanced means of communication. This question leads once more to the figure of Brecht. But before that, it will be useful to discuss briefly the work of Walter Benjamin; Benjamin's theoretical work on the question of a revolutionary art was largely an attempt to systematise and propagate the praxis of Bertolt Brecht, and this constitutes one of Benjamin's lasting contributions to aesthetics. First, however, it is informative to consider some basic differences between Benjamin and the Frankfurt School.

7 Walter Benjamin

The basic difference between Benjamin and Adorno can be summarised as the differing levels of concreteness in their respective work. Adorno's aesthetics reveals a high level of hypostatisation, even unintelligibility, the most blatant example of which is the following passage from the *Aesthetic Theory:*

It is dubious whether works of art intervene politically; if they do, it is usually peripheral to the respective works; and if they strive to, they usually fall short of their own concept (*Begriff*). Their true social impact, or effect, is highly mediate; it is participation in that spirit (*Geist*) which contributes in

136

subterranean processes to the transformation of society and which is concentrated in works of art.[68]

Benjamin, on the other hand, might be considered to have forestalled, and repudiated, this very passage in a lecture of 1934, where he said:

The mind, the spirit that makes itself heard in the name of fascism, *must* disappear. The mind which believes only in its own magic strength (a strength it opposes to fascism) *will* disappear. For the revolutionary struggle is not fought between capitalism and mind. It is fought between capitalism and the proletariat.[69]

This perspective was, in Benjamin's case, not merely a stated methodological imperative (as it was with the Frankfurt School), but actually informed his analyses of specific cultural phenomena, particularly under Brecht's influence.

Like Adorno, Benjamin was very interested in the avant-garde, but he avoided Adorno's passive stance. This was largely due to the influence of Brecht, who, while repudiating Lukács's undialectical attack on the avant-garde, none the less emphasised that it *could* become unrealistic: it could 'march so far ahead that the main body of the army cannot follow it, loses it from sight, and so on'.[70] Benjamin followed this critical perspective, and, in his discussion of the affinity between the anti-mechanistic force of surrealism and the struggle for classless society, stressed:

as Berl puts it, 'even if he has revolutionised art, the artist is not thereby any more revolutionary than Poiret, who, for his part, revolutionised clothing-fashions.' The most advanced, most adventurous products of the avant-garde in all arts have had as their only public, in France, as in Germany, the upper bourgeoisie. This fact contains, if by no means the judgment as to its value, none the less a clue to the political unsurety of the groups behind these manifestations.[71]

Anticipating the later concept of 'one-dimensionality', Benjamin succeeded in revealing the specifically materialist problematic:

For we are confronted with the fact ... that the bourgeois apparatus of production and publication is capable of assimilating, indeed of propagating, an astonishing amount of revolutionary themes without ever seriously putting into question its own continued existence or that of the class which owns it.[72]

Thus, Benjamin explained the rational use of montage in terms of Brecht's epic theatre, where montage did not have the force of titillating the senses but had an 'organising function'.[73] This organising function was not merely the mental labour of artistic 'negation' (as it was with Adorno's Mahler), but aimed, by linking to the realities of class-struggle through discursive communication, at organising the listeners into a 'coherent whole'.[74]

8 Brecht's work in radio

Benjamin's categories of production, distribution and reception have metacritical significance for the Frankfurt School's analysis of 'culture industry'. In this regard, once again, Benjamin's work is largely a theoretical reflection on Brecht's aesthetic praxis: in this case, his practical involvement with the mass media. Whereas the Frankfurt School's first theoretical involvement with the new means of communication came with the emigration to America, and resulted in a subsumption of these media under the derogatory label of 'culture industry', Brecht had been involved with them actively since the late 1920s, attempting to use them in a progressive manner. Brecht refused to be passively critical, and maintained that to write off the new media as 'rubbish' only ensured that rubbish would be produced for them.[75]

Brecht believed that the new media should not be supplied, but 'functionally transformed', or 'subverted' (*umfunktioniert*) in the interests of proletarian communication. Apart from actualisation, Brecht demanded a radical change in the sender-receiver relation:

Radio would be the greatest apparatus of communication imaginable for public life, a massive network, that is, it could be, if it could see its way clear to not merely transmitting, but also receiving, making the listener not just listen, but actually speak, thus not isolating him as a passive object, but putting him in active contact with other listener-speakers. Radio, according to our conception, should become more than a supplier: it should organise the listener as a supplier.[76]

Benjamin emphasised the significance of the Brechtian concept of 'functional transformation',[77] and, examining the general implications of the work of art's technological reproducibility, pointed out the positive development: that the loss of 'aura' meant the definitive emancipation of art from its 'parasitical dependence on ritual'.[78]

This positive evaluation prompted Adorno to a critical reply, and the essay on musical fetishism in the *Zeitschrift* was written, in part, to fulfil this very purpose: to correct the imbalance caused by Benjamin's 'undifferentiated' and 'undialectical' assessment.[79] However, Adorno's own analysis was undialectical in its failure to question whether the new techniques of production could not function differently in a different social context (that is, in different production-relations), and whether those media could not be subverted now, as part of the struggle for social change. And, in addition, Benjamin and Brecht were far from undialectical in their analysis. Benjamin actually anticipated Adorno's critique of pseudo-individualisation and personality-plugging, as well as analysing the fascist abuse of film.[80] And Brecht's repeated tactic of appealing to the radio authorities did not testify to any political naivety, but was intended as a means of giving a public exposé of his own conception of how the media should operate, and thus challenging the authorities to comply with the conception which, so Brecht claimed, was in the best interests of the majority. Brecht emphasised simultaneously that any progressive stand by the radio personnel would provoke repressive radio laws, and that, as a result, only mass working-class support would win the fight. The non-manipulative implementation of the means of communication presupposed a proletarian dictatorship. Thus, the whole debate was both a theoretical anticipation of, and a propaganda campaign for, a society where these media would realise their full potential.[81] Any optimism on Brecht's part was not passive (as was Adorno's pessimism), but the enthusiastic perspective of somebody actually involved in concrete struggles.

In addition, Brecht experimented with the possibility of using radio for direct socialist propaganda, the classic example being the 'Flight of the Lindberghs', later retitled 'The Ocean Flight'.[82] Here, the dramatic representation of a historic one-man flight aimed at activating the audience, who became the main speakers; the radio transmitted the various background voices, while the audience, schoolchildren, recited the lines of the pilot and became 'the pilots'. In the section entitled 'Ideology' the pilots' text juxtaposes technological progress and socio-political chaos, both real and ideational:

In the cities god was created by the chaos
Of social classes, because there are two sorts of people
Exploitation and ignorance, but
The revolution will wipe him out . . .
So join
In the struggle against all that is primitive
In the liquidation of the 'Beyond' and
In the banishing of each and every god wherever
He appears.[83]

In this way, the schoolchildren become the subjects of the action, subjects linked in a group-ego, subjects of a progressive praxis.

9 Brecht's work in agitation songs

This attempt to create an active group-ego via a critical aesthetic praxis was not new, but taken over from the example of workers' songs and choruses, a major feature of the class-struggles of Weimar Germany. Lenin, who had no productive relationship to the avant-garde (admitting he was an 'old fogy'), had maintained that the evaluation of the avant-garde was, in fact, of secondary importance. What was of more importance was that art which 'belongs to the people'. This art must be developed as an agitational weapon, and be 'implanted in the very thick of the labouring masses', so as to 'unite and elevate their feelings, thoughts and will'.[84] In 1913, Lenin actually referred to the 'hearty proletarian song about mankind's coming emancipation from wage-slavery'.[85] This is significant, not for the assertion of the 'orthodox' Leninist line, but because Lenin succeeded in pinpointing the mass art-form which, in Weimar Germany, did indeed serve to elevate the feelings, thoughts and *will* of the class-conscious workers.

Brecht wrote numerous agitation songs with Hanns Eisler at this time; an example is the 'Solidarity Song',[86] the chorus of which runs as follows:

Onwards and no retreating,
Our strength lies in unity!
When we're starving and when we're eating
Onwards and no retreating
In solidarity.

The final chorus is modified:

Onwards, never retreating
And asking defiantly
When we're starving and when we're eating
'Whose tomorrow is tomorrow?
Whose world is the world to be?'

This song linked directly to the class-struggles of Weimar Germany, where mass immiseration of an absolute nature marked the reality of working-class life (see Chapter 1), and where 'when we're starving' was no anachronistic stereotype but a desperately pressing issue that mobilised the masses in a potentially revolutionary, but, unfortunately, disunited struggle.

The correct presentation of the song was an infectious but jagged fusion of chanting and singing. Brecht emphasised that the correct delivery was, simply, the one that best accommodated the current expressions of the class-struggle, which are harsh, rough and aggressive. Regular rhythms with uniform intonation, by contrast, 'do not bite sufficiently', and require circumscriptions.[87] Thus Brecht's repudiation of 'affirmative' art had quite definite practical consequences thanks to his involvement in mass ideological struggle.

At times, Adorno affirms the Brechtian technique of 'brushing taste against the grain', for recognising the complicity of richness in expression with the poverty of reality.[88] However, Adorno questions the efficacy of broken style in an agit-prop chorus of the early 1930s (although the scepticism is 'purely' aesthetic), stating that 'it was always dubious whether the artistic attitude of roughness and growling actually denounced, or identified with, these forces in their social reality'.[89] Thus, Adorno's position remains one of 'total negation' of reification, and precludes concrete agitational struggle. Brecht, by contrast, retained the materialist perspective of the theory-praxis nexus, and stressed the relation of critical theory (and art) to an addressee:

> You cannot just 'write the truth;' you have to write it *for*, and
> *to* somebody, somebody who can do something with it. . . .
> You must address yourself not merely to people of a certain
> disposition, but to those people whom this disposition benefits
> on the basis of their social position.[90]

To this, Adorno replied by applying to Brecht's work the Anglo-Saxon label of 'preaching to the saved'.[91] This reveals Adorno's ignorance of the complex, dynamic nature of class-consciousness. For Brecht, there was no clear line of demarcation between those who were 'saved' and those who were not. Rather, revolutionary art was the art of a period when the masses were already being mobilised on a considerable scale and with progressively critical consciousness; and revolutionary art directed itself to these people in order to carry out the vital task of *strengthening* their will and *clarifying* their consciousness.[92]

Adorno's idealist perspective reveals itself further in his discussion of the crucial question of the potential mediation between art's 'negation' and critical social praxis. Although he states, quite correctly, that the practical impact of any specific work of art is not determined exclusively by the work in itself, but by the historical context, Adorno proceeds to explicate this idea with reference to Beaumarchais's political effect (adding that Brecht was 'socially impotent'). And Adorno then maintains, of works of art in general:

> The effect that they would wish to have is at present absent,
> and they suffer from that absence greatly; but as soon as they
> attempt to attain that effect by accommodating themselves to
> prevailing needs, they deprive men of precisely that which they
> could (to take the phraseology of needs seriously, and to use it
> against itself) give them.[93]

141

To link art, via discursive communication, to actual socio-political struggles, would mean, Adorno believes, abolishing art altogether, not as a sublation, but as a concession to barbarism. Meanwhile, 'true' critical art 'gives' us only necessarily incomprehensible works.

10 Aesthetic elitism and the loss of class praxis

If one examines the various historical periods through which the Frankfurt School have passed during their productive lives, then it must be admitted that the preceding quotation does deserve some sympathy: after all, it was written in the early 1960s, when no mass revolutionary consciousness existed among the working class. Equally, the article on 'Engagement' was written in 1962, with the Cold War at its height, in the face of the total bureaucratic degeneration of the Soviet Union, and with the traumatic memory (particularly for the intellectual of Jewish origins) of Nazi barbarism. Fascism had been defeated in Germany, but the capitalist base that had spawned it was thriving, and no serious anti-capitalist movement was evident among the masses.

However, the aesthetic theory of the Frankfurt School, distilled in Adorno's *Aesthetic Theory*, is far more than the response to an objective diminution of revolutionary class-struggle. On the contrary, this theory has spanned several decades, and during this time has revealed remarkable consistency. Having established the main components of that theory, it is now possible to analyse it in its genesis, and this analysis shows that the loss of praxis in that theory was already evident in the revolutionary period of the Weimar Republic's twilight, when critical aesthetic praxis was no longer a merely theoretical problem, but an active component of a concrete mass ideological struggle.

In his *Zeitschrift* essay of 1932, 'Concerning the Social Position of Music', Adorno maintained that the prevailing consciousness, even the class-consciousness of the proletariat, was deformed because it bore, necessarily, the scars of alienation. This determined Adorno's aesthetics: 'just as theory as a whole goes beyond the prevailing consciousness of the masses, so too must music go beyond it.'[94] But, like 'critical theory of society' as a whole, this aesthetic theory, and the praxis it eulogised, went so far beyond the prevailing consciousness that, to use Brecht's expression, even the most advanced sections of the workers were bound to 'lose it from sight'. This was due to Adorno's formalistic criteria:

Here and now, music can do no more than to present, in its own structure, the social antinomies which, amongst other things, carry the responsibility for music's isolation. It will

succeed all the better, the more deeply it manages to form,
within itself, the force of those contradictions and the need to
resolve them in society, and the more precisely it expresses, in
the antinomies of its own language and forms, the miseries of
the status quo, emphatically calling, through the ciphered
language of suffering, for change.[95]

Paradigmatic is Arnold Schönberg, whose technical solutions in
music are, despite their 'isolation', none the less 'socially of consequence'.[96] As to the concrete 'consequence' of this esoteric music
for social praxis, Adorno is silent. Thereby, his correct materialist
awareness that music's isolation can be resolved 'not in an inner-
musical struggle, but only socially, i.e. by transforming society',[97]
eventually locks him in a vicious circle, upon which his dialectical
thought can reflect only as a pessimistic resignation.

Adorno, in this essay, actually discussed Eisler's agitational music,
and the evaluation is significantly different from Brecht's. To the
latter, Eisler was the most fortunate of the Weimar Republic's
revolutionary artists: in possession of a highly developed technique,
acquired as a pupil of Schönberg, Eisler freed this technique from its
elitism and placed it in the service of the mobilised masses who now
became the active producers.[98] Such an activation would seem to
satisfy, on the aesthetic level, the Frankfurt School's precept that
'in the struggle for classless society, the masses must first organise
themselves, and transform themselves from a mere object into the
active subject of history, thereby throwing off their character of
being masses once and for all' (see Chapter 3); but Adorno actually
accuses Eisler's aesthetic praxis of absolutising the prevailing consciousness, which is deformed:

those very criteria which this production orientates itself to,
singability, simplicity, collective effect as such, are necessarily
tied up with a state of consciousness which is so weighted down
and shackled by class-domination—nobody formulated that
more extremely than Marx—that this consciousness, if it is to
become the one-sided criterion of production, becomes a fetter
on the musical productive force.[99]

Adorno gladly concedes that the agitational value in proletarian
music is indisputable, and that it would be 'utopian' and 'idealist' to
replace this music with one 'which was inwardly more appropriate
to the essential function of the proletariat, but which was unintelli-
gible to that class'. But Adorno's concept of an adequate *aesthetic*
praxis 'transcends' proletarian music in the direction not of a higher
mass ideological struggle but in the direction of the bourgeois avant-
garde. Thus, Adorno says of proletarian music: 'As soon . . . as this
music leaves the front of immediate action, reflects and posits itself

143

as an art-form, it becomes patently obvious that the products cannot hold their own against the advanced bourgeois production. . . .'[100] In this way, the analysis of the avant-garde ceases to be a sublation, and the aesthetic praxis of class-struggle loses all significance for Adorno's theory. Henceforth, even the *memory* of the proletarian art forms of Weimar Germany was doomed to extinction in Adorno's work. In contrast to this, it can be said that while the work of Brecht and Eisler and the entire agit-prop movement cannot be transplanted uncritically into an ever-changing class constellation, a systematic historical materialist study of the theory and praxis of figures like Brecht *will* ensure that the object and categories of a critical aesthetic praxis avoid Adorno's deviations into idealism and cultural elitism.

11 Brecht's attack on the Frankfurt School 'Tuis'

In the last issue of the *Zeitschrift*, Horkheimer summed up the entire Frankfurt School position on aesthetics (in its broadest sense): art had once upheld 'another world', a world 'other' than that of commodity-production; this other world had been repressively eroded by monopoly capitalism and the 'culture industry', and today survived only in works like Picasso's *Guernica* and Joyce's prose:

> The grief and horror such works convey are not identical with the feelings of those who, for rational reasons, are turning away from reality or rising against it. The consciousness behind them is rather one cut off from society as it is, and forced into queer, discordant forms.[101]

Thus, the step from 'total negation' to the *socio-political* negation of class praxis is precluded in art. This finds its antithesis in Brecht's work, which was conceived as 'a call to the oppressed to rise up against the oppressors, and to do so in the name of humanity'. For, as Brecht stressed, 'in times like these, humanity must become warlike, if it is not to be wiped out altogether'.[102] This was Brecht's version of the sublation of the humanist heritage. And if the Frankfurt School were critical of this conception, Brecht in turn was no less critical of the Frankfurt School, whom he branded as 'Tuis'.

A 'Tui' is an intellectual, but of a specific kind: idealist, politically impotent, Social Democratic. Brecht wrote that 'the main cause of non-interventionist thought is the false, non-interventionist democracy', that is, 'political freedom based on economic slavery'.[103] This, of course, is not true of the Frankfurt School, who criticised the SPD for precisely the same reasons (see Chapter 3), and who, in the figure of the Institute's Director, agreed with Brecht that 'now, the literary opponents of the totalitarian society praise the state that spawned it, and deny the theory which revealed the true nature of this state, when there was still time'.[104] But the Frankfurt School's 'critical theory of society' never drew the full consequences in terms of a *practical, materialist* theory, either during the last years of Weimar, the Nazi regime, or ever (apart from Marcuse's work following his break with his former colleagues), and this was why Brecht derided them as 'Tuis'.[105]

What Brecht really despised about Horkheimer's team was their *passive* dialectical critique of culture, which he saw as evidence of their *academic* perspective. He wrote, for example, of a discussion with Adorno in the early 1940s:

> This Frankfurt Institute is a real find for the Tui-Novel. . . . It's really funny when they come up with things like: 'Robert Walser is very important, because he reflects the degeneration of bourgeois society.' What a pity that this bourgeoisie then degenerates into Panzer-divisions and SS-units![106]

Ultimately, the Frankfurt School's differentiated critique of culture collapsed due to its failure to proceed from ideology-critique to the *practical-critical* theory of class praxis. In this sense, Brecht felt that Horkheimer's team were little better than the Social Democrats. And, in fact, Brecht thereby predicted the total theoretical collapse of Horkheimer in later years, as had Korsch (see Chapter 3).

12 The role of aesthetics in Marcuse's radicalised 'critical theory of society'

Benjamin's conception of critical aesthetic praxis was more akin to Brecht's than the Frankfurt School's and thus escaped the pitfall of 'Tui-ism'. Indeed, Adorno himself admits that Benjamin's differences with the Frankfurt School were largely due to Brecht's 'Anti-Tui-ism'.[107] But what of the Marcuse of recent years? Did Marcuse's radicalisation in the late 1960s prompt a fundamental reconsideration of the role of art? The answer is: No! Paradoxically, the area where the Frankfurt School produced their finest dialectical analyses of ideology and manipulation, but where the ultimate weaknesses of 'critical theory of society' manifest themselves most clearly, is the area where Marcuse has remained firmly within the Frankfurt School tradition.

One-Dimensional Man restates the dialectics of affirmation and negation to the decided advantage of the latter: '*artistic alienation* is the conscious transcendence of the alienated existence'. Marcuse speaks of art's 'negation of the order of business'.[108] But although he stresses that 'transcendent' is to be understood in a materialist sense,[109] and although he speaks of 'images of a gratification that

145

would dissolve the society which suppresses it',[110] Marcuse's aesthetic theory pursues the same 'total negation' as Adorno:

> The truly avant-garde works of literature communicate the break with communication. With Rimbaud, and then with dadaism and surrealism, literature rejects the very structure of discourse which, throughout the history of culture, has linked artistic and ordinary language.[111]

An Essay on Liberation, which marked Marcuse's more articulate reception of the student anti-authoritarian movement, reaffirmed the Frankfurt School's aesthetics, stating that 'it is precisely the Form by virtue of which art transcends the given reality, works in the established reality against the established reality'.[112] And *Counterrevolution and Revolt*, for its part, maintained that 'the aesthetic universe *contradicts* reality—a "methodical," intentional contradiction'.[113] This 'negation' cannot be sublated into mass ideological struggle of a coherent discursive nature, because that would make art 'instrumentalist'.[114]

In line with 'critical theory of society' as a whole, art assumes the critical role of a de-ideologising force, dismantling and exposing the manipulative aspects of prevailing discourse. But this de-ideologisation of reality fails to constitute itself as a *practical-critical* force of class praxis. Reality is viewed not, as with Brecht, according to the class constellation, but, as with Adorno, according to the alienation and reification that permeate human society so far. And the artistic struggle becomes a 'total negation'. Thus, 'style, embodiment of the aesthetic form, in subjecting reality to another order, subjects it to the "laws of beauty" '.[115]

This is consistent with Marcuse's thesis that real art 'reveals the human condition as it pertains to the entire history (Marx: prehistory) of mankind over and above any specific conditions', and that art thus 'preserves and *transcends* its class character'.[116] But the implicit conception of a *sublation* is not concretised by Marcuse, and, in reality, he fails to preserve the conscious class content of revolutionary art, opting instead for 'total' transcendence. Thus, Marcuse's claim that 'art can indeed become a weapon in the class struggle by promoting changes in the prevailing consciousness',[117] loses its materialist significance.

'Promoting changes' in consciousness, as an element of ideological struggle, presupposes two things: *effective* communication, and communication to a *revolutionary class*. The first of these is sacrificed, ultimately, by the anti-discursive nature of Marcuse's critical art. The second precondition for creating revolutionary consciousness is also lost, but in a far more complex manner. Paradoxically, this aspect of Marcuse's theory is based on a discussion of

Marx's economic theory, a discussion which does a great deal to remedy the Frankfurt School's failure to provide an articulate analysis of *economic* manipulation. After a detailed exposé of Marx's concept of the 'collective labourer' (*Gesamtarbeiter*), where Marcuse touches on Sohn-Rethel's theory of mental and manual labour, *Counterrevolution and Revolt* concludes that the transfer of power to the proletariat, which is only one component of the productive labour-force, would not alone guarantee the transition to a qualitatively different society. This entire argument is then repeated in the discussion of art, where Marcuse rejects the notion of an agitational art guided by a proletarian world view:

> If the term 'proletarian world view' is to mean the world view that is prevalent among the working class, then it is, in the advanced capitalist countries, a world view shared by a large part of the other classes, especially the middle classes. . . . If the term is to designate *revolutionary* consciousness (latent or actual), then it is today certainly not distinctively or even predominantly 'proletarian'— not only because the revolution against global monopoly capitalism is more and other than a proletarian revolution, but also because its conditions, prospects, and goals cannot be adequately formulated in terms of a proletarian revolution. . . .[118]

Yet despite the stress on the modern concatenation of exploitation, and despite the stress that the proletariat's radicalisation is a sine qua non for revolution, Marcuse does not broach the question of an art geared to an adequate strategy for reconciling mental and manual labour (if only tendentially) *within* class-struggle. Thus, art's 'transcendence' and the concrete negation of capitalism in revolutionary praxis are not mediated in Marcuse's theory any more than they are in Adorno's.

One possible exception is Marcuse's discussion of the rebellious force of black language, which 'strengthens solidarity'.[119] But even here, the stress is essentially on the 'total' rebellion implicit in this development and particularly in its art; the concern is for 'the very existence of the individual and his group as *human beings*'.[120] The *demarcating* force of this art is neglected. Similarly, Marcuse's discussion of the critical aesthetic praxis of the 1920s and 1930s, while focusing on Brecht and Eisler, does not relate positively to what Marcuse would presumably regard as the 'instrumentalist' function of this art: namely, the strengthening of the will and solidarity of the mobilised workers as *class-conscious workers*.

In this way, Marcuse's aesthetics ends up in the same contradiction as Adorno's: while art's 'transcendence' is a 'negation' of alienation and reification, the primary task remains the ideological struggle for the emancipation of consciousness: 'Without it, all emancipation of the senses, all radical activism, remains blind, self-defeating. Political practice still depends on theory. . . . on education, persuasion—on Reason'.[121] Ultimately, art, even for Marcuse, cannot be geared to this task in any significant sense, and the theory-praxis nexus is lost. In conclusion, it can be stated that whereas Adorno and Horkheimer, as they distanced themselves from critical praxis, were consistent in turning their backs on the revolutionary tradition in art, Marcuse, by contrast, in his attempt to overcome the fundamental flaws of the original 'critical theory of society' (as expounded by Horkheimer and implemented by his team in the *Zeitschrift* period), can and must free himself from the hypostatisation, idealism and elitism of mainstream Frankfurt School aesthetics. Otherwise, Marcuse's radicalised theoretical activity since the 1960s will remain, in this crucial area, tied up in the contradictions that have marred the Frankfurt School since its inception.

Notes

Introduction

1 Martin Jay, *The Dialectical Imagination: A History of the Frankfurt School and the Institute of Social Research 1923–1950* (Boston: Little, Brown, 1973).
2 Ibid., p. xiv.
3 Ibid., p. 4.
4 Douglas Kellner, 'The Frankfurt School Revisited: A Critique of Martin Jay's *The Dialectical Imagination*', *New German Critique*, No. 4 (1975).

Chapter 1 The historical background of the Frankfurt School

1 This account is based on four main sources: Paul Kluke, *Die Stiftungs-universität Frankfurt am Main 1914–1932* (Frankfurt: Waldemar Kramer, 1972), pp. 486–513; Max Horkheimer, *Verwaltete Welt* (Zurich: Arche, 1970); interview with Felix Weil, Frankfurt am Main, 25 November 1972; interview with Max Horkheimer, Frankfurt am Main, 27 November 1972.
2 Kluke, op. cit., p. 489.
3 Weil later explained that he would gladly have called the Institute what it was really intended to be, that is, Institut für Marxismus (Institute for Marxism), but that this title was sacrificed in the interest of formal academic recognition (interview with Weil).
4 Kluke, op. cit., p. 489.
5 Ibid., pp. 495–6.
6 Carl Grunberg, 'Festrede gehalten zur Einweihung des Instituts fur Sozialforschung an der Universität Frankfurt a. M. am 22. Juni 1924', *Frankfurter Universitätsreden*, 20 (Frankfurt: Universitäts-Druckerei Werner und Winter, 1924), p. 9.
7 Ibid., p. 15.
8 Ibid., p. 7.
9 Interview with Weil.

10 Grünberg, op. cit., pp. 10–11.
11 Ibid., p. 10. This assertion too was inserted by Weil (interview with Weil).
12 Grünberg, op. cit., p. 13.
13 Ibid., p. 10.
14 Ibid., p. 16.
15 Ibid., pp. 13–14.
16 Ibid., pp. 9, 10.
17 Interview with Weil.
18 Felix Weil, 'Denkschrift über die Arbeit des Instituts für Sozialforschung an der Universität Frankfurt a. M.' For details, see Kluke, op. cit., p. 511.
19 Henryk Grossmann, *Das Akkumulations- und Zusammenbruchsgesetz des kapitalistischen Systems (Zugleich eine Krisentheorie)*, Schriften des Instituts für Sozialforschung an der Universität Frankfurt a. M., 1, ed. Carl Grünberg (Leipzig: Hirschfeld, 1929).
20 Ibid., p. vi.
21 Ibid., pp. vi–vii.
22 Karl Marx, *Capital: A Critique of Political Economy*, III, ed. Frederick Engels (London: Lawrence & Wishart, 1972), pp. 211–66.
23 Ibid., p. 239.
24 Karl Marx, *Grundrisse: Foundations of the Critique of Political Economy (Rough Draft)*, trans. Martin Nicolaus (Harmondsworth: Penguin, 1973), p. 101.
25 Friedrich Pollock, *Die planwirtschaftlichen Versuche in der Sowjetunion 1917–1927*, Schriften des Instituts für Sozialforschung an der Universität Frankfurt a. M., 2, ed. Carl Grünberg (Leipzig: Hirschfeld, 1929).
26 Ibid., p. v.
27 Karl August Wittfogel, *Wirtschaft und Gesellschaft Chinas: Versuch der wissenschaftlichen Analyse einer grossen asiatischen Agrargesellschaft*, Schriften des Instituts für Sozialforschung an der Universität Frankfurt a. M., 3, ed. Carl Grünberg (Leipzig: Hirschfeld, 1931).
28 Ibid., pp. ix, xiii–xiv.
29 Ibid., pp. 16–17, 137.
30 Ibid., pp. 416–60.
31 Carl Grünberg (ed.), *Archiv für die Geschichte des Sozialismus und der Arbeiterbewegung* (Leipzig: Hirschfeld, 1911–30). Henceforth, the abbreviation *Grünberg Archiv* will be used.
32 Felix Weil, 'Rosa Luxemburg über die russische Revolution: Einige unveröffentlichte Manuskripte', *Grunberg Archiv*, 13 (1928), p. 285.
33 Carl Grünberg, 'Vorwort des Herausgebers', *Grünberg Archiv*, 1 (1911), pp. ii–iii.
34 Ibid., p. ii.
35 Ibid., p. iii.
36 Carl Grünberg, 'Der Grundgesetz der russischen Sowjetrepublik', *Grünberg Archiv*, 8 (1919), p. 402.
37 Karl Korsch, *Marxism and Philosophy*, trans. Fred Halliday (London: NLB, 1970) (originally 'Marxismus und Philosophie', 1923).

38 Emil Hammacher, 'Zur Würdigung des 'wahren' Marxismus', *Grünberg Archiv*, 1 (1911), pp. 50–1, 70.

39 Ibid., pp. 96–100.

40 Georg Lukács, 'Moses Hess und die Probleme der idealistischen Dialektik', *Grünberg Archiv*, 12 (1926).

41 Ibid., p. 123.

42 Ibid., p. 140.

43 Ibid., p. 143.

44 Korsch, op. cit., p. 69.

45 Interview with Weil.

46 Kluke, op. cit., p. 505; interview with Weil.

47 Max Horkheimer, 'Die gegenwärtige Lage der Sozialphilosophie und die Aufgaben eines Instituts für Sozialforschung', *Frankfurter Universitätsreden*, 37 (Frankfurt: Englert & Schlosser, 1931).

48 Ibid., p. 3.

49 Ibid., p. 6.

50 Ibid., pp. 8–9.

51 Ibid., p. 11.

52 Ibid., p. 11.

53 Ibid., p. 14.

54 Ibid., pp. 13–14.

55 Ibid., p. 14.

56 Ibid., p. 11.

57 Max Horkheimer, *Anfänge der bürgerlichen Geschichtsphilosophie* (1930; rpt Frankfurt: Fischer, 1971).

58 Ibid., p. 9.

59 Kluke, op. cit., p. 507.

60 Franz Borkenau, *Der Übergang vom feudalen zum bürgerlichen Weltbild: Studien zur Geschichte der Philosophie der Manufakturperiode*, Schriften des Instituts für Sozialforschung, 4, ed. Max Horkheimer (Paris: Alcan, 1934).

61 Max Horkheimer, 'Vorrede des Herausgebers', in ibid., p. v.

62 *Studien über Autorität und Familie: Forschungsberichte aus dem Institut für Sozialforschung* (Paris: Alcan, 1936).

63 Max Horkheimer, 'Vorwort', in ibid., pp. vii–viii.

64 Max Horkheimer, 'Allgemeiner Teil', in ibid., p. 38.

65 Max Horkheimer (ed.), *Zeitschrift für Sozialforschung* (Leipzig: Hirschfeld, 1932–3; Paris: Alcan, 1933–9). The Institute's journal was continued as *Studies in Philosophy and Social Science* (New York: Institute of Social Research, 1939–41). Henceforth, the abbreviations *ZfS* and *SPSS*, respectively, are used.

66 Alfred Schmidt, *Die 'Zeitschrift für Sozialforschung': Geschichte und gegenwärtige Bedeutung* (Munich: Kösel, 1970), inside cover.

67 Max Horkheimer, 'Vorwort', *ZfS*, 1 (1932), p. ii.

68 Ibid., p. iii.

69 Ibid., pp. ii–iii.

70 Max Horkheimer, 'Bemerkungen zur philosophischen Anthropologie', *ZfS*, 4 (1935), p. 9.

71 Max Horkheimer, 'Zum Rationalismusstreit in der gegenwärtigen Philosophie', *ZfS*, 3 (1934), pp. 26–7.

72 Max Horkheimer, 'Geschichte und Psychologie', *ZfS*, 1 (1932), p. 133.

73 Herbert Marcuse, *Reason and Revolution: Hegel and the Rise of Social Theory* (1941; rpt with supplementary chapter 1955; rpt London: Routledge & Kegan Paul, 1967).

74 Ibid., p. 410.

75 Theodor Wiesengrund Adorno (with the assistance of George Simpson), 'On Popular Music', *SPSS*, 9 (1941), p. 29.

76 Theodor Wiesengrund Adorno, 'Spengler Today', *SPSS*, 9 (1941), p. 310.

77 Friedrich Pollock, 'Bemerkungen zur Wirtschaftskrise', *ZfS*, 2 (1933), pp. 329–30.

78 Max Horkheimer and Theodor Wiesengrund Adorno, *Dialectic of Enlightenment*, trans. John Cumming (London: Allen Lane, 1973), p. 160 (originally *Dialektik der Aufklärung: Philosophische Fragmente*, 1947).

79 Herbert Marcuse, *Counterrevolution and Revolt* (London: Allen Lane, 1972), pp. 23–4.

80 Karl Marx, *Capital: A Critique of Political Economy*, I, ed. Frederick Engels (London: Lawrence & Wishart, 1970), p. 763.

81 Max Horkheimer, 'Vorwort zur Neupublikation', in *Kritische Theorie: Eine Dokumentation*, ed. Alfred Schmidt (Frankfurt: Fischer, 1968), I, p. ix.

82 Erich Eyck, *A History of the Weimar Republic*, trans. Harlan P. Hanson and Robert G. L. Waite (Cambridge: Harvard University Press, 1962–4), I, pp. 324–6.

83 Jürgen Kuczynski, *Darstellung der Lage der Arbeiter in Deutschland von 1917/18 bis 1932/33*, Die Geschichte der Lage der Arbeiter unter dem Kapitalismus, Part One, 5 (Berlin: Akademie-Verlag, 1966), pp. 207–8.

84 Ibid., pp. 235–8.

85 Ibid., pp. 238–9.

86 Ibid., p. 222.

87 Ibid., p. 26.

88 Ibid., pp. 196–8.

89 Pollock, 'Bemerkungen zur Wirtschaftskrise', *ZfS*, 2 (1933), p. 324.

90 Kuczynski, *Darstellung . . . 1917/18 bis 1932/33*, p. 197.

91 Helmut Heiber, *Die Republik von Weimar*, dtv-Weltgeschichte des 20. Jahrhunderts, ed. Martin Broszat and Helmut Heiber, 3 (Munich: DTV, 1966), pp. 212, 224–5.

92 Max Horkheimer, 'Montaigne und die Funktion der Skepsis', *ZfS*, 7 (1938), p. 38.

93 Max Horkheimer, 'Die Juden und Europa', *ZfS*, 8 (1939), p. 115.

94 Horkheimer, 'Montaigne und die Funktion der Skepsis', *ZfS*, 7 (1938), p. 31.

95 Friedrich Pollock, 'Die gegenwärtige Lage des Kapitalismus und die Aussichten einer planwirtschaftlichen Neuordnung', *ZfS*, 1 (1932), p. 12.

96 Frederick Pollock, 'State Capitalism: Its Possibilities and Limitations', *SPSS*, 9 (1941), p. 201.
97 Frederick Pollock, 'Is National Socialism a New Order?', *SPSS*, 9 (1941), p. 451.
98 Pollock, 'State Capitalism', *SPSS*, 9 (1941), p. 200.
99 Franz Neumann, *Behemoth: The Structure and Practice of National Socialism* (London: Gollancz, 1942).
100 Ibid., p. 183.
101 Ibid., p. 182.
102 Letter from Felix Weil to Karl Korsch, 15 August 1942. This letter, together with a number of other letters to or from Korsch, is kept in the Internationaal Instituut voor sociale Geschedenis, Amsterdam. I am indebted to Götz Langkau for drawing my attention to these letters, many of which relate to the Franfurt School, and will be discussed in Chapter 3.
103 Herbert Marcuse, 'Some Social Implications of Modern Technology', *SPSS*, 9 (1941), p. 414.
104 Pollock, 'State Capitalism', *SPSS*, 9 (1941), p. 201.
105 Jürgen Kuczynski, *Darstellung der Lage der Arbeiter in Deutschland von 1933 bis 1945*, Die Geschichte der Lage der Arbeiter unter dem Kapitalismus, Part One, 6 (Berlin: Akademie-Verlag, 1964), pp. 154-5, 177, 233-8.
106 Ibid., pp. 183-4.
107 Ibid., pp. 158, 230.
108 Ibid., pp. 102-8.
109 Ibid., pp. 159, 270-3.
110 Marcuse, *Reason and Revolution*, p. 415.
111 Martin Broszat, *Der Staat Hitlers: Grundlegung und Entwicklung seiner inneren Verfassung*, dtv-Weltgeschichte des 20. Jahrhunderts, ed. Martin Broszat and Helmut Heiber, 9 (Munich: DTV, 1969), p. 205.
112 Kuczynski, *Darstellung ... 1933 bis 1945*, pp. 245-7.
113 Horkheimer, 'Die Juden und Europa', *ZfS*, 8 (1939), p. 133.
114 Pollock, 'Is National Socialism a New Order?', *SPSS*, 9 (1941), pp. 450-4.
115 Max Horkheimer, 'Preface', *SPSS*, 9 (1941), p. 198.
116 Horkheimer, 'Die Juden und Europa', *ZfS*, 8 (1939), p. 135.
117 Horkheimer, 'Allgemeiner Teil', in *Studien über Autorität und Familie*, p. 15.
118 Horkheimer, 'Die gegenwärtige Lage der Sozialphilosophie', *Frankfurter Universitätsreden*, 37 (1931), p. 14.
119 Siegfried Kracauer, *Die Angestellten: Aus dem neuesten Deutschland* (1929; rpt Frankfurt: Suhrkamp, 1971).
120 Kuczynski, *Darstellung ... 1917/18 bis 1932/33*, p. 62.
121 Kracauer, op. cit., p. 11.
122 Ibid., pp. 12-13.
123 Ibid., p. 85.
124 Ibid., p. 91.
125 Ibid., p. 38.

126 Ibid., p. 89.
127 Wilhelm Reich, *Massenpsychologie des Faschismus: Zur Sexual-ökonomie der politischen Reaktion und zur proletarischen Sexualpolitik*, 2nd edn (Copenhagen, etc.: Verlag für Sexualpolitik, 1934), p. 36.

2 'Critical theory of society': the historical materialist critique of ideology

1 Max Horkheimer, 'Traditionelle und kritische Theorie', *ZfS*, 6 (1937).
2 Max Horkheimer and Herbert Marcuse, 'Philosophie und kritische Theorie', *ZfS*, 6 (1937). Marcuse's contribution is available in English, as 'Philosophy and Critical Theory', in *Negations: Essays in Critical Theory*, trans. Jeremy J. Shapiro (Harmondsworth: Penguin, 1972).
3 Herbert Marcuse, 'On Hedonism', in *Negations*, p. 282 (originally 'Zur Kritik des Hedonismus', *ZfS*, 7 (1938)).
4 Max Horkheimer, *Kritische Theorie: Eine Dokumentation*, ed. Alfred Schmidt (Frankfurt: Fischer, 1968), I, p. ix.
5 Horkheimer, 'Traditionelle und kritische Theorie', *ZfS*, 6 (1937), p. 261.
6 Horkheimer, 'Philosophie und kritische Theorie', *ZfS*, 6 (1937), p. 625.
7 Horkheimer, 'Traditionelle und kritische Theorie', *ZfS*, 6 (1937), p. 247.
8 Ibid., pp. 250–1.
9 Ibid., pp. 252, 255.
10 Ibid., p. 256.
11 Ibid., p. 254.
12 Ibid., p. 254.
13 Ibid., pp. 261–2.
14 Ibid., p. 272.
15 Ibid., p. 280.
16 Ibid., pp. 279, 278.
17 Ibid., p. 261.
18 Ibid., p. 254.
19 Ibid., p. 277.
20 Ibid., p. 284.
21 Horkheimer, 'Philosophie und kritische Theorie', *ZfS*, 6 (1937), p. 627.
22 Horkheimer, 'Traditionelle und kritische Theorie', *ZfS*, 6 (1937), p. 292.
23 Horkheimer, 'Philosophie und kritische Theorie', *ZfS*, 6 (1937), p. 626.
24 Ibid., p. 626.
25 Ibid., p. 627.
26 Horkheimer, 'Traditionelle und kritische Theorie', *ZfS*, 6 (1937), p. 262.
27 Max Horkheimer, 'Zum Problem der Wahrheit', *ZfS*, 4 (1935), p. 343.
28 Max Horkheimer, 'Zum Rationalismusstreit', *ZfS*, 3 (1934), p. 22.

29 Max Horkheimer, 'Materialismus und Metaphysik', *ZfS*, 2 (1933), p. 12.

30 Max Horkheimer, 'Materialismus und Moral', *ZfS*, 2 (1933), p. 177.

31 Horkheimer, 'Zum Problem der Wahrheit', *ZfS*, 4 (1935), p. 334.

32 Herbert Marcuse, *Reason and Revolution: Hegel and the Rise of Social Theory* (1941; rpt with supplementary chapter 1955; rpt London: Routledge & Kegan Paul, 1967), pp. 252–3.

33 Herbert Marcuse, *Hegels Ontologie und die Theorie der Geschichtlichkeit* (1932; rpt Frankfurt: Klostermann, 1968).

34 Theodor Wiesengrund Adorno, rev. of *Hegels Ontologie und die Theorie der Geschichtlichkeit*, by Herbert Marcuse, *ZfS*, 1 (1932), pp. 409–10. Adorno's assessment could, in fact, be extended to Marcuse's work in the previous four years as a whole, where, in a series of programmatic essays, Marcuse had attempted to go beyond the limits of Heidegger's a-historical ontology. This undertaking is presented with characteristic lucidity and scholarship in Alfred Schmidt's 'Existential-Ontologie und historischer Materialismus bei Herbert Marcuse', in *Antworten auf Herbert Marcuse*, ed. Jürgen Habermas (Frankfurt: Suhrkamp, 1968). The transcendence of ontology was not yet complete (hence the continued concern with the 'Meaning' of Being) but, as Adorno rightly stresses, Marcuse is 'inclining' (*tendiert*) *away* from Heidegger and *towards* historical materialism. Adorno is further correct to view *Hegels Ontologie* as a further step in this general direction, for here Marcuse concentrates on the ambivalent function of 'objectification' in Hegel's work. As shown below, this anticipates the Frankfurt School's concern with a problem that Marx had centralised in his early critique of the Hegelian dialectic.

35 Marcuse, *Hegels Ontologie*, p. 5.

36 Ibid., p. 217.

37 Ibid., p. 280.

38 G. W. F. Hegel, *The Phenomenology of Mind*, trans. J. B. Baillie (London: Allen & Unwin, 1931), pp. 85–6, et passim.

39 Ibid., p. 75.

40 Ibid., p. 83.

41 Ibid., p. 245.

42 Ibid., pp. 426–38.

43 Max Horkheimer, 'Geschichte und Psychologie', *ZfS*, 1 (1932), p. 130.

44 Horkheimer, 'Zum Problem der Wahrheit', *ZfS*, 4 (1935), p. 332.

45 Horkheimer, 'Traditionelle und kritische Theorie', *ZfS*, 6 (1937), p. 259.

46 Herbert Marcuse, 'A Study on Authority', in *Studies in Critical Philosophy*, trans. Joris de Bres (London: NLB, 1972), p. 88 (originally 'Ideengeschichtlicher Teil', in *Studien über Autorität und Familie*, 1936).

47 Hegel, op. cit., pp. 784–5.

48 Ibid., p. 800.

49 Marcuse, *Reason and Revolution*, p. 28.

50 Marcuse, 'Philosophy and Critical Theory', in *Negations*, p. 134.

51 Karl Marx, *Economic and Philosophic Manuscripts of 1844*, ed. Dirk J. Struik (London: Lawrence & Wishart, 1973).
52 Ibid., p. 177.
53 Ibid., pp. 175, 178.
54 Ibid., p. 108.
55 Marcuse, 'Philosophy and Critical Theory', in *Negations*, p. 134.
56 Karl Marx, *Capital: A Critique of Political Economy*, I, ed. Frederick Engels (London: Lawrence & Wishart, 1970), p. 20.
57 Karl Marx, *Critique of Hegel's 'Philosophy of Right'*, ed. Joseph O'Malley (Cambridge University Press, 1970), p. 137.
58 Herbert Marcuse, 'The Foundation of Historical Materialism', in *Studies in Critical Philosophy*, p. 4 (originally 'Neue Quellen zur Grundlegung des historischen Materialismus,' 1932).
59 Marx, *Critique of Hegel's 'Philosophy of Right'*, p. 136.
60 Max Horkheimer, 'Der neueste Angriff auf die Metaphysik', *ZfS*, 6 (1937), p. 44.
61 Vladimir I. Lenin, *Materialism and Empirio-Criticism* (Peking: Foreign Languages Press, 1972) (Russian original 1909).
62 Ibid., p. 56.
63 Ibid., pp. 284–6.
64 Ibid., p. 111.
65 Ibid., p. 14.
66 Ibid., p. 64.
67 Horkheimer, 'Zum Rationalismusstreit', *ZfS*, 3 (1934), p. 19.
68 Lenin, *Materialism and Empirio-Criticism*, p. 289.
69 Karl Korsch, *Marxism and Philosophy*, trans. Fred Halliday (London: NLB, 1970), p. 62.
70 Ibid., p. 83.
71 Karl Korsch, 'The Present State of the Problem of "Marxism and Philosophy": An Anti-Critique', in *Marxism and Philosophy* (originally 'Der gegenwärtige Stand des Problems "Marxismus und Philosophie",' 1930).
72 Ibid., p. 90.
73 Ibid., p. 114.
74 Ibid., p. 115.
75 Herbert Marcuse, 'Das Problem der geschichtlichen Wirklichkeit', *Die Gesellschaft: Internationale Revue für Sozialismus und Politik*, 8 (1931), p. 350.
76 Herbert Marcuse, *Soviet Marxism: A Critical Analysis* (1958; rpt Harmondsworth: Penguin, 1971).
77 Ibid., pp. 123–4.
78 Theodor Wiesengrund Adorno, *Negative Dialectics*, trans. E. B. Ashton (London: Routledge & Kegan Paul, 1973) (originally *Negative Dialektik*, 1966).
79 Ibid., p. 197.
80 Alfred Sohn-Rethel, *Geistige und körperliche Arbeit: Zur Theorie der gesellschaftlichen Synthesis* (Frankfurt: Suhrkamp, 1970), p. 8.
81 Marcuse, 'Foreword', in *Negations*, p. xv.
82 Adorno, *Negative Dialectics*, p. 3.

83 See, for example, Adorno's use of the term 'positivist' in Theodor Wiesengrund Adorno et al., *Der Positivismusstreit in der deutschen Soziologie*, Soziologische Texte, 58, ed. Heinz Maus and Friedrich Fürstenberg (Neuwied: Luchterhand, 1972), p. 7.

84 Marcuse, *Reason and Revolution*, p. 341.

85 Max Horkheimer, 'Bemerkungen über Wissenschaft und Krise', *ZfS*, 1 (1932), p. 3.

86 Max Horkheimer, 'The Social Function of Philosophy', *SPSS*, 8 (1939), p. 327.

87 Marcuse, *Reason and Revolution*, p. 327.

88 Hegel, op. cit., p. 81.

89 Marx, *Capital*, I, p. 373.

90 Frederick Engels, *Herr Eugen Dühring's Revolution in Science (Anti-Dühring)*, Marxist Library, Works of Marxism-Leninism, 18, ed. C. P. Dutt (New York: International Publishers, 1939), p. 19.

91 Marcuse, 'Philosophy and Critical Theory', in *Negations*, pp. 134–5.

92 Frederick Engels, *Dialectics of Nature*, trans. C. P. Dutt (Moscow: Foreign Languages Publishing House, 1954), p. 49.

93 Theodor Wiesengrund Adorno, *Minima Moralia: Reflections from Damaged Life*, trans. E. F. N. Jephcott (London: NLB, 1974), p. 50 (originally *Minima Moralia: Reflexionen aus dem beschädigten Leben*, 1951). All references to this work are to the English translation.

94 Herbert Marcuse, 'A Note on Dialectic', Preface (1960 edn), *Reason and Revolution: Hegel and the Rise of Social Theory* (Boston: Beacon, 1960), p. xiv. Otherwise, in the present study, all reference to *Reason and Revolution* is to the previously cited edition (London: Routledge & Kegan Paul, 1967).

95 Max Horkheimer, 'Montaigne und die Funktion der Skepsis' *ZfS*, 7 (1938), p. 50.

96 Adorno, *Minima Moralia*, p. 44. The political significance of this position is discussed in chapter 3.

97 Albrecht Wellmer, *Critical Theory of Society*, trans. John Cumming (New York: Herder, 1971) (originally *Kritische Gesellschaftstheorie und Positivismus*, 1969). Behind Wellmer's entire argument lies the post-war Frankfurt School figure of Jürgen Habermas (born 1929), particularly the latter's essays collected in the volume entitled *Technik und Wissenschaft als 'Ideologie'* (Frankfurt: Suhrkamp, 1968). The crucial essays are to be found in translation as 'Labor and Inter-action: Remarks on Hegel's Jena *Philosophy of Mind'* and as 'Technology and Science as "Ideology" ', in, respectively, *Theory and Practice*, trans. John Viertel (London: HEB, 1974), and *Toward a Rational Society: Student Protest, Science, and Politics*, trans. Jeremy J. Shapiro (London: HEB, 1972). Habermas's distance from the Frankfurt School of the 1930s is abundantly clear in his assertion that a critical theory of society cannot be founded today on the critique of political economy (Habermas, *Toward a Rational Society*, pp. 101, 113). Habermas is an important commentator on the early Frankfurt School, but since Wellmer co-ordinates and specifies all the relevant criticisms, the present study can rest content with a serious analysis

of Wellmer's arguments, all of which are wrong. This simultaneously implies a criticism of Trent Schroyer's *The Critique of Domination: The Origins and Development of Critical Theory* (New York: Braziller, 1973), where the formative (and most Marxist) years of the Frankfurt School are passed over far too cursorily and treated as merely a prelude to the Frankfurt School's 'climax' in the figure of Habermas. Significantly, Schroyer's evaluation of Marx rests on an uncritical reading of Wellmer. It is clearly high time that Wellmer should be analysed at length, and, above all, critically.

98 Wellmer, op. cit., pp. 54-7.
99 Ibid., pp. 63-5, 70-2.
100 Ibid., p. 74.
101 Marx, *Capital*, I, p. 81.
102 Ibid., p. 538.
103 Wellmer, op. cit., p. 99.
104 Karl Marx, *Grundrisse der Kritik der politischen Ökonomie* (Frankfurt: Europäische Verlagsanstalt, 1972), p. 916. This passage is not included in the English translation of the *Grundrisse*; otherwise in this present study, all reference to this work is to the latter (Harmondsworth: Penguin, 1973).
105 Horkheimer, 'Geschichte und Psychologie', *ZfS*, 1 (1932), pp. 130-1.
106 Marcuse, *Reason and Revolution*, pp. 317-18.
107 Horkheimer, 'Zum Problem der Wahrheit', *ZfS*, 4 (1935), p. 356.
108 Horkheimer, 'Materialismus und Metaphysik', *ZfS*, 2 (1933), p. 12.
109 Wellmer, op. cit., p. 129.
110 Horkheimer, 'Montaigne und die Funktion der Skepsis', *ZfS*, 7 (1938), p. 36.
111 Frederick Engels, *Ludwig Feuerbach and the Outcome of Classical German Philosophy*, ed. C. P. Dutt (London: Martin Lawrence, 1934), pp. 15-16.
112 Marcuse, *Negations*, p. xii.
113 Ernst Bloch, *Erbschaft dieser Zeit*, enlarged edn (1962; rpt Frankfurt: Suhrkamp, 1973). The original version appeared in 1935.
114 Ernst Bloch, 'Vorwort zur Ausgabe 1935', in ibid., p. 16.
115 Horkheimer, 'Zum Rationalismusstreit', *ZfS*, 3 (1934), p. 5.
116 Ibid., p. 32.
117 Max Horkheimer, 'Bemerkungen zur philosophischen Anthropologie', *ZfS*, 4 (1935), p. 24.
118 Horkheimer, 'Der neueste Angriff auf die Metaphysik', *ZfS*, 6 (1937), pp. 4-5.
119 Marx, *Capital*, I, pp. 19-20.
120 Horkheimer, 'Bemerkungen über Wissenschaft und Krise', *ZfS*, 1 (1932), pp. 4-5.
121 Max Horkheimer, 'Art and Mass Culture', *SPSS*, 9 (1941), p. 299.
122 Horkheimer, 'Der neueste Angriff auf die Metaphysik', *ZfS*, 6 (1937), p. 50.
123 Horkheimer, 'Zum Rationalismusstreit', *ZfS*, 3 (1934), p. 20.
124 Max Horkheimer, 'Zu Bergsons Metaphysik der Zeit', *ZfS*, 3 (1934), p. 328.

125 Ernst Bloch, 'Zur Originalgeschichte des Dritten Reiches', in *Erbschaft dieser Zeit*, p. 148. This section is dated 1937.
126 Hans Albert, 'Kleines, verwundertes Nachwort zu einer grossen Einleitung', in Adorno et al., *Der Positivismusstreit in der deutschen Soziologie*, p. 336.
127 Horkheimer, 'Zum Rationalismusstreit', *ZfS*, 3 (1934), p. 30.
128 Marcuse, *Reason and Revolution*, p. 351.
129 Horkheimer, 'Der neueste Angriff auf die Metaphysik', *ZfS*, 6 (1937), p. 13.
130 Ibid., p. 23.
131 Ibid., p. 38.
132 Herbert Marcuse, 'The Struggle Against Liberalism in the Totalitarian View of the State', in *Negations* (originally 'Der Kampf gegen den Liberalismus in der totalitären Staatsauffassung', *ZfS*, 3 (1934)).
133 Marcuse, *Negations*, pp. xi–xii.
134 Marcuse, 'Philosophy and Critical Theory', in *Negations*, p. 158.
135 Herbert Marcuse, 'The Affirmative Character of Culture', in *Negations*, p. 124 (originally 'Über den affirmativen Charakter der Kultur', *ZfS*, 6 (1937)).
136 Horkheimer, 'Materialismus und Moral', *ZfS*, 2 (1933), pp. 184–5.
137 Max Horkheimer, 'Die Philosophie der absoluten Konzentration', *ZfS*, 7 (1938), p. 378.
138 Marcuse, 'Philosophy and Critical Theory', in *Negations*, p. 152.
139 Marx, *Critique of Hegel's 'Philosophy of Right'*, p. 136.
140 Max Horkheimer, 'Egoismus und Freiheitsbewegung: Zur Anthropologie des bürgerlichen Zeitalters', *ZfS*, 5 (1936), p. 220.

3 The historical materialist theory-praxis nexus

1 Max Horkheimer, 'Zum Problem der Wahrheit', *ZfS*, 4 (1935), pp. 335–6.
2 Max Horkheimer, 'Traditionelle und kritische Theorie', *ZfS*, 6 (1937), p. 275.
3 Karl Marx and Frederick Engels, *Manifesto of the Communist Party* (Moscow: Progress Publishers, 1969), p. 62.
4 Vladimir I. Lenin, 'What is to be done? Burning Questions of our Movement', in *Selected Works in Three Volumes* (Moscow: Progress Publishers, 1970–1), I, pp. 143–4.
5 Ibid., p. 226.
6 Horkheimer, 'Traditionelle und kritische Theorie', *ZfS*, 6 (1937), p. 267.
7 Ibid., pp. 290–1.
8 Ibid., p. 269.
9 Ibid., p. 268.
10 Walter Benjamin, 'Ein deutsches Institut freier Forschung', in *Gesammelte Schriften*, III, ed. Hella Tiedemann-Bartels (Frankfurt: Suhrkamp, 1972), p. 522 (original 1938).
11 Horkheimer, 'Traditionelle und kritische Theorie', *ZfS*, 6 (1937), p. 269.

12 Marx and Engels, *Communist Manifesto*, p. 76.

13 Ibid., p. 74.

14 Karl Marx, *Critique of the Gotha Programme* (Moscow: Progress Publishers, 1971), p. 26.

15 Herbert Marcuse, *Soviet Marxism: A Critical Analysis* (1958; rpt Harmondsworth: Penguin, 1971), pp. 24–5.

16 Vladimir I. Lenin, 'The State and Revolution: The Marxist Theory of the State and the Tasks of the Proletariat in the Revolution', in *Selected Works*, II.

17 Edward Hallett Carr, *A History of Soviet Russia. The Interregnum 1923–1924* (Harmondsworth: Penguin, 1969), pp. 47–94.

18 Vladimir I. Lenin, 'Report on the Substitution of a Tax in Kind for the Surplus-Grain Appropriation System', in *Selected Works*, III, p. 569.

19 Joseph Stalin, 'On the Problems of Leninism', in *Problems of Leninism* (Moscow: Foreign Languages Publishing House, 1940), p. 153.

20 Friedrich Pollock, *Die plantwirtschaftlichen Versuche in der Sowjetunion 1917–1927*, Schriften des Instituts für Sozialforschung an der Universität Frankfurt a. M., 2, ed. Carl Grünberg (Leipzig: Hirschfeld, 1929), p. 37.

21 Max Horkheimer (Heinrich Regius), *Dämmerung: Notizen in Deutschland* (Zurich: Oprecht & Helbling, 1934), pp. 152–3.

22 Max Horkheimer, *Verwaltete Welt* (Zurich: Arche, 1970), pp. 21, 27.

23 'Spiegel-Gespräch mit dem Philosophen Max Horkheimer', *Der Spiegel*, 5 January 1970, pp. 79–80.

24 Max Horkheimer, *Kritische Theorie: Eine Dokumentation*, ed. Alfred Schmidt (Frankfurt: Fischer, 1968), I, p. xiii.

25 Horkheimer, *Verwaltete Welt*, p. 32.

26 Max Horkheimer, 'Philosophie und kritische Theorie', *ZfS*, 6 (1937), p. 629.

27 Max Horkheimer, 'Zum Rationalismusstreit', *ZfS*, 3 (1934), p. 36.

28 Max Horkheimer, 'Bemerkungen zur philosophischen Anthropologie', *ZfS*, 4 (1935), p. 16.

29 Horkheimer, 'Traditionelle und kritische Theorie', *ZfS*, 6 (1937), p. 271.

30 Herbert Marcuse, *An Essay on Liberation* (1969; rpt Harmondsworth: Penguin, 1972), p. 87.

31 Herbert Marcuse, *Negations: Essays in Critical Theory*, trans. Jeremy J. Shapiro (Harmondsworth: Penguin, 1972), p. xv.

32 Edward Hallett Carr and R. Davies, *A History of Soviet Russia. Foundations of a Planned Economy 1926–29*, I (London: Macmillan, 1969), pp. 550–6.

33 Interview with Alfred Sohn-Rethel, Birmingham, 2 November 1971.

34 Boris Lifšic (Boris Souvarine), *Staline: Aperçu historique du Bolchévisme* (Leiden: Brill, 1935).

35 Ibid., pp. 477–9.

36 Interview with Horkheimer, Frankfurt am Main, 27 November 1972.

37 Marcuse, *Soviet Marxism*, pp. 65–6.

38 Johannes Heinrich von Heiseler et al. (ed.), *Die 'Frankfurter Schule' im Lichte des Marxismus: Zur Kritik der Philosophie und Soziologie*

von Horkheimer, Adorno, Marcuse, Habermas (Frankfurt: Verlag Marxistische Blätter, 1970), pp. 125–6.

39 Theodor Wiesengrund Adorno, *Minima Moralia: Reflections from Damaged Life*, trans. E. F. N. Jephcott (London: NLB, 1974), p. 51.

40 Horkheimer, *Kritische Theorie*, I, p. xii.

41 Franz Borkenau, *The Communist International* (London: Faber, 1938), p. 88.

42 Martin Jay, *The Dialectical Imagination: A History of the Frankfurt School and the Institute of Social Research 1923–1950* (Boston: Little, Brown, 1973), p. 14.

43 Rosa Luxemburg, *Organisational Questions of Russian Social Democracy* (London, ca. 1935).

44 Ibid., p. 8.

45 Herbert Marcuse, *Counterrevolution and Revolt* (London: Allen Lane, 1972), p. 39.

46 Rosa Luxemburg, *The Russian Revolution* (London: Socialist Review Publishing, 1959), p. 34.

47 Ibid., p. 34.

48 Rosa Luxemburg, *On the Spartacus Programme* (London: Merlin, 1971), p. 27.

49 Luxemburg, *The Russian Revolution*, p. 31.

50 Luxemburg, *On the Spartacus Programme*, p. 14.

51 Max Horkheimer, 'The Authoritarian State', *Telos*, no. 15 (1973), p. 10 (originally 'Autoritärer Staat', 1942).

52 Max Horkheimer, 'Die Philosophie der absoluten Konzentration', *ZfS*, 7 (1938), p. 384.

53 Rosa Luxemburg, *Reform or Revolution*, trans. Integer (New York: Three Arrows Press, 1937), p. 4.

54 Luxemburg, *On the Spartacus Programme*, p. 19.

55 Karl Heinrich Tjaden, *Struktur und Funktion der 'KPD-Opposition' (KPO): Eine organisationssoziologische Untersuchung zur 'Rechts'-Opposition im deutschen Kommunismus zur Zeit der Weimarer Republik* (1964; rpt Erlangen: Politladen, 1970), I, pp. 6–8, 12–13, 17–18, 24–5.

56 Marcuse, *Soviet Marxism*, p. 124.

57 Edward Hallett Carr, *A History of Soviet Russia. The Bolshevik Revolution 1917–1923* (Harmondsworth: Penguin, 1966), III, pp. 390–1.

58 Edward Hallett Carr, *A History of Soviet Russia. Socialism in One Country 1924–1926* (Harmondsworth; Penguin, 1970–2), III, pp. 302–18, 947–8.

59 Tjaden, op. cit., II, pp. 29–33.

60 Ibid., I, pp. 38–9.

61 Ibid., p. 41.

62 'Das XII. Plenum des EKKI und die KPD', *Die Internationale: Zeitschrift für Praxis und Theorie des Marxismus*, 15 (1932), p. 384.

63 Karl Korsch (under the pseudo-initials L. H.), 'Revolution for What? A Critical Comment on Jan Valtin's *Out of the Night*', *Living*

Marxism: International Council Correspondence, Series 1940–1, no. 4, p. 26.

64 Letter from Karl Korsch to Paul Mattick, 6 May 1941.

65 Adorno, *Minima Moralia*, p. 44.

66 Horkheimer, *Kritische Theorie*, I, p. ix.

67 Leon Trotsky, 'What Next? Vital Questions for the German Proletariat', in *The Struggle Against Fascism in Germany*, ed. George Breitman and Merry Maisel (New York: Pathfinder, 1971), pp. 168–9.

68 Leon Trotsky, 'Workers' Control of Production', in ibid., p. 80.

69 Marcuse, *Soviet Marxism*, p. 65.

70 Trotsky, 'What Next? Vital Questions for the German Proletariat', in *The Struggle Against Fascism in Germany*, p. 199.

71 Horkheimer, 'The Authoritarian State', *Telos*, no. 15 (1973), p. 10.

72 Leon Trotsky, 'It is Necessary to Build Communist Parties and an International Anew', in *The Struggle Against Fascism in Germany*, p. 421.

73 Tjaden, op. cit., I, pp. 89–100.

74 'Was wir wollen', *Gegen den Strom*, 17 November 1928, p. 3.

75 Ibid., p. 3.

76 Horkheimer (Regius), *Dämmerung*, p. 130.

77 'Zehn Jahre KPD: 31. Dezember 1918 bis 31. Dezember 1928', *Gegen den Strom*, 29 December 1928, p. 1.

78 'Entwurf von Leitsätzen über das Verhältnis der Internationalen Kommunistischen Opposition (IVKO.) zum Zentrismus und Trotzkismus', *Gegen den Strom*, 18 June 1932, p. 149.

79 'Was wir wollen', *Gegen den Strom*, 17 November 1928, p. 4.

80 Tjaden, op. cit., I, pp. 336–7.

81 'Die politische Lage und die Aufgaben der Kommunisten in Deutschland: Resolution der Reichsleitung für die Reichskonferenz der KPDO', *Gegen den Strom*, 6 December 1930, p. 701.

82 'Abänderungsantrag I: Zu dem Abschnitt V b über "Die Stellung zur KP.d.SU. und zur Sowjetunion" ', *Gegen den Strom*, 6 December 1930, p. 703.

83 Tjaden, op. cit., I, pp. 283–93.

84 Carr, *A History of Soviet Russia. The Bolshevik Revolution 1917–1923*, III, pp. 143–5.

85 Vladimir I. Lenin, ' "Left-Wing" Communism: An Infantile Disorder', in *Selected Works*, III, pp. 364–9.

86 Hanno Drechsler, *Die Sozialistische Arbeiterpartei Deutschlands (SAPD): Ein Beitrag zur Geschichte der Arbeiterbewegung am Ende der Weimarer Republik*, Marburger Abhandlung zur Politischen Wissenschaft, ed. Wolfgang Abendroth (Meisenheim am Glan: Verlag Anton Hain, 1965), p. 292.

87 Anton Pannekoek, *Bolschewismus und Demokratie* (Vienna: Communist Party of German Austria, 1919), p. 5.

88 Anton Pannekoek, *Lenin as Philosopher: A Critical Examination of the Philosophical Basis of Leninism*, New Essays, ed. Paul Mattick (New York, 1948) (German original 1938). The copy of the English

translation (which was undertaken by the author himself), kept in the Internationaal Instituut voor sociale Geschiedenis, Amsterdam, contains Pannekoek's own pencilled modifications.

89 Ibid., p. 51.

90 Ibid., p. 73.

91 Ibid., p. 76.

92 Letter from Karl Korsch to Paul Mattick, 24 August 1938.

93 Letter from Karl Korsch to Paul Mattick, 23 December 1938.

94 Eduard Bernstein, *Die Voraussetzungen des Sozialismus und die Aufgaben der Sozialdemokratie*, ed. Susanne Hillmann (Reinbek: Rowohlt, 1969), p. 156.

95 Ibid., pp. 156–7.

96 Ibid., p. 207.

97 Ibid., p. 53.

98 Ibid., p. 62.

99 Ibid., p. 47.

100 Ibid., pp. 48–52.

101 Herbert Marcuse, *Reason and Revolution: Hegel and the Rise of Social Theory* (1941; rpt with supplementary chapter 1955; rpt London: Routledge & Kegan Paul, 1967), p. 399.

102 Ibid., p. 400.

103 'Für Republik und Arbeiterrecht! Entschliessung der Sozialdemokratischen Reichstagsfraktion', *Vorwärts*, morn. edn, 4 October 1930, p. 1.

104 'An das werktätige Volk!', *Vorwärts*, morn. edn, 29 March 1930, p. 1.

105 Günter Olzog, *Die politischen Parteien in der Bundesrepublik Deutschland*, Geschichte und Staat, 104, 6th edn (Munich: Olzog, 1970), p. 131.

106 Bernstein, op. cit., p. 196.

107 'Eine Million Mitglieder! Die Macht der deutschen Sozialdemokratie', *Vorwärts*, morn. edn, 28 February 1930, p. 1.

108 Horkheimer, 'Die Philosophie der absoluten Konzentration', *ZfS*, 7 (1938), p. 380.

109 Herbert Marcuse, 'The Affirmative Character of Culture', in *Negations*, p. 132.

110 Horkheimer, 'Die Philosophie der absoluten Konzentration', *ZfS*, 7 (1938), p. 384.

111 Max Adler, 'Die Bedeutung Vicos für die Entwicklung des soziologischen Denkens', *Grünberg Archiv*, 14 (1929), p. 303.

112 Ibid., p. 282.

113 Max Adler, *Demokratie und Rätesystem*, Sozialistische Bücherei, 8 (Vienna: Ignaz Brand, 1919), pp. 23–5.

114 Ibid., p. 31.

115 Max Adler, 'Unsere Stellung zu Sowjetrussland: Die hauptsächlichen Fehlerquellen für die Beurteilung der russischen Revolution', in *Unsere Stellung zu Sowjet-Russland: Lehren und Perspektiven der Russischen Revolution*, ed. Max Adler et al., Rote Bücher der 'Marxistischen Büchergemeinde', 3 (Berlin: Verlag der Marxistischen Verlagsgesellschaft, 1931), pp. 164–5.

116 Ibid., pp. 170, 171, 187.
117 Max Adler, *Linkssozialismus: Notwendige Betrachtungen über Reformismus und revolutionären Sozialismus*, Sozialistische Zeit- und Streitfragen, ed. Max Adler (Karlsbad: 'Graphia', 1933), p. 46.
118 Max Adler, 'Wie kommen wir zum Sozialismus', *Der Klassenkampf: Marxistische Blätter*, 6 (1932), pp. 33–4.
119 Drechsler, op. cit., pp. 16–18.
120 Ibid., pp. 70–1.
121 Max Seydewitz, 'Die Rolle des Faschismus: Wie will der Kapitalismus die Krise überwinden?', *Der Klassenkampf*, 5 (1931), p. 163.
122 Drechsler, op. cit., p. 105.
123 'Prinzipienerklärung der SAP', *Das Kampfsignal: Wochenzeitung der Sozialistischen Arbeiterpartei Deutschlands*, 1 April 1932, p. 7.
124 '15 Jahre proletarische Revolution: Bemerkungen über die Oktober-Revolution 1917', *Das Kampfsignal*, 1st week of November 1932, Supplement 1, p. 1.
125 Drechsler, op. cit., pp. 150, 160–3.
126 Ibid., p. 109.
127 Ibid., pp. 300–2.
128 Horkheimer, 'Traditionelle und kritische Theorie', *ZfS*, 6 (1937), p. 291.
129 Hans-Jürgen Krahl, *Konstitution und Klassenkampf: Zur historischen Dialektik von bürgerlicher Emanzipation und proletarischer Revolution (Schriften, Reden und Entwürfe aus den Jahren 1966–1970)* (Frankfurt: Verlag Neue Kritik, 1971), p. 289.
130 Ibid., p. 286.
131 Ibid., p. 241.
132 Manfred Clemenz, 'Theorie als Praxis? Zur Philosophie und Soziologie Theodor W. Adornos', in *Neue politische Literatur: Berichte über das internationale Schrifttum*, 13 (1968), p. 180.
133 Krahl, op. cit., p. 238.
134 Ibid., p. 240
135 Alfred Sohn-Rethel, *Geistige und körperliche Arbeit: Zur Theorie der gesellschaftlichen Synthesis* (Frankfurt: Suhrkamp, 1970), p. 8.
136 Ibid., p. 68.
137 Alfred Sohn-Rethel, 'Zur kritischen Liquidierung des Apriorismus: Eine materialistische Untersuchung', in *Warenform und Denkform: Aufsätze*, Kritische Studien zur Philosophie, ed. Karl Heinz Haag et al. (Frankfurt: Europäische Verlagsanstalt, 1971), p. 70 (original 1937).
138 Ibid., p. 70. Benjamin's marginal notes to the original manuscript are reproduced in the edition cited.
139 Sohn-Rethel, *Warenform und Denkform*, p. 88.
140 Alfred Sohn-Rethel, 'Statt einer Einleitung: Exposé zur Theorie der funktionalen Vergesellschaftung: Ein Brief an Theodor W. Adorno (1936)', in *Warenform und Denkform*.
141 Theodor Wiesengrund Adorno, *Negative Dialectics*, trans. E. B. Ashton (London: Routledge & Kegan Paul, 1973), p. 177.
142 Sohn-Rethel, *Geistige und körperliche Arbeit*, p. 10.

143 Sohn-Rethel, *Warenform und Denkform*, p. 19.
144 Karl Marx and Frederick Engels, *The German Ideology, Part One*, ed. C. J. Arthur (London: Lawrence & Wishart, 1970), p. 51.
145 Marx, *Critique of the Gotha Programme*, pp. 17–18.
146 Marx, *Capital: A Critique of Political Economy*, III, ed. Frederick Engels (London: Lawrence & Wishart, 1972), p. 820.
147 Alfred Sohn-Rethel, *Die ökonomische Doppelnatur des Spätkapitalismus* (Darmstadt: Luchterhand, 1972), p. 24.
148 Herbert Marcuse, 'Some Social Implications of Modern Technology', *SPSS*, 9 (1941), p. 422.
149 Max Horkheimer and Theodor Wiesengrund Adorno, *Dialectic of Enlightenment*, trans. John Cumming (London: Allen Lane, 1973), pp. 36–7.
150 Kurt Mandelbaum and Gerhard Meyer, 'Zur Theorie der Planwirtschaft', *ZfS*, 3 (1934), p. 234.
151 Sohn-Rethel, *Geistige und körperliche Arbeit*, p. 176.
152 Heiseler (ed.), *Die 'Frankfurter Schule'*, p. 134.
153 Max Horkheimer, 'Montaigne und die Funktion der Skepsis', *ZfS*, 7 (1938), p. 42.
154 Sohn-Rethel, *Die ökonomische Doppelnatur*, p. 26.
155 Horkheimer, 'Die Philosophie der absoluten Konzentration', *ZfS*, 7 (1938), p. 378.
156 Horkheimer and Adorno, *Dialectic of Enlightenment*, p. xiv.
157 Ibid., p. xv.
158 Albrecht Wellmer, *Critical Theory of Society*, trans. John Cumming (New York: Herder, 1971), pp. 129–30.
159 Krahl, op. cit., p. 231.
160 Horkheimer, *Kritische Theorie*, I, p. xii.
161 'Spiegel-Gespräch mit dem Philosophen Max Horkheimer', *Der Spiegel*, 5 January 1970, p. 80.
162 Ibid., p. 79.
163 Interview with Herbert Marcuse, London, 12 June 1974.
164 In fairness to Professor Marcuse, I should state that while rightly regarding his recent work as the legitimate heir of the Institute's work of the 1930s, he does not believe that Horkheimer's volte-face is in any sense an outcome of inherent contradictions in the Frankfurt School's first major period of production. At the same time, Professor Marcuse has revealed that he did have some fundamental criticisms to make of the Institute's work in this period (as related below).
165 Interview with Marcuse, 12 June 1974.
166 Herbert Marcuse, 'A Study on Authority', in *Studies in Critical Philosophy*, trans. Joris de Bres (London: NLB, 1972), p. 130.
167 Ibid., p. 135.
168 Marcuse, 'Some Social Implications of Modern Technology', *SPSS*, 9 (1941), p. 422.
169 Marcuse, *Soviet Marxism*, p. 89.
170 Herbert Marcuse, *One-Dimensional Man* (1964; rpt London: Sphere, 1968), pp. 199–200.
171 Ibid., p. 200.

172 Marcuse, *An Essay on Liberation*, p. 59.
173 Ibid., p. 66.
174 Ibid., p. 59.
175 Marcuse, *Soviet Marxism*, p. 32.
176 Marcuse, *Counterrevolution and Revolt*, pp. 40–1.
177 Marcuse, *One-Dimensional Man*, p. 201.
178 Paul Mattick, *Critique of Marcuse: One-dimensional Man in Class Society* (London: Merlin, 1972) (originally *Kritik an Herbert Marcuse: Der eindimensionale Mensch in der Klassengesellschaft*, 1969).
179 Ibid., p. 106.
180 Interview with Marcuse, 12 June 1974.
181 Marcuse, *Counterrevolution and Revolt*, pp. 44–5.
182 Krahl, op. cit., p. 234.
183 Horkheimer, *Kritische Theorie*, II, p. ix.
184 Horkheimer, 'Traditionelle und kritische Theorie', *ZfS*, 6 (1937), p. 291.

4 Historical materialist psychology: the psychic dimension of manipulation and revolt

1 Max Horkheimer, 'Geschichte und Psychologie', *ZfS*, 1 (1932), p. 134.
2 Max Horkheimer, 'Die gegenwärtige Lage der Sozialphilosophie', *Frankfurter Universitätsreden*, 37 (1931), p. 15.
3 Georg Lukács, *History and Class Consciousness: Studies in Marxist Dialectics*, trans. Rodney Livingstone (London: Merlin, 1971), p. 1 (originally *Geschichte und Klassenbewusstsein: Studien über marxistische Dialektik*, 1923).
4 Walter Jopke, 'Grundlagen der Erkenntnis- und Gesellschaftstheorie Adornos und Horkheimers', in *Die 'Frankfurter Schule' im Lichte des Marxismus: Zur Kritik der Philosophie und Soziologie von Horkheimer, Adorno, Marcuse, Habermas*, ed. Johannes Heinrich von Heiseler (Frankfurt: Verlag Marxistische Blätter, 1970), p. 54.
5 Robert Steigerwald, 'Wie kritisch ist Herbert Marcuses "kritische Theorie"?', in ibid., p. 96.
6 Heiseler (ed.), op. cit., p. 168.
7 Letter from Herbert Marcuse to me, 16 November 1971.
8 Erich Fromm, *Die Entwicklung des Christusdogmas: Eine psychoanalytische Studie zur sozialpsychologischen Funktion der Religion* (Vienna: Internationaler Psychoanalytischer Verlag, 1931).
9 Franz Borkenau, review of *Die Entwicklung des Christusdogmas*, by Erich Fromm, *ZfS*, 1 (1932), p. 174.
10 Erich Fromm, 'The Method and Function of an Analytic Social Psychology: Notes on Psychoanalysis and Historical Materialism', in *The Crisis of Psychoanalysis: Essays on Freud, Marx and Social Psychology* (Harmondsworth: Penguin, 1973) (originally 'Über Methode und Aufgabe einer analytischen Sozialpsychologie', *ZfS*, 1 (1932)).
11 Fromm, 'Über Methode und Aufgabe einer analytischen Sozialpsychologie', *ZfS*, 1 (1932), p. 46. This footnote is not in the English

translation. Otherwise, all reference to this essay is to the latter.

12 Fromm, 'Analytic Social Psychology', in *The Crisis of Psychoanalysis*, p. 174.

13 Ibid., pp. 150, 152, 154–7.

14 Ibid., p. 152.

15 Karl Marx, *Economic and Philosophic Manuscripts of 1844*, ed. Dirk J. Struik (London: Lawrence & Wishart, 1973), p. 181.

16 Karl Marx, *Capital: A Critique of Political Economy*, I, ed. Frederick Engels (London: Lawrence & Wishart, 1970), p. 609.

17 Karl Marx and Frederick Engels, *The German Ideology, Part One*, ed. C. J. Arthur (London: Lawrence & Wishart, 1970), p. 49.

18 Karl Marx, *Grundrisse: Foundations of the Critique of Political Economy*, trans. Martin Nicolaus (Harmondsworth: Penguin, 1973), p. 92.

19 Marx and Engels, op. cit., p. 47.

20 Fromm, 'Analytic Social Psychology', in *The Crisis of Psychoanalysis*, p. 156.

21 Ibid., p. 153.

22 Ibid., p. 154.

23 Ibid., p. 172.

24 Erich Fromm, 'Sozialpsychologischer Teil', in *Studien über Autorität und Familie: Forschungsberichte aus dem Institut für Sozialforschung* (Paris: Alcan, 1936), p. 80.

25 Leo Löwenthal, 'Zur gesellschaftlichen Lage der Literatur', *ZfS*, 1 (1932), p. 89.

26 Herbert Marcuse, *Eros and Civilization: A Philosophical Inquiry into Freud* (1955; rpt with a Political Preface 1966; rpt London: Sphere, 1969), p. 191.

27 Carl Gustav Jung, 'Concerning the Archetypes, with special Reference to the Anima Concept', in *The Collected Works of C. G. Jung*, ed. Herbert Read et al. (London: Routledge & Kegan Paul, 1953–), IX, Part One, p. 58.

28 Carl Gustav Jung, 'Prefaces to *Collected Papers on Analytical Psychology*', in *Collected Works*, IV, p. 292.

29 Carl Gustav Jung, 'Archetypes of the Collective Unconscious', in *Collected Works*, IX, Part One, p. 7.

30 Sigmund Freud, 'The Future of an Illusion', in *The Standard Edition of the Complete Psychological Works of Sigmund Freud*, ed. James Strachey (London: Hogarth, 1953–), XXI, pp. 44, 81.

31 Theodor Wiesengrund Adorno, 'Fragmente über Wagner', *ZfS*, 8 (1939), p. 27.

32 Marcuse, op. cit., p. 191.

33 Fromm, 'Analytic Social Psychology', in *The Crisis of Psychoanalysis*, p. 171.

34 Heiseler (ed.), op. cit., p. 168.

35 Sigmund Freud, 'Group Psychology and the Analysis of the Ego', in *Works*, XVIII, p. 122.

36 Sigmund Freud, 'Civilization and its Discontents', in *Works*, XXI, p. 80.

37 Marx, *Grundrisse: Foundations of the Critique of Political Economy*, p. 611.
38 Max Horkheimer, 'Bemerkungen zur philosophischen Anthropologie', *ZfS*, 4 (1935), p. 11.
39 Fromm, 'Analytic Social Psychology', in *The Crisis of Psychoanalysis*, p. 150.
40 Sigmund Freud, 'Beyond the Pleasure Principle', in *Works*, XVIII, p. 38.
41 Ibid., p. 40.
42 Fromm, 'Analytic Social Psychology', in *The Crisis of Psychoanalysis*, p. 151.
43 Horkheimer, 'Geschichte und Psychologie', *ZfS*, 1 (1932), p. 139.
44 Max Horkheimer, 'Egoismus und Freiheitsbewegung', *ZfS*, 5 (1936), pp. 225–6.
45 Fromm, 'Analytic Social Psychology', in *The Crisis of Psychoanalysis*, p. 151.
46 Freud, 'Beyond the Pleasure Principle', in *Works*, XVIII, p. 54.
47 Horkheimer, 'Egoismus und Freiheitsbewegung', *ZfS*, 5 (1936), p. 226.
48 Freud, 'Civilization and its Discontents', in *Works*, XXI, p. 108.
49 Ibid., p. 112.
50 Ibid., pp. 113–14.
51 Sigmund Freud, 'The Ego and the Id', in *Works*, XIX.
52 Ibid., p. 17.
53 Ibid., p. 35.
54 Freud, 'Group Psychology and the Analysis of the Ego', in *Works*, XVIII, p. 116.
55 Freud, 'The Future of an Illusion', in *Works*, XXI, p. 13.
56 Freud, 'The Ego and the Id', in *Works*, XIX, pp. 45–6.
57 Freud, 'Civilization and its Discontents', in *Works*, XXI, p. 123.
58 Freud, 'Beyond the Pleasure Principle', in *Works*, XVIII, p. 53.
59 Wilhelm Reich, *Die Funktion des Orgasmus: Zur Psychopathologie und zur Soziologie des Geschlechtslebens* (1927; rpt Amsterdam: Thomas de Munter, 1965), p. 162.
60 Fromm, 'Analytic Social Psychology', in *The Crisis of Psychoanalysis*, pp. 155, 159.
61 Ibid., p. 155.
62 Ibid., p. 155.
63 Horkheimer, 'Geschichte und Psychologie', *ZfS*, 1 (1932), pp. 135–6.
64 Erich Fromm, 'Zum Gefühl der Ohnmacht', *ZfS*, 6 (1937), p. 96.
65 Wilhelm Reich, *What is Class Consciousness?*, 2nd edn (London: Socialist Reproduction, 1973), p. 35 (originally *Was ist Klassenbewusstsein? Ein Beitrag zur Diskussion über die Neuformierung der Arbeiterbewegung*, 1934).
66 Ibid., pp. 68–9.
67 Ibid., p. 22.
68 Max Horkheimer, 'Allgemeiner Teil', in *Studien über Autorität und Familie*, p. 9.
69 Max Horkheimer, 'Vorwort', in ibid., p. ix.
70 Horkheimer, 'Allgemeiner Teil', in ibid., p. 31.

71 Ibid., p. 75.
72 'Erhebungen', in ibid., pp. 315–16.
73 Horkheimer, 'Allgemeiner Teil', in ibid., p. 38.
74 Theodor Wiesengrund Adorno and Peter von Haselberg, 'Über die geschichtliche Angemessenheit des Bewusstseins' (A discussion), *Akzente*, 12 (1965), p. 497.
75 Herbert Marcuse, 'A Study on Authority', in *Studies in Critical Philosophy*, trans. Joris de Bres (London: NLB, 1972), p. 136.
76 Horkheimer, 'Allgemeiner Teil', in *Studien über Autorität und Familie*, p. 48.
77 Fromm, 'Sozialpsychologischer Teil', in ibid., pp. 130–2.
78 Horkheimer, 'Allgemeiner Teil', in ibid., p. 55.
79 Ibid., p. 58.
80 'Erhebungen', in ibid., pp. 321, 421.
81 Ibid., p. 421.
82 Horkheimer, 'Allgemeiner Teil', in ibid., p. 71.
83 'Erhebungen', in ibid., pp. 333–4.
84 Marcuse, 'A Study on Authority', in *Studies in Critical Philosophy*, p. 142.
85 Horkheimer, 'Allgemeiner Teil', in *Studien über Autorität und Familie*, p. 63.
86 Theodor Wiesengrund Adorno, *Minima Moralia: Reflections from Damaged Life*, trans. E. F. N. Jephcott (London, NLB, 1974), p. 23.
87 Horkheimer, 'Allgemeiner Teil', in *Studien über Autorität und Familie*, p. 72.
88 Ibid., p. 76.
89 Ibid., p. 59.
90 Reich, *Die Funktion des Orgasmus*, p. 187.
91 Ibid., p. 192.
92 Fromm, 'Analytic Social Psychology', in *The Crisis of Psychoanalysis*, pp. 153–4.
93 Wilhelm Reich, *Charakteranalyse: Technik und Grundlagen für studierende und praktizierende Analytiker* (Copenhagen: privately published, 1933).
94 Freud, 'Beyond the Pleasure Principle', in *Works*, XVIII, p. 23.
95 Reich, *Charakteranalyse*, p. 184.
96 Sigmund Freud, 'Three Essays on the Theory of Sexuality', in *Works*, VII, p. 158.
97 Reich, *Charakteranalyse*, p. 286.
98 Sigmund Freud, 'The Economic Problem of Masochism', in *Works*, XIX, p. 161.
99 Reich, *Charakteranalyse*, pp. 239–41.
100 Ibid., p. 241.
101 Wilhelm Reich, *Massenpsychologie des Faschismus: Zur Sexual-ökonomie der politischen Reaktion und zur proletarischen Sexualpolitik*, 2nd edn (Copenhagen, etc.: Verlag für Sozialpolitik, 1934), p. 50.
102 Fromm, 'Sozialpsychologischer Teil', in *Studien über Autorität und Familie*, p. 113.
103 Freud, 'The Economic Problem of Masochism', in *Works*, XIX, p. 170.

104 Fromm, 'Zum Gefühl der Ohnmacht', *ZfS*, 6 (1937), p. 102.
105 Fromm, 'Sozialpsychologischer Teil', in *Studien über Autorität und Familie*, p. 113.
106 Horkheimer, 'Allgemeiner Teil', in ibid., p. 21.
107 Ibid., pp. 14–15.
108 Wilhelm Reich, *Dialectical Materialism and Psychoanalysis*, trans. from the 2nd edn of 1934 (London: Socialist Reproduction, ca. 1972), pp. 53–4 (originally *Dialektischer Materialismus und Psychoanalyse*, 1929).
109 Wilhelm Reich, *Geschlechtsreife, Enthaltsamkeit, Ehemoral* (1930; rpt Berlin: Underground Press, 1968).
110 Wilhelm Reich, *Einbruch der Sexualmoral*, 2nd edn (1935; rpt Graz: Verlag für autoritätsfremdes Denken, 1971), p. 1.
111 Reich, *What is Class Consciousness?*, p. 23.
112 Fromm, 'Sozialpsychologischer Teil', in *Studien über Autorität und Familie*, p. 92.
113 Horkheimer, 'Geschichte und Psychologie', *ZfS*, 1 (1932), p. 133.
114 Theodor Wiesengrund Adorno, 'Veblen's Attack on Culture', *SPSS*, 9 (1941), pp. 409–10.
115 Max Horkheimer, 'Materialismus und Moral', *ZfS*, 2 (1933), p. 191.
116 Martin Jay, *The Dialectical Imagination: A History of the Frankfurt School and the Institute of Social Research 1923–1950* (Boston: Little, Brown, 1973), p. 116.
117 Interview with Marcuse, London, 12 June 1974.
118 Marcuse, *Eros and Civilization*, p. 187.
119 'Spiegel-Gespräch mit dem Philosophen Max Horkheimer', *Der Spiegel*, 5 January 1970, p. 84.
120 Herbert Marcuse, *An Essay on Liberation* (1969; rpt Harmondsworth: Penguin, 1972), pp. 56–7.
121 Herbert Marcuse, *Counterrevolution and Revolt* (London: Allen Lane, 1972), p. 48.
122 Ibid., pp. 48–9.
123 For the subsequent attacks by Horkheimer's team on their former colleague, see Jay, op. cit., pp. 101–5.
124 Herbert Marcuse, *One-Dimensional Man* (1964: rpt London: Sphere, 1968), p. 25.
125 Ibid., p. 25.
126 Max Horkheimer and Theodor Wiesengrund Adorno, *Dialectic of Enlightenment*, trans. John Cumming (London: Allen Lane, 1973), pp. 120–67.
127 Marcuse's subsequent work in psychology has already been discussed; for Fromm's revision of the Institute's original work, see Jay, op. cit., pp. 99–100; for Horkheimer's and Adorno's own departure from a radically anti-capitalist psychology, see ibid., p. 227.

5 Historical materialist aesthetics: art as 'affirmation', 'culture industry', and 'negation'

1 Max Horkheimer, 'Die gegenwärtige Lage der Sozialphilosophie', *Frankfurter Universitätsreden*, 37 (1931), p. 13.

2 Leo Löwenthal, 'Zur gesellschaftlichen Lage der Literatur', *ZfS*, 1 (1932), p. 92.

3 Ibid., pp. 94–5.

4 Ibid., p. 93.

5 Theodor Wiesengrund Adorno, *Ästhetische Theorie*, Gesammelte Schriften, VII, ed. Gretel Adorno and Rolf Tiedemann (Frankfurt: Suhrkamp, 1970), pp. 11–12.

6 Herbert Marcuse, 'The Affirmative Character of Culture', in *Negations: Essays in Critical Theory*, trans. Jeremy J. Shapiro (Harmondsworth: Penguin, 1972), p. 95.

7 Ibid., pp. 108, 121.

8 Ibid., pp. 102–3.

9 Ibid., p. 131.

10 Max Horkheimer, 'Art and Mass Culture', *SPSS*, 9 (1941), pp. 302–3.

11 Max Horkheimer and Theodor Wiesengrund Adorno, *Dialectic of Enlightenment*, trans. John Cumming (London: Allen Lane: 1973), pp. 135, 160.

12 Theodor Wiesengrund Adorno, 'Wissenschaftliche Erfahrungen in Amerika, in *Stichworte: Kritische Modelle 2* (Frankfurt: Suhrkamp, 1969), pp. 118–19.

13 Theodor Wiesengrund Adorno, 'Über den Fetischcharakter in der Musik und die Regression des Hörens', *ZfS*, 7 (1938).

14 Ibid., pp. 330–1.

15 Theodor Wiesengrund Adorno (with the assistance of George Simpson), 'On Popular Music', *SPSS*, 9 (1941).

16 Ibid., p. 25.

17 Ibid., p. 27.

18 Ibid., p. 38.

19 Ibid., p. 31.

20 Horkheimer and Adorno, op. cit., p. 159.

21 Vladimir I. Lenin, 'Party Organisation and Party Literature', in *V. I. Lenin on Literature and Art* (Moscow: Progress Publishers, 1970), p. 26.

22 Vladimir I. Lenin, 'On Proletarian Culture', in ibid., p. 154.

23 Lenin, 'Party Organisation and Party Literature', in ibid., p. 24.

24 Lenin, 'On Proletarian Culture', in ibid., p. 155.

25 Ibid., p. 155.

26 Adorno, *Ästhetische Theorie*, p. 251.

27 Leon Trotsky, 'From *Literature and Revolution*', in *Leon Trotsky on Literature and Art*, ed. Paul N. Siegel, 2nd edn (New York: Pathfinder, 1972), p. 42.

28 Ibid., p. 60.

29 Georg Lukács, 'Tendenz oder Parteilichkeit?', in *Schriften zur Literatursoziologie*, Werkauswahl, I, ed. Peter Ludz (Neuwied: Luchterhand, 1961), p. 118 (original 1932).

30 Georg Lukács, 'Reportage oder Gestaltung? Kritische Bemerkungen anlässlich eines Romans von Ottwalt', in ibid., p. 128 (original 1932).

31 Theodor Wiesengrund Adorno, *Kierkegaard: Konstruktion des Ästhetischen*, Beiträge zur Philosophie und ihrer Geschichte, 2 (Tübingen: Mohr, 1933), p. 20.

32 Theodor Wiesengrund Adorno, 'Erpresste Versöhnung: Zu Georg Lukács' *Wider den missverstandenen Realismus*', in *Noten zur Literatur*, II (Frankfurt: Suhrkamp, 1961), p. 180 (original 1958).
33 Adorno, *Ästhetische Theorie*, p. 213.
34 Ibid., p. 147.
35 Georg Lukács, 'Zur Ideologie der deutschen Intelligenz in der imperialistischen Periode', in *Schriften zur Literatursoziologie*, p. 324 (original 1934).
36 Adorno, *Ästhetische Theorie*, p. 218.
37 Ibid., p. 87.
38 Ibid., p. 203.
39 Ibid., pp. 336–7.
40 Bertolt Brecht, '[Der Weg zum zeitgenössischen Theater, 1927 bis 1931]', in *Gesammelte Werke* (Frankfurt: Suhrkamp, 1967), XV, p. 225, and '[Über den Realismus, 1937 bis 1941]', in *Gesammelte Werke*, XIX, p. 326. Henceforth, Brecht's collected works are abbreviated to '*GW*'.
41 Brecht, '[Über den Realismus]', in *GW*, XIX, p. 310.
42 Ernst Bloch, 'Diskussionen über Expressionismus (1938)', in *Erbschaft dieser Zeit* (1962; rpt Frankfurt: Suhrkamp, 1973), p. 270.
43 Brecht, '[Über den Realismus]', in *GW*, XIX, p. 298.
44 Ibid., p. 317.
45 Brecht, '[Der Weg zum zeitgenössischen Theater]', in *GW*, XV, pp. 152–3.
46 Bertolt Brecht, '[Neue Technik der Schauspielkunst, ca. 1935 bis 1941]', in *GW*, XV, p. 355.
47 Bertolt Brecht, '[Über eine nichtaristotelische Dramatik, 1933 bis 1941]', in *GW*, XV, p. 303.
48 Max Horkheimer (Regius), in *Dämmerung: Notizen in Deutschland* (Zurich: Oprecht & Helbling, 1934), p. 108.
49 Bertolt Brecht, 'Anmerkungen zur "Mutter" ', in *GW*, XVII, pp. 1062–3 (original 1932–6).
50 Theodor Wiesengrund Adorno, 'Engagement', in *Noten zur Literatur*, III (Frankfurt: Suhrkamp, 1965), p. 112 (original 1962).
51 Adorno, *Ästhetische Theorie*, p. 152.
52 Ibid., p. 336.
53 Bertolt Brecht, *Arbeitsjournal 1938–1942/1942–1955* (Berlin, etc.: Auf- und Abbau-Verlag, 1973), p. 19.
54 Ernst Bloch, 'Ein Leninist der Schaubühne (1938)', in *Erbschaft dieser Zeit*, p. 253.
55 Adorno, 'Über den Fetischcharakter', *ZfS*, 6 (1937), p. 354.
56 Adorno, *Ästhetische Theorie*, p. 345.
57 Ibid., p. 292.
58 Ibid., pp. 183–4.
59 Ibid., p. 217.
60 Theodor Wiesengrund Adorno, 'Zur gesellschaftlichen Lage der Musik', *ZfS*, 1 (1932), p. 106, and Theodor Wiesengrund Adorno, 'Voraussetzungen: Aus Anlass einer Lesung von Hans G. Helms', in *Noten zur Literatur*, III, pp. 136, 139 (original 1960).

61 Horkheimer, 'Art and Mass Culture', *SPSS*, 9 (1941), p. 296.
62 Adorno, *Ästhetische Theorie*, p. 310.
63 Ibid., p. 358.
64 Martin Jay, *The Dialectical Imagination: A History of the Frankfurt School and the Institute of Social Research 1923–1950* (Boston: Little, Brown, 1973), p. 23.
65 Ibid., p. 192.
66 Adorno, 'On Popular Music', *SPSS*, 9 (1941), pp. 45, 47.
67 Horkheimer, 'Art and Mass Culture', *SPSS*, 9 (1941), p. 304.
68 Adorno, *Ästhetische Theorie*, p. 359.
69 Walter Benjamin, 'The Author as Producer', in *Understanding Brecht*, trans. Anna Bostock (London: NLB, 1973), p. 103 (originally 'Der Autor als Produzent', 1934).
70 Brecht, '[Über den Realismus]', in *GW*, XIX, p. 302.
71 Walter Benjamin, 'Zum gegenwärtigen gesellschaftlichen Standort des französischen Schriftstellers', *ZfS*, 3 (1934), pp. 73–4.
72 Benjamin, 'The Author as Producer', in *Understanding Brecht*, p. 94.
73 Ibid., p. 100.
74 Walter Benjamin, 'A Study on Brecht: What is Epic Theatre? (First Version)', in *Understanding Brecht*, p. 10 (originally 'Was ist das epische Theater? Eine Studie zu Brecht', ca. 1939).
75 Bertolt Brecht, '[Über Film, 1922 bis 1933]', in *GW*, XVIII, p. 156.
76 Bertolt Brecht, '[Radiotheorie, 1927 bis 1932]', in *GW*, XVIII, p. 129.
77 Benjamin, 'The Author as Producer', in *Understanding Brecht*, p. 93.
78 Walter Benjamin, 'The Work of Art in the Age of Mechanical Reproduction', in *Illuminations*, trans. Harry Zohn (London: Fontana, 1973), p. 226 (originally 'L'oeuvre d'art à l'époque de sa reproduction mécanisée', *ZfS*, 5 (1936)).
79 Theodor Wiesengrund Adorno, 'Wissenschaftliche Erfahrungen in Amerika', in *Stichworte*, p. 117.
80 Benjamin, 'The Work of Art in the Age of Mechanical Reproduction', in *Illuminations*, pp. 233, 243.
81 Brecht, '[Radiotheorie]', in *GW*, XVIII, pp. 121–2, 133–4.
82 Bertolt Brecht, 'Der Ozeanflug: Radiolehrstück für Knaben und Mädchen', in *GW*, II (originally 'Der Flug der Lindberghs', 1929).
83 Ibid., pp. 576–7.
84 Clara Zetkin, 'My Recollections of Lenin (An Excerpt)', in *V. I. Lenin on Literature and Art*, p. 251.
85 Vladimir I. Lenin, 'The Development of Workers' Choirs in Germany', in ibid., p. 79.
86 Bertolt Brecht, 'Solidaritätslied', in *GW*, VIII, pp. 369–70 (original 1932).
87 Bertolt Brecht, '[Anmerkungen zur literarischen Arbeit, 1935 bis 1941]', in *GW*, XIX, p. 403.
88 Adorno, *Ästhetische Theorie*, pp. 60, 66.
89 Ibid., p. 341.
90 Bertolt Brecht, '[Kunst und Politik, 1933 bis 1938]', in *GW*, XVIII, p. 230.
91 Adorno, *Ästhetische Theorie*, p. 360.

92 Brecht, '[Anmerkungen zur literarischen Arbeit]', in *GW*, XIX, p. 405.
93 Adorno, *Ästhetische Theorie*, p. 361.
94 Adorno, 'Zur gesellschaftlichen Lage der Musik', *ZfS*, 1 (1932), p. 106.
95 Ibid., p. 105.
96 Ibid., p. 111.
97 Ibid., p. 104.
98 Brecht, '[Über den Realismus]', in *GW*, XIX, pp. 336–7.
99 Adorno, 'Zur gesellschaftlichen Lage der Musik', *ZfS*, 1 (1932), p. 123.
100 Ibid., p. 124.
101 Horkheimer, 'Art and Mass Culture', *SPSS*, 9 (1941), p. 294.
102 Brecht, '[Kunst und Politik]', in *GW*, XVIII, p. 252.
103 Bertolt Brecht, 'Der Tui-Roman (Fragment)', in *GW*, XII, p. 590.
104 Max Horkheimer, 'Die Juden und Europa', *ZfS*, 8 (1939), p. 115.
105 Brecht, *Arbeitsjournal*, pp. 161, 291.
106 Ibid., p. 307.
107 Adorno, *Ästhetische Theorie*, p. 377.
108 Herbert Marcuse, *One-Dimensional Man* (1964; rpt London: Sphere, 1968), p. 60.
109 Ibid., p. 10.
110 Ibid., p. 61.
111 Ibid., p. 66.
112 Herbert Marcuse, *An Essay on Liberation* (1969; rpt Harmondsworth: Penguin, 1972), p. 46.
113 Herbert Marcuse, *Counterrevolution and Revolt* (London: Allen Lane, 1972), p. 86.
114 Ibid., p. 107.
115 Ibid., pp. 98–9.
116 Ibid., pp. 87–8.
117 Ibid., p. 125.
118 Ibid., pp. 123–4.
119 Ibid., p. 80.
120 Ibid., p. 128.
121 Ibid., p. 132.

Bibliography

Publications of the Institute

Studien über Autorität und Familie: Forschungsberichte aus dem Institut für Sozialforschung, Paris: Alcan, 1936.

Zeitschrift für Sozialforschung, Leipzig: Hirschfeld, 1932–3; Paris: Alcan, 1933–9; continued as *Studies in Philosophy and Social Science*, New York: Institute of Social Research, 1939–41.

Publications of the four major Frankfurt School figures

Theodor Wiesengrund Adorno

Ästhetische Theorie, Gesammelte Schriften, VII, ed. Gretel Adorno and Rolf Tiedemann, Frankfurt: Suhrkamp, 1970.

Et al., *Der Positivismusstreit in der deutschen Soziologie*, Neuwied: Luchterhand, 1972.

With Max Horkheimer, *Dialectic of Enlightenment*, trans. John Cumming, London: Allen Lane, 1973.

'Engagement', in *Noten zur Literatur*, III, Frankfurt: Suhrkamp, 1965.

'Erpresste Versöhnung: Zu Georg Lukács' *Wider den missverstandenen Realismus*', in *Noten zur Literatur*, II, Frankfurt: Suhrkamp, 1961.

'Fragmente über Wagner', *ZfS*, 8 (1939).

Kierkegaard: Konstruktion des Ästhetischen, Beiträge zur Philosophie und ihrer Geschichte, 2, Tübingen: Mohr, 1933.

Minima Moralia: Reflections from Damaged Life, trans. E. F. N. Jephcott, London: NLB, 1974.

Negative Dialectics, trans. E. B. Ashton, London: Routledge & Kegan Paul, 1973.

With the assistance of George Simpson, 'On Popular Music', *SPSS*, 9 (1941).

'Spengler Today', *SPSS*, 9 (1941).

'Über den Fetischcharakter in der Musik und die Regression des Hörens', *ZfS*, 7 (1938).

175

With Peter von Haselberg, 'Über die geschichtliche Angemessenheit des Bewusstseins', *Akzente*, 12 (1965).
'Veblen's Attack on Culture', *SPSS*, 9 (1941).
'Voraussetzungen: Aus Anlass einer Lesung von Hans G. Helms', in *Noten zur Literatur*, III, Frankfurt: Suhrkamp, 1965.
'Wissenschaftliche Erfahrungen in Amerika', in *Stichworte: Kritische Modelle 2*, Frankfurt: Suhrkamp, 1969.
'Zur gesellschaftlichen Lage der Musik', *ZfS*, 1 (1932).

Erich Fromm

Die Entwicklung des Christusdogmas: Eine psychoanalytische Studie zur sozialpsychologischen Funktion der Religion, Vienna: Internationaler Psychoanalytischer Verlag, 1931.
'Sozialpsychologischer Teil', in *Studien über Autorität und Familie*, Paris: Alcan, 1936.
The Crisis of Psychoanalysis: Essays on Freud, Marx and Social Psychology, Harmondsworth: Penguin, 1973.
'Über Methode und Aufgabe einer analytischen Sozialpsychologie', *ZfS*, 1 (1932).
'Zum Gefühl der Ohnmacht', *ZfS*, 6 (1937).

Max Horkheimer

'Allgemeiner Teil', in *Studien über Autorität und Familie*, Paris: Alcan, 1936.
Anfänge der bürgerlichen Geschichtsphilosophie, 1930; rpt Frankfurt: Fischer, 1971.
'Art and Mass Culture', *SPSS*, 9 (1941).
'Bemerkungen über Wissenschaft und Krise', *ZfS*, 1 (1932).
'Bemerkungen zur philosophischen Anthropologie', *ZfS*, 4 (1935).
(Under the pseudonym Heinrich Regius), *Dämmerung: Notizen in Deutschland*, Zurich: Oprecht & Helbling, 1934.
'Der neueste Angriff auf die Metaphysik', *ZfS*, 6 (1937).
With Theodor Wiesengrund Adorno, *Dialectic of Enlightenment*, trans. John Cumming, London: Allen Lane, 1973.
'Die gegenwärtige Lage der Sozialphilosophie und die Aufgaben eines Instituts für Sozialforschung', *Frankfurter Universitätsreden*, 37, Frankfurt: Englert & Schlosser, 1931.
'Die Juden und Europa', *ZfS*, 8 (1939).
'Die Philosophie der absoluten Konzentration', *ZfS*, 7 (1938).
'Egoismus und Freiheitsbewegung; Zur Anthropologie des bürgerlichen Zeitalters', *ZfS*, 5 (1936).
'Geschichte und Psychologie', *ZfS*, 1 (1932).
Kritische Theorie: Eine Dokumentation, ed. Alfred Schmidt, Frankfurt: Fischer, 1968.
'Materialismus und Metaphysik', *ZfS*, 2 (1933).
'Materialismus und Moral', *ZfS*, 2 (1933).
'Montaigne und die Funktion der Skepsis', *ZfS*, 7 (1938).
With Herbert Marcuse, 'Philosophie und kritische Theorie', *ZfS*, 6 (1937).

'Spiegel-Gespräch mit dem Philosophen Max Horkheimer', *Der Spiegel*, 5 January 1970.
'The Authoritarian State', *Telos*, no. 15 (1973).
'The Social Function of Philosophy', *SPSS*, 8 (1939).
'Traditionelle und kritische Theorie', *ZfS*, 6 (1937).
Verwaltete Welt, Zurich: Arche, 1970.
'Zu Bergsons Metaphysik der Zeit', *ZfS*, 3 (1934).
'Zum Problem der Wahrheit', *ZfS*, 4 (1935).
'Zum Rationalismusstreit in der gegenwärtigen Philosophie', *ZfS*, 3 (1934).

Herbert Marcuse

'A Note on Dialectic', Preface (1960 edn), in *Reason and Revolution: Hegel and the Rise of Social Theory*, Boston: Beacon, 1960.
An Essay on Liberation, 1969; rpt Harmondsworth: Penguin, 1972.
Counterrevolution and Revolt, London: Allen Lane, 1972.
'Das Problem der geschichtlichen Wirklichkeit', *Die Gesellschaft*, 8 (1931).
'Der Kampf gegen den Liberalismus in der totalitären Staatsauffassung', *ZfS*, 3 (1934).
Eros and Civilization: A Philosophical Inquiry into Freud, 1955; rpt with a Political Preface 1966; rpt London: Sphere, 1969.
Hegels Ontologie und die Theorie der Geschichtlichkeit, 1932; rpt Frankfurt: Klostermann, 1968.
'Ideengeschichtlicher Teil', in *Studien über Autorität und Familie*, Paris: Alcan, 1936.
Negations: Essays in Critical Theory, trans. Jeremy J. Shapiro, Harmondsworth: Penguin, 1972.
'Neue Quellen zur Grundlegung des Historischen Materialismus', *Die Gesellschaft*, 7 (1932).
One-Dimensional Man, 1964; rpt London: Sphere, 1968.
With Max Horkheimer, 'Philosophie und kritische Theorie', *ZfS*, 6 (1937).
Reason and Revolution: Hegel and the Rise of Social Theory, 1941; rpt with supplementary chapter 1955; rpt London: Routledge & Kegan Paul, 1967.
'Some Social Implications of Modern Technology', *SPSS*, 9 (1941).
Soviet Marxism: A Critical Analysis, 1958; rpt. Harmondsworth: Penguin, 1971.
Studies in Critical Philosophy, trans. Joris de Bres, London: NLB, 1972.
'Über den affirmativen Charakter der Kultur', *ZfS*, 6 (1937).
'Zur Kritik des Hedonismus', *ZfS*, 7 (1938).

Publications by other members and associates of the Institute

BENJAMIN, WALTER, 'Ein deutsches Institut freier Forschung', in *Gesammelte Schriften*, III, ed. Hella Tiedemann-Bartels, Frankfurt: Suhrkamp, 1972.
—— *Illuminations*, trans. Harry Zohn, London: Fontana, 1973.
—— 'L'oeuvre d'art à l'époque de sa reproduction mécanisée', *ZfS*, 5 (1936).

—— *Schriften*, ed. Theodor W. Adorno a. Gershom Scholem, Frankfurt: Suhrkamp, 1955.

—— *Understanding Brecht*, trans. Anna Bostock, London: NLB, 1973.

—— 'Zum gegenwärtigen gesellschaftlichen Standort des französischen Schriftstellers', *ZfS*, 3 (1934).

BORKENAU, FRANZ, *Der Übergang vom feudalen zum bürgerlichen Weltbild: Studien zur Geschichte der Philosophie der Manufakturperiode*, Schriften des Instituts für Sozialforschung, 4, ed. Max Horkheimer, Paris: Alcan, 1934.

—— *The Communist International*, London: Faber, 1938.

GROSSMANN, HENRYK, *Das Akkumulations- und Zusammenbruchsgesetz des kapitalistischen Systems (Zugleich eine Krisentheorie)*, Schriften des Instituts für Sozialforschung an der Universität Frankfurt a. M., 1, ed. Carl Grünberg, Leipzig: Hirschfeld, 1929.

GRÜNBERG, CARL (ed.), *Archiv für die Geschichte des Sozialismus und der Arbeiterbewegung*, Leipzig: Hirschfeld, 1911–31.

—— 'Festrede gehalten zur Einweihung des Instituts für Sozialforschung an der Universität Frankfurt a. M. am 22. Juni 1924', *Frankfurter Universitätsreden*, 20, Frankfurt: Universitäts-Druckerei Werner und Winter, 1924.

LÖWENTHAL, LEO, 'Zur gesellschaftlichen Lage der Literatur', *ZfS*, 1 (1932).

MANDELBAUM, KURT and MEYER, GERHARD, 'Zur Theorie der Planwirtschaft', *ZfS*, 3 (1934).

NEUMANN, FRANZ, *Behemoth: The Structure and Practice of National Socialism*, London: Gollancz, 1942.

POLLOCK, FRIEDRICH, 'Bemerkungen zur Wirtschaftskrise', *ZfS*, 2 (1933).

—— 'Die gegenwärtige Lage des Kapitalismus und die Aussichten einer planwirtschaftlichen Neuordnung', *ZfS*, 1 (1932).

—— *Die planwirtschaftlichen Versuche in der Sowjetunion 1917–1927*, Schriften des Instituts für Sozialforschung an der Universität Frankfurt a. M., 2, ed. Carl Grünberg, Leipzig: Hirschfeld, 1929.

—— 'Is National Socialism a New Order?', *SPSS*, 9 (1941).

—— 'State Capitalism: Its Possibilities and Limitations', *SPSS*, 9 (1941).

WITTFOGEL, KARL AUGUST, *Wirtschaft und Gesellschaft Chinas: Versuch der wissenschaftlichen Analyse einer grossen asiatischen Agrargesellschaft*, Schriften des Instituts für Sozialforschung an der Universität Frankfurt a. M., 3, ed. Carl Grünberg, Leipzig: Hirschfeld, 1931.

Works on the Frankfurt School

CLEMENZ, MANFRED, 'Theorie als Praxis? Zur Philosophie und Soziologie Theodor W. Adornos', *Neue politische Literatur*, 13 (1968).

HABERMAS, JÜRGEN (ed.), *Antworten auf Herbert Marcuse*, Frankfurt: Suhrkamp, 1968.

HEISELER, JOHANNES HEINRICH VON, et al. (ed.), *Die 'Frankfurter Schule' im Lichte des Marxismus: Zur Kritik der Philosophie und Soziologie von Horkheimer, Adorno, Marcuse, Habermas*, Frankfurt: Verlag Marxistische Blätter, 1970.

JAY, MARTIN, *The Dialectical Imagination: A History of the Frankfurt School and the Institute of Social Research 1923–1950*, Boston: Little Brown, 1973.

KELLNER, DOUGLAS, 'The Frankfurt School Revisited: A Critique of Martin Jay's *The Dialectical Imagination*', *New German Critique*, no. 4 (1975).

KLUKE, PAUL, *Die Stiftungsuniversität Frankfurt am Main 1914–1932*, Frankfurt: Waldemar Kramer, 1972.

KRAHL, HANS-JÜRGEN, *Konstitution und Klassenkampf: Zur historischen Dialektik von bürgerlicher Emanzipation und proletarischer Revolution* (*Schriften, Reden und Entwürfe aus den Jahren 1966–1970*), Frankfurt: Verlag Neue Kritik, 1971.

MATTICK, PAUL, *Critique of Marcuse: One-dimensional Man in Class Society*, London: Merlin, 1972.

SCHMIDT, ALFRED, *Die 'Zeitschrift für Sozialforschung': Geschichte und gegenwärtige Bedeutung*, Munich: Kösel, 1970.

SCHROYER, TRENT, *The Critique of Domination: The Origins and Development of Critical Theory*, New York: Braziller, 1973.

WELLMER, ALBRECHT, *Critical Theory of Society*, trans. John Cumming, New York: Herder, 1971.

Other works

ADLER, MAX, *Demokratie und Rätesytem*, Sozialistische Bücherei, 8, Vienna: Ignaz Brand, 1919.

—— *Linkssozialismus: Notwendige Betrachtungen über Reformismus und revolutionären Sozialismus*, Sozialistische Zeit- und Streitfragen, ed. Max Adler, Karlsbad: 'Graphia', 1933.

——et al. (ed.), *Unsere Stellung zu Sowjet-Russland: Lehren und Perspektiven der Russischen Revolution*, Rote Bücher der 'Marxistischen Büchergemeinde', 3, Berlin: Verlag der Marxistischen Verlagsgesellschaft, 1931.

—— 'Wie kommen wir zum Sozialismus', *Der Klassenkampf*, 6 (1932).

BERNSTEIN, EDUARD, *Die Voraussetzungen des Sozialismus und die Aufgaben der Sozialdemokratie*, ed. Susanne Hillmann, Reinbek: Rowohlt, 1969.

BLOCH, ERNST, *Erbschaft dieser Zeit*, enlarged edn, 1962; rpt Frankfurt: Suhrkamp, 1973.

BRECHT, BERTOLT, *Arbeitsjournal 1938–1942/1942–1955*, Berlin, etc.: Auf- und Abbau-Verlag, 1973.

—— *Gesammelte Werke*, Frankfurt: Suhrkamp, 1967.

BROSZAT, MARTIN, *Der Staat Hitlers: Grundlegung und Entwicklung seiner inneren Verfassung*, dtv-Weltgeschichte des 20. Jahrhunderts, 9, ed. Martin Broszat and Helmut Heiber, Munich: DTV, 1969.

CARR, EDWARD HALLETT, *A History of Soviet Russia. The Bolshevik Revolution 1917–1923*, Harmondsworth: Penguin, 1966.

—— *A History of Soviet Russia. The Interregnum 1923–1924*, Harmondsworth: Penguin, 1969.

—— *A History of Soviet Russia. Socialism in One Country 1924–1926*, Harmondsworth: Penguin, 1970–2.

179

—— and DAVIES, R. W., *A History of Soviet Russia. Foundations of a Planned Economy 1926–1929*, I, London: Macmillan, 1969.

DRESCHSLER, HANNO, *Die Sozialistische Arbeiterpartei Deutschlands (SAPD): Ein Beitrag zur Geschichte der Arbeiterbewegung am Ende der Weimarer Republik*, Marburger Abhandlung zur Politischen Wissenschaft, ed. Wolfgang Abendroth, Meisenheim am Glan: Verlag Anton Hain, 1965.

ENGELS, FREDERICK, *Dialectics of Nature*, trans. C. P. Dutt, Moscow: Foreign Languages Publishing House, 1954.

—— *Herr Eugen Dühring's Revolution in Science (Anti-Dühring)*, Marxist Library, Works of Marxism-Leninism, 18, ed. C. P. Dutt, New York: International Publishers, 1939.

—— *Ludwig Feuerbach and the Outcome of Classical German Philosophy*, ed. C. P. Dutt, London: Martin Lawrence, 1934.

—— and MARX, KARL, *Manifesto of the Communist Party*, Moscow: Progress Publishers, 1969.

—— and MARX, KARL, *The German Ideology, Part One*, ed. C. J. Arthur, London: Lawrence & Wishart, 1970.

EYCK, ERICH, *A History of the Weimar Republic*, trans. Harlan P. Hanson and Robert G. L. Waite, Cambridge: Harvard University Press, 1962–4.

FREUD, SIGMUND, *The Standard Edition of the Complete Psychological Works of Sigmund Freud*, ed. James Strachey, London: Hogarth, 1953–.

HABERMAS, JÜRGEN, *Theory and Practice*, trans. John Viertel, London: HEB, 1974.

—— *Toward a Rational Society: Student Protest, Science, and Politics*, trans. Jeremy J. Shapiro, London: HEB, 1972.

HEGEL, GEORG WILHELM FRIEDRICH, *The Phenomenology of Mind*, trans. J. B. Baillie, London: Allen & Unwin, 1931.

—— 'Wissenschaft der Logik', Erster Teil, in *Werke*, V, Frankfurt: Suhrkamp, 1969.

HEIBER, HELMUT, *Die Republik von Weimar*, dtv-Weltgeschichte des 20. Jahrhunderts, 3, ed. Martin Broszat and Helmut Heiber, Munich: DTV, 1966.

JUNG, CARL GUSTAV, *The Collected Works of C. G. Jung*, ed. Herbert Read et al., London: Routledge & Kegan Paul, 1953–.

KORSCH, KARL, *Marxism and Philosophy*, trans. Fred Halliday, London: NLB, 1970.

—— (under the pseudo initials L. H.), 'Revolution for What? A Critical Comment on Jan Valtin's *Out of the Night*', *Living Marxism*, series 1940–1, no. 4.

KRACAUER, SIEGFRIED, *Die Angestellten: Aus dem neuesten Deutschland*, 1929; rpt Frankfurt: Suhrkamp, 1971.

KUCZYNSKI, JÜRGEN, *Darstellung der Lage der Arbeiter in Deutschland von 1917/18 bis 1932/33*, Die Geschichte der Lage der Arbeiter unter dem Kapitalismus, Part One, 5, Berlin: Akademie-Verlag, 1966.

—— *Darstellung der Lage der Arbeiter in Deutschland von 1933 bis 1945*, Die Geschichte der Lage der Arbeiter unter dem Kapitalismus, Part One, 6, Berlin: Akademie-Verlag, 1964.

LENIN, VLADIMIR, ' "Left-Wing" Communism: An Infantile Disorder', in *Selected Works*, III, Moscow: Progress Publishers, 1971.

—— *Materialism and Empirio-Criticism*, Peking: Foreign Languages Press, 1972.

—— *On Literature and Art*, Moscow: Progress Publishers, 1970.

—— 'Report on the Substitution of a Tax in Kind for the Surplus-Grain Appropriation System', in *Selected Works*, III, Moscow: Progress Publishers, 1971.

—— 'The State and Revolution: The Marxist Theory of the State and the Tasks of the Proletariat in the Revolution', in *Selected Works*, II, Moscow: Progress Publishers, 1970.

—— 'What is to be done? Burning Questions of our Movement', in *Selected Works*, I, Moscow: Progress Publishers, 1970.

LIFŠIC, BORIS (under the pseudonym Boris Souvarine), *Staline: Aperçu historique du Bolchévisme*, Leiden: Brill, 1935.

LUKÁCS, GEORG, *History and Class Consciousness: Studies in Marxist Dialectics*, trans. Rodney Livingstone, London: Merlin, 1971.

—— *Schriften zur Literatursoziologie*, Werkauswahl, I, ed. Peter Ludz, Neuwied: Luchterhand, 1961.

LUXEMBURG, ROSA, *On the Spartacus Programme*, London: Merlin, 1971.

—— *Organisational Questions of Russian Social Democracy*, London, ca. 1935.

—— *Reform or Revolution*, trans. Integer, New York: Three Arrows Press, 1937.

—— *The Russian Revolution*, London: Socialist Review Publishing, 1959.

MARX, KARL, *Capital: A Critique of Political Economy*, I, ed. Frederick Engels, London: Lawrence & Wishart, 1970.

—— *Capital: A Critique of Political Economy*, III, ed. Frederick Engels, London: Lawrence & Wishart, 1972.

—— *Critique of Hegel's 'Philosophy of Right'*, ed. Joseph O'Malley, Cambridge University Press, 1970.

—— *Critique of the Gotha Programme*, Moscow: Progress Publishers, 1971.

—— *Grundrisse der Kritik der politischen Ökonomie*, Frankfurt: Europäische Verlagsanstalt, 1972.

—— *Grundrisse: Foundations of the Critique of Political Economy* (*Rough Draft*), trans. Martin Nicolaus, Harmondsworth: Penguin, 1973.

—— and ENGELS, FREDERICK, *Manifesto of the Communist Party*, Moscow: Progress Publishers, 1969.

—— and ENGELS, FREDERICK, *The German Ideology, Part One*, ed. C. J. Arthur, London: Lawrence & Wishart, 1970.

OLZOG, GÜNTER, *Die politischen Parteien in der Bundesrepublik Deutschland*, Geschichte und Staat, 104, 6th edn, Munich: Olzog, 1970.

PANNEKOEK, ANTON, *Bolschewismus und Demokratie*, Vienna: Communist Party of German Austria, 1919.

—— *Lenin as Philosopher: A Critical Examination of the Philosophical Basis of Leninism*, New Essays, ed. Paul Mattick, New York, 1948.

REICH, WILHELM, *Charakteranalyse: Technik und Grundlagen für studierende und praktizierende Analytiker*, Copenhagen: privately published, 1933.

—— *Dialectical Materialism and Psychoanalysis,* trans. from the 2nd edn of 1934, London: Socialist Reproduction, ca. 1972.

—— *Die Funktion des Orgasmus: Zur Psychopathologie und zur Soziologie des Geschlechtslebens,* 1927; rpt Amsterdam: Thomas de Munter, 1965.

—— *Einbruch der Sexualmoral,* 2nd edn, 1935; rpt Graz: Verlag für autoritätsfremdes Denken, 1971.

—— *Geschlechtsreife, Enthaltsamkeit, Ehemoral: Eine Kritik der bürgerlichen Sexualmoral,* 1930; rpt Berlin: Underground Press, 1968.

—— *Massenpsychologie des Faschismus: Zur Sexualökonomie der politischen Reaktion und zur proletarischen Sexualpolitik,* 2nd edn, Copenhagen, etc.: Verlag für Sexualpolitik, 1934.

—— *What is Class Consciousness?,* 2nd edn, London: Socialist Reproduction, 1973.

SEYDEWITZ, MAX, 'Die Rolle des Faschismus: Wie will der Kapitalismus die Krise überwinden?', *Der Klassenkampf,* 5 (1931).

SOHN-RETHEL, ALFRED, *Die ökonomische Doppelnatur des Spätkapitalismus,* Darmstadt: Luchterhand, 1972.

—— *Geistige und körperliche Arbeit: Zur Theorie der gesellschaftlichen Synthesis,* Frankfurt: Suhrkamp, 1970.

—— *Warenform und Denkform: Aufsätze,* Kritische Studien zur Philosophie, ed. Karl Heinz Haag et al., Frankfurt: Europäische Verlagsanstalt, 1971.

STALIN, JOSEPH, *Problems of Leninism,* Moscow: Foreign Languages Publishing House, 1940.

TJADEN, KARL HEINRICH, *Struktur und Funktion der 'KPD-Opposition' (KPO): Eine organisationssoziologische Untersuchung zur 'Rechts'-Opposition im deutschen Kommunismus zur Zeit der Weimarer Republik,* 1964; rpt Erlangen: Politladen, 1970.

TROTSKY, LEON, *On Literature and Art,* ed. Paul N. Siegel, 2nd edn, New York: Pathfinder, 1972.

—— *The Struggle Against Fascism in Germany,* ed. George Breitman and Merry Maisel, New York: Pathfinder, 1971.

Index

Routledge Social Science Series

Routledge & Kegan Paul   London and Boston

68–74 Carter Lane London EC4V 5EL
9 Park Street Boston Mass 02108

Contents

Authors wishing to submit manuscripts for any series in
this catalogue should send them to the Social Science Editor,
Routledge & Kegan Paul Ltd, 68–74 Carter Lane,
London EC4V 5EL

●*Books so marked are available in paperback*
All books are in Metric Demy 8vo format (216 × 138mm approx.)

International Library of Sociology

General Editor John Rex

GENERAL SOCIOLOGY

Barnsley, J. H. The Social Reality of Ethics. *464 pp.*

Belshaw, Cyril. The Conditions of Social Performance. *An Exploratory Theory. 144 pp.*

Brown, Robert. Explanation in Social Science. *208 pp.*

● Rules and Laws in Sociology. *192 pp.*

Bruford, W. H. Chekhov and His Russia. *A Sociological Study. 244 pp.*

Cain, Maureen E. Society and the Policeman's Role. *326 pp.*

Gibson, Quentin. The Logic of Social Enquiry. *240 pp.*

Glucksmann, M. Structuralist Analysis in Contemporary Social Thought. *212 pp.*

Gurvitch, Georges. Sociology of Law. *Preface by Roscoe Pound. 264 pp.*

Hodge, H. A. Wilhelm Dilthey. *An Introduction. 184 pp.*

Homans, George C. Sentiments and Activities. *336 pp.*

Johnson, Harry M. Sociology: *a Systematic Introduction. Foreword by Robert K. Merton. 710 pp.*

Mannheim, Karl. Essays on Sociology and Social Psychology. *Edited by Paul Kecskemeti. With Editorial Note by Adolph Lowe. 344 pp.*

Systematic Sociology: *An Introduction to the Study of Society. Edited by J. S. Erös and Professor W. A. C. Stewart. 220 pp.*

Martindale, Don. The Nature and Types of Sociological Theory. *292 pp.*

●**Maus, Heinz.** A Short History of Sociology. *234 pp.*

Mey, Harald. Field-Theory. *A Study of its Application in the Social Sciences. 352 pp.*

Myrdal, Gunnar. Value in Social Theory: *A Collection of Essays on Methodology. Edited by Paul Streeten. 332 pp.*

Ogburn, William F., and **Nimkoff, Meyer F.** A Handbook of Sociology. *Preface by Karl Mannheim. 656 pp. 46 figures. 35 tables.*

Parsons, Talcott, and **Smelser, Neil J.** Economy and Society: *A Study in the Integration of Economic and Social Theory. 362 pp.*

●**Rex, John.** Key Problems of Sociological Theory. *220 pp.*

Discovering Sociology. *278 pp.*

Sociology and the Demystification of the Modern World. *282 pp.*

●**Rex, John** (Ed.) Approaches to Sociology. *Contributions by Peter Abell, Frank Bechhofer, Basil Bernstein, Ronald Fletcher, David Frisby, Miriam Glucksmann, Peter Lassman, Herminio Martins, John Rex, Roland Robertson, John Westergaard and Jock Young. 302 pp.*

Rigby, A. Alternative Realities. *352 pp.*

Roche, M. Phenomenology, Language and the Social Sciences. *374 pp.*

Sahay, A. Sociological Analysis. *220 pp.*

Urry, John. Reference Groups and the Theory of Revolution. *244 pp.*

Weinberg, E. Development of Sociology in the Soviet Union. *173 pp.*

FOREIGN CLASSICS OF SOCIOLOGY

●**Durkheim, Emile.** Suicide. *A Study in Sociology. Edited and with an Introduction by George Simpson. 404 pp.*
Professional Ethics and Civic Morals. *Translated by Cornelia Brookfield. 288 pp.*
●**Gerth, H. H.,** and **Mills, C. Wright.** From Max Weber: *Essays in Sociology. 502 pp.*
●**Tönnies, Ferdinand.** Community and Association. (*Gemeinschaft und Gesellschaft.*) *Translated and Supplemented by Charles P. Loomis. Foreword by Pitirim A. Sorokin. 334 pp.*

SOCIAL STRUCTURE

Andreski, Stanislav. Military Organization and Society. *Foreword by Professor A. R. Radcliffe-Brown. 226 pp. 1 folder.*
Coontz, Sydney H. Population Theories and the Economic Interpretation. *202 pp.*
Coser, Lewis. The Functions of Social Conflict. *204 pp.*
Dickie-Clark, H. F. Marginal Situation: *A Sociological Study of a Coloured Group. 240 pp. 11 tables.*
Glaser, Barney, and **Strauss, Anselm L.** Status Passage. *A Formal Theory. 208 pp.*
Glass, D. V. (Ed.) Social Mobility in Britain. *Contributions by J. Berent, T. Bottomore, R. C. Chambers, J. Floud, D. V. Glass, J. R. Hall, H. T. Himmelweit, R. K. Kelsall, F. M. Martin, C. A. Moser, R. Mukherjee, and W. Ziegel. 420 pp.*
Jones, Garth N. Planned Organizational Change: *An Exploratory Study Using an Empirical Approach. 268 pp.*
Kelsall, R. K. Higher Civil Servants in Britain: *From 1870 to the Present Day. 268 pp. 31 tables.*
König, René. The Community. *232 pp. Illustrated.·*
●**Lawton, Denis.** Social Class, Language and Education. *192 pp.*
McLeish, John. The Theory of Social Change: *Four Views Considered. 128 pp.*
Marsh, David C. The Changing Social Structure of England and Wales, 1871-1961. *288 pp.*
Mouzelis, Nicos. Organization and Bureaucracy. *An Analysis of Modern Theories. 240 pp.*
Mulkay, M. J. Functionalism, Exchange and Theoretical Strategy. *272 pp.*
Ossowski, Stanislaw. Class Structure in the Social Consciousness. *210 pp.*
Podgórecki, Adam. Law and Society. *About 300 pp.*

SOCIOLOGY AND POLITICS

Acton, T. A. Gypsy Politics and Social Change. *316 pp.*
Hechter, Michael. Internal Colonialism. *The Celtic Fringe in British National Development, 1536–1966. About 350 pp.*
Hertz, Frederick. Nationality in History and Politics: *A Psychology and Sociology of National Sentiment and Nationalism. 432 pp.*

Kornhauser, William. The Politics of Mass Society. *272 pp. 20 tables.*

Laidler, Harry W. History of Socialism. *Social-Economic Movements: An Historical and Comparative Survey of Socialism, Communism, Co-operation, Utopianism; and other Systems of Reform and Reconstruction. 992 pp.*

Lasswell, H. D. Analysis of Political Behaviour. *324 pp.*

Mannheim, Karl. Freedom, Power and Democratic Planning. *Edited by Hans Gerth and Ernest K. Bramstedt. 424 pp.*

Mansur, Fatma. Process of Independence. *Foreword by A. H. Hanson. 208 pp.*

Martin, David A. Pacifism: *an Historical and Sociological Study. 262 pp.*

Myrdal, Gunnar. The Political Element in the Development of Economic Theory. *Translated from the German by Paul Streeten. 282 pp.*

Wootton, Graham. Workers, Unions and the State. *188 pp.*

FOREIGN AFFAIRS: THEIR SOCIAL, POLITICAL AND ECONOMIC FOUNDATIONS

Mayer, J. P. Political Thought in France from the Revolution to the Fifth Republic. *164 pp.*

CRIMINOLOGY

Ancel, Marc. Social Defence: *A Modern Approach to Criminal Problems. Foreword by Leon Radzinowicz. 240 pp.*

Cain, Maureen E. Society and the Policeman's Role. *326 pp.*

Cloward, Richard A., and Ohlin, Lloyd E. Delinquency and Opportunity: *A Theory of Delinquent Gangs. 248 pp.*

Downes, David M. The Delinquent Solution. *A Study in Subcultural Theory. 296 pp.*

Dunlop, A. B., and McCabe, S. Young Men in Detention Centres. *192 pp.*

Friedlander, Kate. The Psycho-Analytical Approach to Juvenile Delinquency: *Theory, Case Studies, Treatment. 320 pp.*

Glueck, Sheldon, and Eleanor. Family Environment and Delinquency. *With the statistical assistance of Rose W. Kneznek. 340 pp.*

Lopez-Rey, Manuel. Crime. *An Analytical Appraisal. 288 pp.*

Mannheim, Hermann. Comparative Criminology: *a Text Book. Two volumes. 442 pp. and 380 pp.*

Morris, Terence. The Criminal Area: *A Study in Social Ecology. Foreword by Hermann Mannheim. 232 pp. 25 tables. 4 maps.*

Rock, Paul. Making People Pay. *338 pp.*

●**Taylor, Ian, Walton, Paul, and Young, Jock.** The New Criminology. *For a Social Theory of Deviance. 325 pp.*

SOCIAL PSYCHOLOGY

Bagley, Christopher. The Social Psychology of the Epileptic Child. *320 pp.*

Barbu, Zevedei. Problems of Historical Psychology. *248 pp.*

Blackburn, Julian. Psychology and the Social Pattern. *184 pp.*

●**Brittan, Arthur.** Meanings and Situations. *224 pp.*

Carroll, J. Break-Out from the Crystal Palace. *200 pp.*

●**Fleming, C. M.** Adolescence: Its Social Psychology. *With an Introduction to recent findings from the fields of Anthropology, Physiology, Medicine, Psychometrics and Sociometry. 288 pp.*

● The Social Psychology of Education: *An Introduction and Guide to Its Study. 136 pp.*

Homans, George C. The Human Group. *Foreword by Bernard DeVoto. Introduction by Robert K. Merton. 526 pp.*

● Social Behaviour: *its Elementary Forms. 416 pp.*

●**Klein, Josephine.** The Study of Groups. *226 pp. 31 figures. 5 tables.*

Linton, Ralph. The Cultural Background of Personality. *132 pp.*

●**Mayo, Elton.** The Social Problems of an Industrial Civilization. *With an appendix on the Political Problem. 180 pp.*

Ottaway, A. K. C. Learning Through Group Experience. *176 pp.*

Ridder, J. C. de. The Personality of the Urban African in South Africa. *A Thematic Apperception Test Study. 196 pp. 12 plates.*

●**Rose, Arnold M.** (Ed.) Human Behaviour and Social Processes: *an Interactionist Approach. Contributions by Arnold M. Rose, Ralph H. Turner, Anselm Strauss, Everett C. Hughes, E. Franklin Frazier, Howard S. Becker, et al. 696 pp.*

Smelser, Neil J. Theory of Collective Behaviour. *448 pp.*

Stephenson, Geoffrey M. The Development of Conscience. *128 pp.*

Young, Kimball. Handbook of Social Psychology. *658 pp. 16 figures. 10 tables.*

SOCIOLOGY OF THE FAMILY

Banks, J. A. Prosperity and Parenthood: *A Study of Family Planning among The Victorian Middle Classes. 262 pp.*

Bell, Colin R. Middle Class Families: *Social and Geographical Mobility. 224 pp.*

Burton, Lindy. Vulnerable Children. *272 pp.*

Gavron, Hannah. The Captive Wife: *Conflicts of Household Mothers. 190 pp.*

George, Victor, and **Wilding, Paul.** Motherless Families. *220 pp.*

Klein, Josephine. Samples from English Cultures.

1. Three Preliminary Studies and Aspects of Adult Life in England. *447 pp.*

2. Child-Rearing Practices and Index. *247 pp.*

Klein, Viola. Britain's Married Women Workers. *180 pp.*

The Feminine Character. *History of an Ideology. 244 pp.*

McWhinnie, Alexina M. Adopted Children. *How They Grow Up. 304 pp.*

● **Myrdal, Alva,** and **Klein, Viola.** Women's Two Roles: *Home and Work. 238 pp. 27 tables.*

Parsons, Talcott, and **Bales, Robert F.** Family: Socialization and Interaction Process. *In collaboration with James Olds, Morris Zelditch and Philip E. Slater. 456 pp. 50 figures and tables.*

SOCIAL SERVICES

Bastide, Roger. The Sociology of Mental Disorder. *Translated from the French by Jean McNeil. 260 pp.*

Carlebach, Julius. Caring For Children in Trouble. *266 pp.*

Forder, R. A. (Ed.) Penelope Hall's Social Services of England and Wales. *352 pp.*

George, Victor. Foster Care. *Theory and Practice. 234 pp.*
Social Security: *Beveridge and After. 258 pp.*

George, V., and **Wilding, P.** Motherless Families. *248 pp.*

● **Goetschius, George W.** Working with Community Groups. *256 pp.*

Goetschius, George W., and **Tash, Joan.** Working with Unattached Youth. *416 pp.*

Hall, M. P., and **Howes, I. V.** The Church in Social Work. *A Study of Moral Welfare Work undertaken by the Church of England. 320 pp.*

Heywood, Jean S. Children in Care: *the Development of the Service for the Deprived Child. 264 pp.*

Hoenig, J., and **Hamilton, Marian W.** The De-Segregation of the Mentally Ill. *284 pp.*

Jones, Kathleen. Mental Health and Social Policy, 1845-1959. *264 pp.*

King, Roy D., Raynes, Norma V., and **Tizard, Jack.** Patterns of Residential Care. *356 pp.*

Leigh, John. Young People and Leisure. *256 pp.*

Morris, Mary. Voluntary Work and the Welfare State. *300 pp.*

Morris, Pauline. Put Away: *A Sociological Study of Institutions for the Mentally Retarded. 364 pp.*

Nokes, P. L. The Professional Task in Welfare Practice. *152 pp.*

Timms, Noel. Psychiatric Social Work in Great Britain (1939-1962). *280 pp.*

● Social Casework: *Principles and Practice. 256 pp.*

Young, A. F. Social Services in British Industry. *272 pp.*

Young, A. F., and **Ashton, E. T.** British Social Work in the Nineteenth Century. *288 pp.*

SOCIOLOGY OF EDUCATION

Banks, Olive. Parity and Prestige in English Secondary Education: a Study in Educational Sociology. *272 pp.*

Bentwich, Joseph. Education in Israel. *224 pp. 8 pp. plates.*

● **Blyth, W. A. L.** English Primary Education. *A Sociological Description.*
1. Schools. *232 pp.*
2. Background. *168 pp.*

Collier, K. G. The Social Purposes of Education: *Personal and Social Values in Education. 268 pp.*

7

Dale, R. R., and **Griffith, S.** Down Stream: *Failure in the Grammar School.* *108 pp.*

Dore, R. P. Education in Tokugawa Japan. *356 pp. 9 pp. plates.*

Evans, K. M. Sociometry and Education. *158 pp.*

● **Ford, Julienne.** Social Class and the Comprehensive School. *192 pp.*

Foster, P. J. Education and Social Change in Ghana. *336 pp. 3 maps.*

Fraser, W. R. Education and Society in Modern France. *150 pp.*

Grace, Gerald R. Role Conflict and the Teacher. *About 200 pp.*

Hans, Nicholas. New Trends in Education in the Eighteenth Century. *278 pp. 19 tables.*

● Comparative Education: *A Study of Educational Factors and Traditions.* *360 pp.*

Hargreaves, David. Interpersonal Relations and Education. *432 pp.*

● Social Relations in a Secondary School. *240 pp.*

Holmes, Brian. Problems in Education. *A Comparative Approach. 336 pp.*

King, Ronald. Values and Involvement in a Grammar School. *164 pp.*

School Organization and Pupil Involvement. *A Study of Secondary Schools.*

● **Mannheim, Karl,** and **Stewart, W. A. C.** An Introduction to the Sociology of Education. *206 pp.*

Morris, Raymond N. The Sixth Form and College Entrance. *231 pp.*

● **Musgrove, F.** Youth and the Social Order. *176 pp.*

● **Ottaway, A. K. C.** Education and Society: An Introduction to the Sociology of Education. *With an Introduction by W. O. Lester Smith. 212 pp.*

Peers, Robert. Adult Education: *A Comparative Study. 398 pp.*

Pritchard, D. G. Education and the Handicapped: *1760 to 1960. 258 pp.*

Richardson, Helen. Adolescent Girls in Approved Schools. *308 pp.*

Stratta, Erica. The Education of Borstal Boys. *A Study of their Educational Experiences prior to, and during, Borstal Training. 256 pp.*

Taylor, P. H., Reid, W. A., and **Holley, B. J.** The English Sixth Form. *A Case Study in Curriculum Research. 200 pp.*

SOCIOLOGY OF CULTURE

Eppel, E. M., and **M.** Adolescents and Morality: *A Study of some Moral Values and Dilemmas of Working Adolescents in the Context of a changing Climate of Opinion. Foreword by W. J. H. Sprott. 268 pp. 39 tables.*

● **Fromm, Erich.** The Fear of Freedom. *286 pp.*

● The Sane Society. *400 pp.*

Mannheim, Karl. Essays on the Sociology of Culture. *Edited by Ernst Mannheim in co-operation with Paul Kecskemeti. Editorial Note by Adolph Lowe. 280 pp.*

Weber, Alfred. Farewell to European History: *or The Conquest of Nihilism. Translated from the German by R. F. C. Hull. 224 pp.*

SOCIOLOGY OF RELIGION

Argyle, Michael and **Beit-Hallahmi, Benjamin.** The Social Psychology of Religion. *About 256 pp.*

Nelson, G. K. Spiritualism and Society. *313 pp.*

Stark, Werner. The Sociology of Religion. *A Study of Christendom.*
  Volume I. *Established Religion. 248 pp.*
  Volume II. *Sectarian Religion. 368 pp.*
  Volume III. *The Universal Church. 464 pp.*
  Volume IV. *Types of Religious Man. 352 pp.*
  Volume V. *Types of Religious Culture. 464 pp.*

Turner, B. S. Weber and Islam. *216 pp.*

Watt, W. Montgomery. Islam and the Integration of Society. *320 pp.*

SOCIOLOGY OF ART AND LITERATURE

Jarvie, Ian C. Towards a Sociology of the Cinema. *A Comparative Essay on the Structure and Functioning of a Major Entertainment Industry. 405 pp.*

Rust, Frances S. Dance in Society. *An Analysis of the Relationships between the Social Dance and Society in England from the Middle Ages to the Present Day. 256 pp. 8 pp. of plates.*

Schücking, L. L. The Sociology of Literary Taste. *112 pp.*

Wolff, Janet. Hermeneutic Philosophy and the Sociology of Art. *About 200 pp.*

SOCIOLOGY OF KNOWLEDGE

Diesing, P. Patterns of Discovery in the Social Sciences. *262 pp.*

●**Douglas, J. D.** (Ed.) Understanding Everyday Life. *370 pp.*

●**Hamilton, P.** Knowledge and Social Structure. *174 pp.*

Jarvie, I. C. Concepts and Society. *232 pp.*

Mannheim, Karl. Essays on the Sociology of Knowledge. *Edited by Paul Kecskemeti. Editorial Note by Adolph Lowe. 353 pp.*

Remmling, Gunter W. (Ed.) Towards the Sociology of Knowledge. *Origin and Development of a Sociological Thought Style. 463 pp.*

Stark, Werner. The Sociology of Knowledge: *An Essay in Aid of a Deeper Understanding of the History of Ideas. 384 pp.*

URBAN SOCIOLOGY

Ashworth, William. The Genesis of Modern British Town Planning: *A Study in Economic and Social History of the Nineteenth and Twentieth Centuries. 288 pp.*

Cullingworth, J. B. Housing Needs and Planning Policy: *A Restatement of the Problems of Housing Need and 'Overspill' in England and Wales. 232 pp. 44 tables. 8 maps.*

Dickinson, Robert E. City and Region: *A Geographical Interpretation* *608 pp. 125 figures.*

The West European City: *A Geographical Interpretation. 600 pp. 129 maps. 29 plates.*

● The City Region in Western Europe. *320 pp. Maps.*

Humphreys, Alexander J. New Dubliners: *Urbanization and the Irish Family. Foreword by George C. Homans. 304 pp.*

Jackson, Brian. Working Class Community: *Some General Notions raised by a Series of Studies in Northern England. 192 pp.*

Jennings, Hilda. Societies in the Making: *a Study of Development and Re-development within a County Borough. Foreword by D. A. Clark. 286 pp.*

●**Mann, P. H.** An Approach to Urban Sociology. *240 pp.* .

Morris, R. N., and **Mogey, J.** The Sociology of Housing. *Studies at Berinsfield. 232 pp. 4 pp. plates.*

Rosser, C., and **Harris, C.** The Family and Social Change. *A Study of Family and Kinship in a South Wales Town. 352 pp. 8 maps.*

RURAL SOCIOLOGY

Chambers, R. J. H. Settlement Schemes in Tropical Africa: *A Selective Study. 268 pp.*

Haswell, M. R. The Economics of Development in Village India. *120 pp.*

Littlejohn, James. Westrigg: *the Sociology of a Cheviot Parish. 172 pp. 5 figures.*

Mayer, Adrian C. Peasants in the Pacific. *A Study of Fiji Indian Rural Society. 248 pp. 20 plates.*

Williams, W. M. The Sociology of an English Village: *Gosforth. 272 pp. 12 figures. 13 tables.*

SOCIOLOGY OF INDUSTRY AND DISTRIBUTION

Anderson, Nels. Work and Leisure. *280 pp.*

●**Blau, Peter M.,** and **Scott, W. Richard.** Formal Organizations: *a Comparative approach. Introduction and Additional Bibliography by J. H. Smith. 326 pp.*

Eldridge, J. E. T. Industrial Disputes. *Essays in the Sociology of Industrial Relations. 288 pp.*

Hetzler, Stanley. Applied Measures for Promoting Technological Growth. *352 pp.*

Technological Growth and Social Change. *Achieving Modernization. 269 pp.*

Hollowell, Peter G. The Lorry Driver. *272 pp.*

Jefferys, Margot, *with the assistance of Winifred Moss.* Mobility in the Labour Market: *Employment Changes in Battersea and Dagenham. Preface by Barbara Wootton. 186 pp. 51 tables.*

Millerson, Geoffrey. The Qualifying Associations: *a Study in Professionalization. 320 pp.*

Smelser, Neil J. Social Change in the Industrial Revolution: *An Application of Theory to the Lancashire Cotton Industry, 1770-1840. 468 pp. 12 figures. 14 tables.*

Williams, Gertrude. Recruitment to Skilled Trades. *240 pp.*

Young, A. F. Industrial Injuries Insurance: *an Examination of British Policy. 192 pp.*

DOCUMENTARY

Schlesinger, Rudolf (Ed.) Changing Attitudes in Soviet Russia.
   2. The Nationalities Problem and Soviet Administration. *Selected Readings on the Development of Soviet Nationalities Policies. Introduced by the editor. Translated by W. W. Gottlieb. 324 pp.*

ANTHROPOLOGY

Ammar, Hamed. Growing up in an Egyptian Village: *Silwa, Province of Aswan. 336 pp.*

Brandel-Syrier, Mia. Reeftown Elite. *A Study of Social Mobility in a Modern African Community on the Reef. 376 pp.*

Crook, David, and **Isabel.** Revolution in a Chinese Village: *Ten Mile Inn. 230 pp. 8 plates. 1 map.*

Dickie-Clark, H. F. The Marginal Situation. *A Sociological Study of a Coloured Group. 236 pp.*

Dube, S. C. Indian Village. *Foreword by Morris Edward Opler. 276 pp. 4 plates.*
   India's Changing Villages: *Human Factors in Community Development. 260 pp. 8 plates. 1 map.*

Firth, Raymond. Malay Fishermen. *Their Peasant Economy. 420 pp. 17 pp. plates.*

Firth, R., Hubert, J., and **Forge, A.** Families and their Relatives. *Kinship in a Middle-Class Sector of London: An Anthropological Study. 456 pp.*

Gulliver, P. H. Social Control in an African Society: a Study of the Arusha, Agricultural Masai of Northern Tanganyika. *320 pp. 8 plates. 10 figures.*
   Family Herds. *288 pp.*

Ishwaran, K. Shivapur. *A South Indian Village. 216 pp.*
   Tradition and Economy in Village India: *An Interactionist Approach. Foreword by Conrad Arensburg. 176 pp.*

Jarvie, Ian C. The Revolution in Anthropology. *268 pp.*

Jarvie, Ian C., and **Agassi, Joseph.** Hong Kong. *A Society in Transition. 396 pp. Illustrated with plates and maps.*

Little, Kenneth L. Mende of Sierra Leone. *308 pp. and folder.*
   Negroes in Britain. *With a New Introduction and Contemporary Study by Leonard Bloom. 320 pp.*

Lowie, Robert H. Social Organization. *494 pp.*

Mayer, Adrian. C. Caste and Kinship in Central India: *A Village and its Region. 328 pp. 16 plates. 15 figures. 16 tables.*
  Peasants in the Pacific. *A Study of Fiji Indian Rural Society. 248 pp.*

Smith, Raymond T. The Negro Family in British Guiana: *Family Structure and Social Status in the Villages. With a Foreword by Meyer Fortes. 314 pp. 8 plates. 1 figure. 4 maps.*

SOCIOLOGY AND PHILOSOPHY

Barnsley, John H. The Social Reality of Ethics. *A Comparative Analysis of Moral Codes. 448 pp.*

Diesing, Paul. Patterns of Discovery in the Social Sciences. *362 pp.*

● **Douglas, Jack D.** (Ed.) Understanding Everyday Life. *Toward the Reconstruction of Sociological Knowledge. Contributions by Alan F. Blum. Aaron W. Cicourel, Norman K. Denzin, Jack D. Douglas, John Heeren, Peter McHugh, Peter K. Manning, Melvin Power, Matthew Speier, Roy Turner, D. Lawrence Wieder, Thomas P. Wilson and Don H. Zimmerman. 370 pp.*

Jarvie, Ian C. Concepts and Society. *216 pp.*

Pelz, Werner. The Scope of Understanding in Sociology. *Towards a more radical reorientation in the social humanistic sciences. 283 pp.*

Roche, Maurice. Phenomenology, Language and the Social Sciences. *371 pp.*

Sahay, Arun. Sociological Analysis. *212 pp.*

Sklair, Leslie. The Sociology of Progress. *320 pp.*

International Library of Anthropology

General Editor   Adam Kuper

Brown, Paula. The Chimbu. *A Study of Change in the New Guinea Highlands. 151 pp.*

Lloyd, P. C. Power and Independence. *Urban Africans' Perception of Social Inequality. 264 pp.*

Pettigrew, Joyce. Robber Noblemen. *A Study of the Political System of the Sikh Jats. 284 pp.*

Van Den Berghe, Pierre L. Power and Privilege at an African University. *278 pp.*

International Library of Social Policy

General Editor   Kathleen Jones

Bayley, M. Mental Handicap and Community Care. *426 pp.*

Butler, J. R. Family Doctors and Public Policy. *208 pp.*

Holman, Robert. Trading in Children. *A Study of Private Fostering. 355 pp.*

Jones, Kathleen. History of the Mental Health Service. *428 pp.*

Thomas, J. E. The English Prison Officer since 1850: *A Study in Conflict.* *258 pp.*

Woodward, J. To Do the Sick No Harm. *A Study of the British Voluntary Hospital System to 1875. About 220 pp.*

International Library of Welfare and Philosophy

General Editors Noel Timms and David Watson

● **Plant, Raymond.** Community and Ideology. *104 pp.*

Primary Socialization, Language and Education

General Editor Basil Bernstein

Bernstein, Basil. Class, Codes and Control. *2 volumes.*
   1. *Theoretical Studies Towards a Sociology of Language. 254 pp.*
   2. *Applied Studies Towards a Sociology of Language. About 400 pp.*

Brandis, W., and **Bernstein, B.** Selection and Control. *176 pp.*

Brandis, Walter, and **Henderson, Dorothy.** Social Class, Language and Communication. *288 pp.*

Cook-Gumperz, Jenny. Social Control and Socialization. *A Study of Class Differences in the Language of Maternal Control. 290 pp.*

● **Gahagan, D. M.,** and **G. A.** Talk Reform. *Exploration in Language for Infant School Children. 160 pp.*

Robinson, W. P., and **Rackstraw, Susan D. A.** A Question of Answers. *2 volumes. 192 pp. and 180 pp.*

Turner, Geoffrey J., and **Mohan, Bernard A.** A Linguistic Description and Computer Programme for Children's Speech. *208 pp.*

Reports of the Institute of Community Studies

Cartwright, Ann. Human Relations and Hospital Care. *272 pp.*

● Parents and Family Planning Services. *306 pp.*

Patients and their Doctors. *A Study of General Practice. 304 pp.*

● **Jackson, Brian.** Streaming: *an Education System in Miniature. 168 pp.*

Jackson, Brian, and **Marsden, Dennis.** Education and the Working Class: *Some General Themes raised by a Study of 88 Working-class Children in a Northern Industrial City. 268 pp. 2 folders.*

Marris, Peter. The Experience of Higher Education. *232 pp. 27 tables.*

Loss and Change. *192 pp.*

Marris, Peter, and **Rein, Martin.** Dilemmas of Social Reform. *Poverty and Community Action in the United States. 256 pp.*

Marris, Peter, and **Somerset, Anthony.** African Businessmen. *A Study of Entrepreneurship and Development in Kenya. 256 pp.*

Mills, Richard. Young Outsiders: *a Study in Alternative Communities. 216 pp.*

Runciman, W. G. Relative Deprivation and Social Justice. *A Study of Attitudes to Social Inequality in Twentieth-Century England. 352 pp.*

Willmott, Peter. Adolescent Boys in East London. *230 pp.*

Willmott, Peter, and **Young, Michael.** Family and Class in a London Suburb. *202 pp. 47 tables.*

Young, Michael. Innovation and Research in Education. *192 pp.*

●**Young, Michael,** and **McGeeney, Patrick.** Learning Begins at Home. *A Study of a Junior School and its Parents. 128 pp.*

Young, Michael, and **Willmott, Peter.** Family and Kinship in East London. *Foreword by Richard M. Titmuss. 252 pp. 39 tables.*
　The Symmetrical Family. *410 pp.*

Reports of the Institute for Social Studies in Medical Care

Cartwright, Ann, Hockey, Lisbeth, and **Anderson, John L.** Life Before Death. *310 pp.*

Dunnell, Karen, and **Cartwright, Ann.** Medicine Takers, Prescribers and Hoarders. *190 pp.*

Medicine, Illness and Society

General Editor　W. M. Williams

Robinson, David. The Process of Becoming Ill. *142 pp.*

Stacey, Margaret, *et al.* Hospitals, Children and Their Families. *The Report of a Pilot Study. 202 pp.*

Monographs in Social Theory

General Editor　Arthur Brittan

●**Barnes, B.** Scientific Knowledge and Sociological Theory. *About 200 pp.*

Bauman, Zygmunt. Culture as Praxis. *204 pp.*

●**Dixon, Keith.** Sociological Theory. *Pretence and Possibility. 142 pp.*

●**Smith, Anthony D.** The Concept of Social Change. *A Critique of the Functionalist Theory of Social Change. 208 pp.*

Routledge Social Science Journals

The British Journal of Sociology. *Edited by Terence P. Morris. Vol. 1, No. 1,*
March 1950 and Quarterly. Roy. 8vo. Back numbers available. An inter-
national journal with articles on all aspects of sociology.
Economy and Society. *Vol. 1, No. 1. February 1972 and Quarterly. Metric*
Roy. 8vo. A journal for all social scientists covering sociology, philosophy,
anthropology, economics and history. Back numbers available.
Year Book of Social Policy in Britain, The. *Edited by Kathleen Jones. 1971.*
Published annually.